"This book is a withering and unrelentir
tic enthusiasts such as Tim LaHaye ar
demonstrates the tenuousness of their vi
even Armageddon, but he shows us the
early dispensationalism. Every fan of LaHaye's Left Behind series or Lindsey's
Apocalypse Code owes it to himself to read this book. The fog will clear and common sense will return to our reading of the Bible."

—GARY M. BURGE

Professor of New Testament,
Wheaton College and Graduate School

"This is a very readable and well-argued book which deserves the widest possible circulation. With all that is unfolding in the Middle East at the present time, the stakes could hardly be higher, and what Christians believe about the interpretation of the book of Revelation has profound implications for the peace of that region and the world. The people who don't want to read this book are probably the people who need to read it most!"

—COLIN CHAPMAN

Former lecturer, Near East School of
Theology, Beirut; and Author of *Whose
Promised Land?*

"The study of the history of prophetic speculation will demonstrate to any care ful reader that accuracy takes a back seat to sensationalism when it comes to matching the Bible's prophetic passages to current events. Hank Hanegraaff's *The Apocalypse Code* outlines a sound interpretive methodology that all Christians can follow and apply so they won't ever be fooled by anyone who claims to know what's on the prophetic horizon."

—GARY DEMAR

President of American Vision
and author of *Last Days Madness*
and *Is Jesus Coming Soon?*

"*The Apocalypse Code* is at once a manual on responsible hermeneutics and also a cogent refutation of the bizarre system of end-times speculation that has become the benchmark of orthodoxy in the minds of many evangelicals. Thus Hank Hanegraaff has given the body of Christ two valuable books in one—both greatly needed in this age of biblical illiteracy and eschatological naiveté."

—STEVE GREGG

Host of *The Narrow Path* radio
broadcast and Author of *Revelation:
Four Views: A Parallel Commentary*

"Provocative and passionate, this fascinating book is a must-read for everyone who's interested in end-times controversies."

—LEE STROBEL

Author of *The Case for the Real Jesus*

"Throughout the history of the Christian church, wrongheaded teachings have appeared that temporarily attracted a large following, only to become fading fads once the light of proper biblical interpretation illuminated their error. A current example is the dispensational, pretribulational-rapture theology promoted by such prophecy pundits as Hal Lindsey, Tim LaHaye, John Walvoord, Thomas Ice, John Hagee, and others. For years now, I've been wondering what might convince such prophecy specialists to recognize that the eschatology they are foisting on the world is simply embarrassing to the church, and so prompt them to back out of their dispensational cul-de-sac. Hank Hanegraaff's *The Apocalypse Code* may well be the answer. In brilliant fashion, the Bible Answer Man not only dismantles the fantastic claims made by these errorists, but supplies a healthy corrective by presenting proper methods of biblical interpretation that resonate so handsomely with what the church has always taught through the ages. I cannot recommend this book highly enough!"

—PAUL L. MAIER
Professor of Ancient History, Western
Michigan University; and coauthor of
The Da Vinci Code: Fact or Fiction?

"*The Apocalypse Code* is that rare combination of theologically complex discussion and practical, concise exposition that provides even novice readers of prophetic scripture with the sound biblical principles that reveal the plan of redemption and kingdom fulfillment in the fullness of God's glory. Without sacrificing crucial scriptural teaching for simplistic imagining, Hanegraaff has brought the excitement of historical, apocalyptic theology into the twenty-first-century church. Readers will especially appreciate his willingness to engage popular—but misguided—speculations about the last days with firm but fair criticism."

—GRETCHEN PASSANTINO
Cofounder and Director, Answers In
Action

"Hank Hanegraaff has done it again. What his *Christianity in Crisis* did for charismania, *The Apocalypse Code* will do for armaggedonites. Hank exposes how dangerous and destructive faulty exegesis really is—inviting not only bad theology but dangerous politics—and, in this very readable book, shows us all, from the young believer to the scholar, how to handle Scripture accurately and reverently and not to be afraid of the apocalyptic Scriptures."

—STEPHEN SIZER
Vicar of Christ Church, Virginia Water;
Chairman of the International Bible
Society UK; and Author of *Christian
Zionism: Roadmap or Armageddon?*

THE APOCALYPSE CODE

OTHER BOOKS BY HANK HANEGRAAFF

Nonfiction

Fiction

THE APOCALYPSE CODE

*Find Out What the Bible Really Says About
the End Times and Why It Matters Today*

HANK HANEGRAAFF

THOMAS NELSON
Since 1798

NASHVILLE   DALLAS   MEXICO CITY   RIO DE JANEIRO

Published in Nashville, Tennessee, by Thomas Nelson. Thomas Nelson is a registered trademark of Thomas Nelson, Inc.

Thomas Nelson, Inc. titles may be purchased in bulk for educational, business, fund-raising, or sales promotional use. For information, please e-mail SpecialMarkets@ThomasNelson.com.

Unless otherwise noted, Scripture quotations are taken from the Holy Bible, New International Version®, NIV®. © 1973, 1978, 1984 by Biblica, Inc.™ Used by permission of Zondervan. All rights reserved worldwide. Italics added to NIV quotations indicate the author's emphasis.

Other Scripture references are from the King James Version of the Bible (KJV).

ISBN 978-0-8499-1991-6 (trade paper)

Library of Congress Cataloging-in-Publication Data

Hanegraaff, Hank.
    The apocalypse code : find out what the Bible really says about the end times . . . and why it matters today / Hank Hanegraaff.
        p. cm.
    Includes bibliographical references.
    ISBN 978-0-8499-0184-3 (hardcover)
    1. Eschatology—Biblical teaching. I. Title.
BS680.E8H36 2007
236'.9—dc22   2007004633

Printed in the United States of America

10   11   12   13   14   RRD   5   4   3   2   1

To Brian and Kay Mulvaney—
with deep appreciation for your friendship and faithfulness.

THE APOCALYPSE CODE

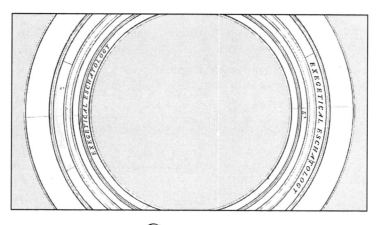

Contents

CONTENTS

Acknowledgments

⟞⟝⟞⟝⟞

FIRST AND FOREMOST, I AM INDEBTED TO MY colleague and comrade, Stephen Ross, who assisted me in the formulation of Exegetical Eschatology or e^2. Your faithfulness and friendship over the last fifteen years has been indispensable—I look forward to the next fifteen! I am also deeply grateful for the staff and support network of the Christian Research Institute, particularly Elliot Miller, Paul Young, Sam Wall, Warren Nozaki, Andy Milliken and Bob Eaton. A special thanks to Adam Pelser who contributed significantly to the finished manuscript—your insights and input during the final stages of the writing process were invaluable. I would also like to acknowledge Sigmund Brouwer, coauthor of *Fuse of Armageddon* and *The Last Disciple* series, for helping me communicate Exegetical Eschatology through the power of story.

Furthermore, I would like to express my deep appreciation for the insights I garnered through such intellects as N. T. Wright, Gary Burge, Stephen Sizer, Colin Chapman, Timothy Weber, R. C. Sproul, Gary DeMar, Kenneth Gentry Jr., David Chilton, Steve Gregg, Dennis Johnson, Gene Edward Veith Jr., Gordon Fee, Keith Mathison, Richard Bauckham, and Gretchen Passantino. I am likewise indebted to Michael Hyatt and the Thomas Nelson team—particularly David Moberg, Jack Countryman, Greg Daniel, and Thom Chittom.

Finally, I want to thank Kathy and the kids—Michelle, Katie, David, John Mark, Hank Jr., Christina, Paul, Faith—

for their patience and understanding during the three-year-plus writing process. You are the love of my life. Above all I am supremely grateful to the Lord Jesus Christ without whom I am nothing.

Introduction

━━◦◦◦━━

In reality the code breaker for apocalypse passages does not reside in "special insight," unbridled speculation, or subjective flights of fancy. Rather, "the code" is decoded by reading Scripture in light of Scripture. The real code breaker for the apocalypse "of Jesus Christ which God gave him to show his servants what must soon take place" (Revelation 1:1) is the Old Testament. Indeed, more than two-thirds of Revelation's four hundred four verses allude to Old Testament passages. The reason we often cannot make heads or tails out of them is that we have not sufficiently learned to read the Bible for all it is worth. When our interpretations are tethered to the hottest sensation rather than to the Holy Scripture, we are apt to grab at anything—and usually miss.

—HANK HANEGRAAFF, *THE APOCALYPSE CODE*

IN 1997 HAL LINDSEY PUBLISHED *APOCALYPSE CODE*. IT was released replete with the promise that God had privileged him to do what had never been done before. For two millennia the book of Revelation had remained shrouded in mystery. August Christian intellects— Athanasius, Augustine, Anselm—had all attempted to decode its meaning, but to no avail. Until the present generation, the encrypted message of the Apocalypse[1] had remained unrealized as had the blessings promised to "those who hear it and take to heart what is written in it" (Revelation 1:3). At long last, promises *Apocalypse*

Code, "the father of modern-day Bible prophecy cracks the 'Apocalypse Code' and deciphers long-hidden messages about man's future and the fate of the earth."[2] Says Lindsey, "The Spirit of God gave me a special insight, not only into how John described what he actually experienced, but also into how this whole phenomenon encoded the prophecies so that they could be fully understood *only* when their fulfillment drew near."[3]

One of the significant insights claimed by Lindsey is that the apostle John, author of the Apocalypse, wrote "about only the things to which he was a personal eyewitness."[4] This, says Lindsey, raises a question that "I pondered over and prayed about for a long time . . . how would a first-century prophet describe, much less understand, the incredible advances in science and technology that exist at the end of the 20th and the beginning of the 21st centuries?"[5] The key to Lindsey's conundrum was time travel. Says Lindsey, "The unique concept of a 'first-century time traveler' accelerated up to the beginning of the 21st century; of being vividly shown all the phenomena of a global war fought with weapons of unimaginable power, speed and lethality; of being brought back to the first century and told to write an accurate eyewitness account of this terrifying future time—*is the essence of understanding his code.*"[6]

The first example of decoding the apocalypse code provided by Lindsey involves chapter 9 of Revelation. He decodes the following description given by the apostle John.

The locusts *looked like* horses prepared for battle. On their heads they wore *something like* crowns of gold, and their faces *resembled* human faces. Their hair was *like* women's hair, and their teeth were *like* lions' teeth.

They had breastplates *like* breastplates of iron, and the sound of their wings was *like* the thundering of many horses and chariots rushing into battle. They had tails and stings like scorpions, and in their tails they had power to torment people for five months.[7]

Through "special insight" Lindsey determined that the locusts were "attack helicopters," the crowns of gold were "the elaborate helmets worn by helicopter pilots," and the women's hair was "the whirling propeller."[8]

This description of Apache, Cobra, and Comanche helicopters, says Lindsey,

is just a sample of the kind of descriptions John recorded in this mysterious book of prophecy. It is my belief that current events and technology can give us insights into the amazing Book of the Apocalypse that couldn't have been discerned in other generations. . . . This is the code that most effectively kept prophecy concealed until the time of the end. . . . All of these symbols helped to so encode the message that only a spiritually alive person guided by the Spirit of God has been able to unlock its prophetic content.[9]

While Lindsey, as "the best-known prophecy teacher in the world"[10] and coauthor of *The Late Great Planet Earth*,[11] is certainly a force to contend with, in reality the code breaker for apocalypse passages does not reside in "special insight," unbridled speculation, or subjective flights of fancy. Rather, "the code" is decoded by reading Scripture in light of Scripture. The real code breaker for the apocalypse "of Jesus

Christ which God gave him to show his servants what must soon take place" (Revelation 1:1) is the Old Testament. Indeed, more than two-thirds of Revelation's four hundred four verses allude to Old Testament passages.[12] The reason we often cannot make heads or tails out of them is that we have not sufficiently learned to read the Bible for all it is worth. When our interpretations are tethered to the hottest sensation rather than to the Holy Scripture, we are apt to grab at anything—and usually miss.

A decade after the publication of *Apocalypse Code*, I am releasing *The Apocalypse Code* in hopes that you, and multitudes like you, will be equipped to read the Scriptures for all they're worth. As you continue reading, you will discover that I reference the writings of Dr. Tim LaHaye more than any other modern prophecy pundit. While I could have centered on the writings of numerous authors, Dr. LaHaye, more than anyone else in contemporary church history, has become the standard-bearer for Lindsey's brand of eschatology. The mantle of Lindsey has fallen squarely on his shoulders. Like Lindsey, who claims to interpret prophecy "in the most literal futuristic sense possible,"[13] LaHaye takes great pains to emphasize that, unlike the "false teacher" who traffics in the "bizarre," he is deeply committed to the *literal* principle as conceived of in the dispensationalist mind-set.[14]

Make no mistake: this is not the stuff of ivory-tower debates. The stakes for Christianity and the culture in the controversy surrounding eschatology are enormous! Not only are great and glorious passages believed throughout church history to refer directly to the blessed hope of resurrection arrogated for the dispensational pretribulational rapture theory first popularized in the nineteenth century by a priest named John

Nelson Darby, but by logical extension the uniqueness and significance of Christ's resurrection are undermined.

Resurrection of Antichrist

A classic case in point is LaHaye's depiction of the Antichrist. In *The Indwelling*, volume seven of LaHaye's Left Behind series,[15] Nicolae Carpathia, the novel's Antichrist character, dies and is resurrected physically in order to vindicate his claim to be God. Just like Christ, LaHaye's Antichrist dies on a Friday and rises from the dead on the first day of the week. And like Christ, he has the power over "earth and sky."[16] LaHaye's belief in the resurrection of the Antichrist is driven in part by a literalistic interpretation of Revelation 13. The apostle John says the "fatal wound" of the Beast "had been healed" (v. 3). Therefore, to LaHaye's way of thinking, the Antichrist, like Christ, will one day be empowered to lay down his life and take it up again. What is not accounted for by LaHaye's literalism is the fact that Revelation 13 also clearly communicates that the Beast had seven heads and only one of his seven heads "seemed" to be fatally wounded (vv. 1, 3). Moreover, the Beast is described as having "ten horns," resembling "a leopard," having "feet like those of a bear," and boasting "a mouth like that of a lion" (vv. 1–2).

While LaHaye's interpretation of Revelation is no doubt driven by a desire to be biblical, it nonetheless erodes epistemic warrant for the resurrection and ultimately the deity of our Lord.[17] If the Antichrist could rise from the dead and control the earth and sky as LaHaye contends, Christianity would lose the basis for believing that Christ's resurrection vindicated his claim to deity. In a Christian worldview, Satan can parody the work of Christ through "all kinds of counterfeit miracles, signs and wonders" (2 Thessalonians 2:9), but he cannot perform the truly miraculous as Christ did. If Satan possesses the creative power of God, he could have masqueraded as the resurrected Christ. Moreover, the notion that Satan can perform acts that are indistinguishable from genuine miracles suggests a dualistic worldview in which God and Satan are equal and opposite powers competing for dominance.[18]

Racial Discrimination

Furthermore, there is the very real problem of *racial discrimination*. Biblical theology knows nothing of racism. Nor would it ever justify ethnic cleansing based on the pretext of a promise made to Abraham. Rather, according to Scripture, there is neither "Jew nor Greek." Neither is there a distinction between Israel and the church based on race. As the apostle Paul explains, "You are all sons of God through faith in Christ Jesus. . . . If you belong to Christ, then you are Abraham's seed, and heirs according to the promise" (Galatians 3:26–29). Scripture emphasizes *faith* not genealogy. Thus, historic Christianity has always believed in one people of God based on *relationship* rather than race.

In sharp distinction, LaHaye divides people into two categories on the basis of race rather than relationship. In his view, God has two "classes" of people. The first class consists of Jews. The second class consists of Gentiles. In LaHaye's words, "Jacob had 12 sons, who became the heads of the 12 tribes of Israel. They began the Jewish nation, and since then the human race has been divided into *Jews and Gentiles*. . . . Israel began with 'Father Abraham' and will continue as a distinct entity throughout the rest of history."[19]

One of the ways by which LaHaye distinguishes between

these two classes is temperament: "As a student of human temperament for many years, I have been intrigued by the Jewish temperament. After carefully analyzing the temperament of the first Israelite as he is described in the Bible, I have found Jacob to be a 'dead ringer' for the twentieth-century residents of Israel."[20] Therefore, according to LaHaye, the two classes can rightly be distinguished and divided on the basis of personal characteristics.

The good news for Jews is that LaHaye believes that on the basis of their race they have a divine right to the land of Palestine. The bad news is that, as a direct result of the crucifixion of Christ, twenty-first-century Jews will soon die in an Armageddon that will make the Nazi Holocaust pale by comparison. So, before "all Israel will be saved" (Romans 11:26), a majority of Israelis must be slaughtered.

According to *The End Times Controversy*, edited by LaHaye, when Jacob's descendants rejected and crucified Christ, they suffered two distinct consequences. The first consequence was that "the flock of Israel was dispersed." The second consequence will be "the death of two-thirds of the flock. This will be fulfilled during the Great Tribulation when Israel will suffer tremendous persecution (Matthew 24:15–28; Revelation 12:1-17). As a result of this persecution of the Jewish people, two-thirds are going to be killed."[21]

LaHaye predicts that this Jewish holocaust is right around the corner. In his words, there is "ample reason to conclude that the Austrian declaration of war in July of 1914 began to fulfill *the sign* of the end of the age as given by our Lord."[21] LaHaye spends several chapters in *The Beginning of the End* seeking to demonstrate from our Lord's own words that the generation that saw World War I will not pass away before Jesus returns.[23] Since "no other explanation fits the context,"[24] LaHaye says that he is certain that "we can thus know the season of his return."[25] While LaHaye has had to make numerous revisions and disclaimers over the years, he continues to insist that there is more reason now than ever to believe we are living in the shadow of the greatest apocalypse in human history.[26]

LaHaye's theory of two peoples of God has had chilling consequences not only for Jews, but for Palestinian Arabs as well. Unlike early dispensationalists, who believed that the Jews would be regathered in Palestine because of *belief* in their Redeemer, LaHaye holds to the theory that Jews must initially be regathered in *unbelief* solely on the basis of race.[27] Such unbiblical notions put Christian Zionists in the untenable position of condoning the displacement of Palestinian Christians from their homeland in order to facilitate an occupation based on unbelief and racial affiliation.

The tragic consequence is that Palestinians today form the largest displaced people group in the world.[28] As Dr. Gary Burge, professor of New Testament at Wheaton College and Graduate School, explains, "Israeli historians now talk about the mass and planned expulsion of the Palestinians, an early form of 'ethnic cleansing.' The most troubling national confession has been the destruction of at least four hundred Palestinian villages, the ruin of dozens of Arab urban neighborhoods, and several massacres that would motivate the Arab population to flee."[29]

If America required people of African descent to carry special ID cards or to leave the country to make way for people of European ancestry, we would be condemned as a nation that promoted racism and apartheid. Attempting to justify our actions on the basis of biblical proscriptions is even more unthinkable. Says Burge, "Any country that de facto excludes a segment of its society from its national benefits on the basis of race can hardly qualify as democratic."[30]

This is precisely why Zionism has been labeled a racist political philosophy. As Burge notes, "In 1998, the Association for Civil Rights in Israel accused the government of race-based discrimination and 'creating a threatening atmosphere that makes violations of human rights more acceptable.'"[31]

Far from facilitating race-based discrimination on the basis of our eschatological presuppositions, Christians must be equipped to communicate that Christianity knows nothing of dividing people on the basis of race. Just as evangelicalism now universally repudiates the once-common appeal to Genesis 9:27 in support of slavery of blacks, we must thoroughly and finally put to rest any thought that the Bible supports the horrors of racial discrimination wherever and in whatever form we encounter it, whether within the borders of the United States or in the hallowed regions of the Middle East.

Real Estate

Finally, at issue is an explosive debate over *real estate*. Eight years before Israel was formally founded in 1948, Joseph Weitz, director of the Jewish National Land Fund, defined the debate over real estate when he declared that there was not enough room in Palestine for both Jews and Arabs. "If the Arabs leave the country, it will be broad and wide open for us. If the Arabs stay, the country will remain narrow and miserable. The only solution is Israel without Arabs. There is no room for compromise on this point."[32] Israel's first prime minister, David Ben-Gurion, was equally direct when he wrote, "We will expel the Arabs and take their place."[33]

Thus, scarcely three years after the Nazi Holocaust ended in 1945, a Holy Land holocaust was initiated. Brother Andrew, best known for smuggling Bibles to Christians living behind the Iron Curtain, recalls the well-known 1948 massacre of Deir Yassin in which an entire village of two hundred fifty men, women, children, and babies were brutally slaughtered by the Israeli paramilitary: "A few men were left alive and driven around to other villages to tell the story; then those men were killed too. The result was a panic. That's why so many Palestinians fled. Entire villages were emptied, which is exactly what the Israelis wanted. They just took over those people's homes."[34]

In *Whose Land? Whose Promise?* Gary Burge provides names and faces for many of the victims and villages that were uprooted at gunpoint:

> Na'im Stifan Ateek was eleven years old in 1948. He and his family belonged to the Anglican Christian community in Beisan. Their home was a locus of Christian activity: Bible studies, visiting missionaries, and Sunday school classes met there. His father even helped build an Anglican Church for Beisan. In the absence of a resident Anglican pastor (who came from Nazareth once a month for Holy Communion), Na'im's father served as the church's lay reader.
>
> On May 12, 1948 (two days before the state of Israel was declared), Israeli soldiers occupied Beisan. There was no fighting, no resistance, no killing. The town was simply taken over. After searching the homes for weapons and radios, on May 26 they rounded up the leading men of the town to make an important

announcement. Everyone would have to leave their homes in a few hours. "If you do not leave, we will have to kill you," they said.

When the people had gathered in the center of town, the soldiers separated the Muslims from the Christians. The Muslims were sent east to Jordan, and the Christians were put on buses and deposited on the outskirts of Nazareth. Within a few hours, Na'im's mother, father, seven sisters, and two brothers were refugees. They had lost everything except the things they could carry. In Nazareth they joined some friends, and seventeen of them lived in two rooms near "Mary's Well." Na'im's father went to work at once helping relief efforts for the countless Christians and Muslims flooding Nazareth daily as refugees.

Ten years later, in 1958, the government permitted many of the Palestinian families to travel for one day without restriction. Na'im's father was eager to bring his children to Beisan so that they could see their "home." The Anglican Church had become a storehouse. The Roman Catholic Church was a school. The Greek Orthodox church was in ruins. Na'im remembers the moment his father stepped up to the door of his home, the one he had built with his own hands. He wanted to see it one last time. But his request was refused. The new Israeli occupant said, "This is not your house. It is ours."[35]

Burge goes on to recount the story of an Arab peasant making an inquiry of an official at the Israel Lands Administration.

"How do you deny my right to this land? It is my property. I inherited it from my parents and grandparents, and I have the deed of ownership." The official replied, "Ours is a more impressive deed; we have the deed for the land from Dan [in the far north] to Elat [in the far south]." Another official was paying a peasant a token sale price for his land. Holding the peasant's property deed, the official remarked, "This is not your land; it is ours, and we are paying you 'watchman's wages,' for that is what you are. You have watched our land for two thousand years, and now we are paying your fee. But the land has always been ours."[36]

Former Israeli prime minister Benjamin Netanyahu put it plainly: "Our claim to this land is based on the greatest and most incontrovertible document in creation—the Holy Bible."[37]

The debate over who owns the land takes on heightened significance with the city of Jerusalem. No piece of real estate in Israel is more coveted. And in Jerusalem no property is more precious than the Temple Mount. LaHaye calls Mount Moriah, site of the ancient Jewish temple, "the most coveted ground in the world." As he explains, "The deep significance of the 1967 Six-Day War is seen in the prospect that at long last Israel can rebuild its temple. This is not just a national yearning—but a prophetic requirement of God's Word."[38]

LaHaye goes on to underscore what he considers to be the major dilemma: "The Muslims' multimillion-dollar Dome of the Rock is located on the spot where the temple should be."[39] He takes issue with those who suggest that the Jewish temple could coexist with the Muslim mosque. "Some have tried to suggest that perhaps this location is not the only place in Jerusalem the temple could be built, and thus the Muslim mosque and the Jewish temple could coexist. No careful Bible student would accept that reasoning. . . . There is no substitute on the face of the earth for that spot."[40] According to LaHaye, "there is no other single factor so likely to unite the Arabs in starting a holy war as the destruction of the Dome of the Rock."[41]

Such inflammatory rhetoric raises a host of troubling questions. Does the Bible indeed prophesy a rebuilt temple with reinstituted temple sacrifices that are *"for atonement* rather than a memorial"[42] on the exact piece of land on which the sacred mosque of the Muslims has stood for centuries? Is there truly a need to rebuild a temple and inflame the fires of Armageddon in the twenty-first century in light of our Messiah's first-century reminder that the time had come when true worshipers would no longer worship on a mountain in Samaria or in a temple in Jerusalem (John 4:21–22)? Ultimately, we must decide whether the land is the focus of the Lord or the Lord the locus of the land.

In the pages that follow, you will answer these and a host of other questions by internalizing and applying the principles of a methodology called Exegetical Eschatology or $\boxed{e^2}$. In the process you will not only be equipped to interpret the Bible for all it's worth but you may well discover that you hold the key to the problem of terrorism in one hand and the fuse of Armageddon in the other.

I

⸻ꝏꝏ⸻

EXEGETICAL ESCHATOLOGY $\boxed{e^2}$:
Method vs. Model

Dispensationalism is essential to correctly understand the Bible, especially Bible prophecy.

—TIM LAHAYE AND ED HINDSON, EDITORS,
THE POPULAR ENCYCLOPEDIA OF BIBLE PROPHECY

I coined the phrase Exegetical Eschatology $\boxed{e^2}$ *to underscore that above all else I am deeply committed to a proper method of biblical interpretation rather than to any particular model of eschatology.*

—HANK HANEGRAAFF, *THE APOCALYPSE CODE*

AS YOU HAVE NO DOUBT GUESSED, *THE APOCALYPSE Code* is about the end times. But it is about much more than simply the end times. It is about learning to read the Bible correctly. It's about learning to read the Bible for all it's worth! The backbone of the book is a principle I call Exegetical Eschatology. While the word *exegetical* may at first sound daunting, its meaning is easy to comprehend. *Exegesis* is the method by which a student seeks to uncover what an author intended his or her original audience to understand.[1] In sharp contrast, *eisegesis* is reading into the biblical text something that simply isn't there.

Like *exegetical*, the word *eschatology* is an intimidating word with a simple meaning—the study of end times. While the meaning of eschatology is simple to grasp, its importance is difficult to overemphasize. Far from being a mere branch in the theological tree, eschatology is the root that provides life and luster to every fiber of its being. Put another way, eschatology is the thread that weaves the tapestry of Scripture into a harmonious pattern. It is the study of everything we long and hope for.[2]

Early in Genesis, Adam and Eve fell into lives of habitual sin terminated by death. The rest of Scripture chronicles God's unfolding plan of redemption, culminating in the book of Revelation where Paradise lost becomes Paradise restored. Jesus returns. The dead in Christ are resurrected. And the problem of sin is fully and finally resolved.

I coined the phrase Exegetical Eschatology e^2 to underscore that above all else I am deeply committed to a proper *method* of biblical interpretation rather than to any particular *model* of eschatology. The plain and proper meaning of a biblical passage must always take precedence over a particular eschatological presupposition or paradigm.

To highlight the significance of proper methodology, I use the symbol e^2 interchangeably with the phrase Exegetical Eschatology. Just as in mathematics the squaring of a number increases its value exponentially, so too, perceiving eschatology through the prism of biblical exegesis will increase its value exponentially.

Ultimately, e^2 has its basis in a discipline known as hermeneutics. In Greek mythology, the task of the god Hermes was to interpret the will of the gods. In biblical hermeneutics, the task is to interpret the Word of God. Simply stated, hermeneutics is the art and science of biblical interpretation. It is a science in that certain rules apply. It is an art in that the more you apply these rules, the better you get at it.

My goal in the following pages is to put hermeneutical tools into your hands so that you can draw from Scripture what God intends you to understand rather than uncritically accepting end-time models that may well be foreign to the text. Dr. Tim LaHaye may sincerely believe that the Left Behind eschatology model is the result of faithful exegesis. However, with Exegetical Eschatology in hand, you will be the judge. In the final analysis, my purpose is not to entice you to embrace a particular model of eschatology but to employ a proper method of biblical interpretation.

I have organized the principles that are foundational to e^2 around the acronym LIGHTS. Just as helmet lights assist miners in discovering gold beneath the surface of the earth, so the acronym LIGHTS will aid you in drawing out of Scripture what God intends you to understand regarding the end times.[3]

Literal Principle

The *L* in LIGHTS will serve to remind you of the *literal principle* of Exegetical Eschatology. Simply put, this means that we are to interpret the Word of God just as we interpret other forms of communication—in the most obvious and natural sense. And when Scripture uses a metaphor or a figure of speech, we should interpret it accordingly.

For example, the Bible says that at Armageddon the blood of Christ's enemies will rise "as high as the horses' bridles for a distance of 1,600 stadia" (Revelation 14:20). Does Scripture intend to convey, as LaHaye contends, that Palestine will literally be submerged in a five-foot-deep river of blood that stretches the length of Palestine from north to south[4]—or is the apostle John simply using a common apocalyptic motif to convey massive wartime death and slaughter?

Conversely, when Daniel was instructed to seal up prophecy because the time of fulfillment was in the *far future* (Daniel 8:26; 12:4, 9; cf. 9:24), and John was told not to seal up his prophecy because its fulfillment was *near* (Revelation 22:10), are we to accept LaHaye's interpretation that by "near" John really intends to communicate "far"?[5] Or, for that matter, might we rightly suppose that the word "far" in Daniel really means "near"? Likewise, could John's repeated use of such words and phrases as "soon" or "the time is near," in reality indicate that he had the twenty-first century in mind?[6] Armed with the principles embodied in Exegetical Eschatology, you will be the judge.

Illumination Principle

The *I* in LIGHTS represents the *illumination principle* of Exegetical Eschatology. "We have not received the spirit of the world but the Spirit who is from God, that we may understand what God has freely given us" (1 Corinthians 2:12). The Spirit of truth not only provides insights that permeate the mind, but also provides illumination that penetrates the heart. Clearly, however, the Holy Spirit does not supplant the scrupulous study of Scripture. Rather, he provides us with insights that can only be spiritually discerned. Put another way, the Holy Spirit illumines what is *in* the text; illumination does not *go beyond* the text.

To underscore the significance of the illumination principle of Exegetical Eschatology, I will shine this principle

EXEGETICAL ESCHATOLOGY e²

on beliefs such as dispensational eschatology's cardinal doctrine—the pretribulational rapture. As we will see, prior to the nineteenth century, all Christians—including all premillennialists—believed the rapture or the resurrection of believers and the visible bodily return of Christ were simultaneous events. By the twenty-first century, however, Christian beliefs had experienced a radical transformation.

Due in part to the popularity of the Left Behind novels, multiplied millions are now convinced that Jesus will come back secretly and silently to rapture his church. Approximately seven years later he will come again with his church to establish a thousand-year semi-golden age replete with temple sacrifices. According to Tim LaHaye, "The Rapture was not a major teaching of our Lord except in John 14:1–3";[7] however, the pretribulational rapture doctrine is "taught clearly in 1 Thessalonians 4:13–18, where the apostle Paul provides us with most of the available details."[8]

In chapter 3 you will be equipped to determine whether the pretribulational rapture is the product of faithful illumination or the by-product of a fertile imagination.

Grammatical Principle

The *G* in LIGHTS represents the *grammatical principle* of Exegetical Eschatology. As with any literature, a thorough understanding of the Bible cannot be attained without a grasp of the basic rules that govern the relationships and usages of words.

For example, all scholars agree that in Matthew 23 Jesus is pronouncing judgment on the Jewish leaders when he says:

> Woe to *you*, teachers of the law and Pharisees, *you* hypocrites. . . . *You* snakes! *You* brood of vipers! How

5

will *you* escape being condemned to hell? Therefore I am sending *you* prophets and wise men and teachers. Some of them *you* will kill and crucify: others *you* will flog in *your* synagogues and pursue from town to town. And so upon *you* will come all the righteous blood that has been shed on earth, from the blood of righteous Abel to the blood of Zechariah son of Berekiah, whom *you* murdered between the temple and the altar. *I tell you the truth, all this will come upon this generation.* (vv. 29, 33–36)[9]

Grammatically, scholars see no option. "You" could not possibly refer to a future generation. And when Jesus says all this will come upon "this generation," he could not possibly have a future generation in mind.

In Matthew 24 Jesus continues to speak of the judgment that is about to fall on Jerusalem as well as on the very temple that gave the Jews their theological and sociological identity. Using final consummation language to characterize a near-future event, Jesus continues using the pronoun *you*:

You will hear of wars and rumors of wars. . . . Then *you* will be handed over to be persecuted and put to death, and *you* will be hated by all nations because of me. . . . When *you* see standing in the holy place "the abomination that causes desolation,". . . Pray that *your* flight will not take place in winter or on the Sabbath. . . . So if anyone tells *you*, "There he is, out in the desert," do not go out. . . . when *you* see all these things, *you* know that it is near, right at the door. I tell *you* the truth, *this generation* will certainly not pass away until all these things have happened. (Matthew 24:6–34)

Question: To whom is Jesus speaking in Matthew 24? Does Jesus have his first-century audience in mind as he does in Matthew 23? Or does Jesus have a twenty-first-century audience in mind? Again, when Jesus says, "I tell *you* the truth, *this generation* will certainly not pass away until all *these* things have happened" (Matthew 24:34), does he have a present generation or a future generation in mind?

Scholars such as D. A. Carson are convinced that the grammatical principle dictates that " 'this generation' . . . can only with the greatest difficulty be made to mean anything other than the generation living when Jesus spoke."[10] In sharp distinction, Tim LaHaye believes that by *this* generation our Lord had a future generation in mind. As the *Tim LaHaye Prophecy Study Bible* puts it, "This is a reference to the *future generation* that will live to see all the signs listed in the previous verses fulfilled in *their* lifetime."[11]

Are scholars like Carson properly applying the grammatical principle of biblical interpretation, or are prophecy experts such as LaHaye on target? Armed with the grammatical principle of Exegetical Eschatology, you (I mean *you*, not a future generation) will be an effective judge.

Historical Principle

The letter *H* in LIGHTS represents the *historical principle*. The Christian faith is historical and evidential. Thus, the biblical text is best understood when one is familiar with the customs, culture, and historical context of biblical times. Such background information is crucial in fully grasping what is going on in any given book of the Bible. In light of Exegetical Eschatology, it is particularly helpful to understand the historical context during which the book of Revelation was written. Was it written in the midsixties during the reign of the Roman emperor Nero, or was it written in the midnineties during the reign of Domitian?

The Left Behind series is based on the assumption that Revelation was written by the apostle John in AD 95. Thus, according to LaHaye, Revelation describes events that will take place in the twenty-first century rather than events that took place in the first century. In his words, "Revelation was written by John in AD 95, which means the book of Revelation describes yet future events of the last days just before Jesus comes back to this earth."[12] LaHaye goes on to argue that the Beast of Revelation is a twenty-first-century character. He is so certain of his position that he dismisses the notion that Nero was the Beast of Revelation and that the book of Revelation was written before AD 70 as "historically ridiculous."[13]

Placing the Beast in the twenty-first century, however, may well pose insurmountable historical difficulties. For example, the apostle John tells his first-century audience that with "wisdom" and "insight" they can "calculate the number of the beast, for it is man's number. His number is 666" (Revelation 13:18). Obviously no amount of wisdom would have enabled a first-century audience to figure out the number of a twenty-first-century Beast.

Again, you will be equipped to make a right judgment. Armed with Exegetical Eschatology, you will be enabled to discern whether or not LaHaye's late dating can stand in light of historical evidence.

Typology Principle

The *T* in the LIGHTS acronym represents the principle of *typology*. In terms of a proper end-times paradigm, this principle is of paramount importance. Persons, places, events, or things in redemptive history serve as types of Christ or spiritual realities pertaining to Christ. Palestine is typological of paradise. As Joshua led the people of Israel into the Promised Land, so too Jesus will lead his people into paradise. In our Lord's theology, there is no preoccupation with borders and boundaries. In LaHaye's theology, the physical land is of paramount importance.[14] Thus, we ask, Should we fixate on Palestine regained? Or should we, like our Lord, focus on Paradise restored? Armed with Exegetical Eschatology's *typology principle*, you will make a right judgment (cf. John 7:24).

Scriptural Synergy

Finally, the *S* in LIGHTS represents the principle of *scriptural synergy*. Simply stated, this means that the whole of Scripture is greater than the sum of its individual passages. You cannot comprehend the Bible as a whole without comprehending its individual parts, and you cannot comprehend its individual parts without comprehending the Bible as a whole. Individual passages of Scripture are synergistic rather than deflective with respect to the whole of Scripture.

Scriptural synergy demands that individual Bible passages may never be interpreted in such a way as to conflict with the whole of Scripture. Nor may we assign arbitrary meanings to words or phrases that have their referent in biblical history. The biblical interpreter must keep in mind that all Scripture, though communicated through various human instruments, has one single Author. And that Author does not contradict himself, nor does he confuse his servants.

As mentioned, the book of Revelation contains more than four hundred verses. More than two-thirds of these verses contain symbols that have a referent in Old Testament history. As a picture is worth a thousand words, so such symbols are worth a thousand passages. So, when John uses symbolism such as the mark of the Beast, is his intention to give twenty-first-century Christians a heads-up on the nefarious use of social security cards or computer chips? Or is he drawing our attention to "a thousand" biblical allusions ranging from Genesis to Ezekiel? With the principle of *scriptural synergy* in hand, you will be equipped to make a right judgment.

A final note before we move on: Each of the principles of Exegetical Eschatology is a category unto itself but is seldom applied in isolation. The application of each letter in the LIGHTS acronym is required to determine what John, for example, means when he says that the Beast "forced everyone, small and great, rich and poor, free and slave, to receive a mark on his right hand or on his forehead" (Revelation 13:16).

The literal principle demands that this text be interpreted in the sense in which it is intended rather than in a literalistic sense. If I tell you that it is raining cats and dogs, my intent is to convey that it is raining hard—not that cats and dogs are literally falling from the sky. Likewise, the context of Revelation leads to the inevitable conclusion that the mark of the Beast is symbolic language intended to convey identification with the Beast.

The illumination principle adds clarity in that the Holy Spirit illumines what is in the text; illumination does not go beyond the text. Thus the notion that the mark of the Beast is Sunday worship, a social security number, or a silicon microchip is the product of a fertile imagination rather than faithful illumination.

The grammatical principle precludes LaHaye's interpretation that the mark is a biochip physically imbedded *in* the body.[15] By LaHaye's own standard, a grammatically accurate interpretation would require that the mark is specifically placed *on* the right hand and forehead rather than being scientifically implanted *in* the body (see Revelation 13:16).

The historical principle similarly precludes LaHaye's notion that the mark of the Beast is the physical implantation of a biochip. In context John tells first-century readers that with "wisdom" and "insight" they can "calculate the number of the beast." No amount of wisdom and insight would have allowed John's first-century audience to calculate the number of a twenty-first century Beast. Nor would a first-century Beast have been able to employ twenty-first century biochip technology.

The typology principle adds to our understanding by underscoring that the mark of the Beast is simply a parody of the mark of the Lamb. Just as the mark written on the foreheads of the 144,000 in Revelation 14 symbolizes identity with the Lamb, so the mark on the right hand and the forehead in Revelation 13 symbolizes identity with the Beast.

Finally, *the principle of scriptural synergy* warns us not to interpret the mark of the Beast in a way that conflicts with Scripture as a whole. Thus, saying that the 144,000 have the Lamb's name written on their foreheads is a symbolic way of identifying them with Christ. Likewise, when Jesus says, "I will write on him [the one who overcomes] the name of my God, and the name of the city of my God . . . and I will also write on him my new name" (Revelation 3:12), we intuitively realize that Jesus does not have a Magic Marker in mind.

In short, the principles of Exegetical Eschatology taken as a whole preclude the possibility that followers of the Beast are twenty-first-century characters with biochip technology implanted in their bodies. Might it be therefore that John's symbolism points to a far more graphic reality? Could it be that our right hand symbolizes what we do and our forehead symbolizes what we think? Might the mark metaphorically identify us as either belonging to the Beast or belonging to the Lamb—to the Christ or to the Antichrist? Again, armed with Exegetical Eschatology, you will be empowered to make a right judgment.

2

—◈◈◈—

LITERAL PRINCIPLE:
Reading the Bible as Literature

But even if you believe the Bible—the people who wrote the Bible—it was not meant to be history. It was not meant to be literal. They were parables. People read it back then and read into it something that was not literal. We're the dummies who read it literally.

—BILL MAHER, HOST OF ABC'S
POLITICALLY INCORRECT

Many teachers today are confusing Christians by teaching that Scripture was never intended to be interpreted literally. Instead, they call for a spiritualizing or allegorizing of the Bible's prophecies. This only leads to confusion!

—TIM LAHAYE, *CHARTING THE END TIMES*

FOR MORE THAN A DECADE NOW, POPULAR TV personality Bill Maher has made a cottage industry out of ridiculing religion. "I believed all this stuff when I was young," quips Maher. "I believed there was a virgin birth, I believed a man lived inside of a whale, and I believed that the Earth was five thousand years old. But then something very important happened to me—I graduated sixth grade." In an interview with the *Chicago Sun-Times*, Maher went on to pontificate dogmatically that the Bible was "written in parables. It's the idiots today who take it literally."[1]

Tim LaHaye is of an opposite persuasion. He goes to great lengths to emphasize that, unlike "the false teacher" who traffics in the "bizarre," he is deeply committed to the literal principle of biblical interpretation. According to LaHaye, "readers take Scripture literally whenever possible—unless some false teacher has clouded their thinking, rendering prophecy virtually impossible to understand by trying to interpret it through symbols or confusing allegories."[2]

Although Bill Maher and Tim LaHaye are polar extremes, they have one thing in common. They both misconstrue the literal principle of biblical interpretation. Theologian R. C. Sproul has aptly said, "To interpret the Bible literally is to interpret it as literature."[3] Simply put, this means that we are to interpret the Word of God just as we interpret other forms of communication—in its most obvious and natural sense.[4] Thus, when a biblical writer uses a symbol or an allegory, we do violence to his intentions if we interpret it in a strictly literal manner. For example, when the apostle John describes Satan as a "dragon" and an "ancient serpent," we would be seriously mistaken to suppose that he intends to communicate that Satan is literally a smoke-spouting snake.

Conversely, it would be peculiarly prejudicial to pontificate that Dr. Luke is intending to pen a parable when he begins his gospel narrative with words such as the following:

> Many have undertaken to *draw up an account* of the things that have been fulfilled among us, just as they were handed down to us by those who from the first

were *eyewitnesses* and servants of the word. Therefore, since I myself have *carefully investigated everything from the beginning*, it seemed good also to me *to write an orderly account* for you, most excellent Theophilus, so that you may know the certainty of the things you have been taught. (Luke 1:1–4)

Even a cursory reading reveals that Scripture is a treasury replete with a wide variety of literary styles, ranging from poetry, proverbs, and psalms to historical narratives, didactic epistles, and apocalyptic revelations. To dogmatically assert that the Bible was written in parables and that those who read it literally must be "idiots" is at best an idiosyncratic form of fundamentalism and at worst a serious misunderstanding of the literal principle of biblical interpretation.

The Bible does contain parables (as should be obvious to those who have "graduated sixth grade"), but it is not entirely parabolic. The virgin birth account, for example, is clearly presented in Scripture as a historical narrative rather than a parable. If Maher had read Scripture with an open mind— paying attention to genre, grammar, syntax, semantics, and context—he would have recognized that his faith was placed in a dogmatic assertion rather than a defensible argument. As apologetics is the means by which the validity of the virgin birth is historically established, so literary analysis is the method by which the virgin birth account is established as a historical narrative.

While Bill Maher obviously misunderstands what it means to read the Bible literally, Tim LaHaye's definition of literalism is virtually meaningless. He calls it the "Golden Rule of Biblical Interpretation" and warns that "to depart from this rule opens the student to all forms of confusion and sometimes even heresy."⁵

He defines the Golden Rule of Biblical Interpretation as follows: "When the plain sense of Scripture makes common sense, seek no other sense, but take every word at its primary, literal meaning unless the facts of the immediate context clearly indicate otherwise."⁶ Not only is there nothing distinctive about this definition, but it is so vague as to be utterly useless. Plain sense to a first-century Jew is clearly not plain sense to LaHaye. And common sense to LaHaye is clearly not common sense to those he dismisses as "false teachers."

Take, for example, our Lord's words in John 14:1–3: "Do not let your hearts be troubled. Trust in God; trust also in me. In my Father's house are many rooms; if it were not so, I would have told you. I am going there to prepare a place for you. And If I go and prepare a place for you, I will come back, and take you to be with me that you also may be where I am." According to the *Tim LaHaye Prophecy Study Bible*, this is "the first teaching on the Rapture in Scripture."⁷

Despite the fact that the majority of Christians, past and present, do not believe that the plain sense of this passage points to a pretribulational rapture, LaHaye writes:

> Most believers find it easier to take Bible prophecies *literally* whenever possible, believing that Christ will indeed rapture His church to heaven, just as He promised in John 14:1–3. They believe that the earth will go through a seven-year Tribulation, as described in Revelation 6–18. And they believe that Christ will return in glory, set up His promised earthly kingdom for one thousand years (Revelation 19–20), and then

take all believers to heaven to live with Him forever (Revelation 21–22). Obviously this *literal* interpretation is much easier to understand—and gives greater hope for humankind's future.[8]

Prior to the nineteenth century, all Christians, futurists included, believed that a commonsense reading of Scripture inevitability led to the conclusion that the second coming/ bodily return of Christ and the rapture/resurrection of believers are simultaneous events.[9] Thus, a plain-sense or commonsense reading of passages like John 14:1–3 did not lead believers to believe in a pretribulational rapture. Indeed, John Nelson Darby, the father of dispensationalism himself, did not derive the pretribulational rapture theory on the basis of a commonsense reading of Scripture. Rather, as historian Timothy Weber points out, Darby perceived the pretribulational rapture teaching in Scripture only after he presupposed "the absolute distinction between Israel and the church in the prophetic plans of God."[10]

It should also be noted that LaHaye does not live up to his own standard of taking "every word at its primary, literal meaning unless the facts of the *immediate* context clearly indicate otherwise." For example, when our Lord says "the time is *near*," LaHaye says the time is far off; when our Lord says the apocalypse "must *soon* take place," LaHaye says the apocalypse is in the distant future; and when our Lord says to his disciples, "I tell you the truth, some who are standing here will not taste death before they see the Son of Man coming in his kingdom" (Matthew 16:28), LaHaye says our Lord is speaking of "the second coming," even though every one of the disciples would have long ago tasted death. Many other examples could be cited, including our Lord's words recorded in Matthew 10:23, "I tell you the truth, you will not finish going through the cities of Israel before the Son of Man *comes.*"[11]

What is particularly disturbing is the rhetoric LaHaye reserves for those who do not subscribe to his understanding of what is and is not literal. According to LaHaye, "Readers take Scripture literally whenever possible—unless some false teacher has clouded their thinking, rendering prophecy virtually impossible to understand by trying to interpret it through symbols or confusing allegories."[12]

After judging the motives of his critics, LaHaye comments on their methods:

> One thing most of the detractors of our books have in common is a tendency to allegorize or spiritualize prophecy. Some take the rest of Scripture *literally*, but insist that prophecy is somehow different. According to them, we need to be looking for some deeper, "secret meaning" other than the *literal* message conveyed by the words on the page. Once you begin heading down that road, however, everything is up for grabs. You can invent any kind of "interpretation" you want.[13]

Ironically, by LaHaye's standards, our Lord and his disciples could easily be pawned off as false teachers who allegorize or spiritualize prophecy. Consider our Lord's words in John 2:19: "Destroy this temple, and I will raise it again in three days." The Jews interpreted Jesus in a wooden, literal fashion. They understood the plain-sense or commonsense meaning of Jesus's words to refer directly and specifically to the destruction of their temple, which had taken "forty-six years to build" (John 2:20). Jesus, however, spiritualized his prophecy. As the apostle John explains, "The temple he had spoken of was his body" (v. 21).[14]

Ultimately the "deeper" meaning of this passage points to the fact that after our Lord's sacrifice and subsequent resurrection, the temple would no longer have substantial significance. When the types and shadows of temple sacrifices were supplanted by the substance of the Savior's sacrifice, the temple could forever be dispensed with. Additionally, the very notion of sacrifice is in itself metaphorical with respect to the crucifixion of Christ. G. B. Caird goes so far as to say: "The death of Christ was no sacrifice, but a criminal execution, regarded by the one side as a political necessity and by the other as a miscarriage of justice. But because Christ himself chose to regard his death as a sacrifice, and by his words at the Last Supper taught his disciples so to do, he transformed its tragedy into something he could offer to God to be used in the service of his purpose." Caird goes on to say that since the metaphor of Christ's death as a sacrifice has "manifestly changed the shape of history, it serves as a rebuke to those who talk carelessly of 'mere metaphor.'"[15]

LaHaye's misunderstanding of the cardinal truth of Christ's sacrifice has serious ramifications. The writer of Hebrews explicitly says that in Christ the old covenant order, including temple sacrifices, are "obsolete" and "will soon disappear" (Hebrews 8:13). In direct contradiction to the literal meaning of this passage, LaHaye teaches that the temple must be rebuilt and that temple sacrifices must be reinstituted. Even more troubling is the fact that LaHaye's literalism forces him to conclude that such temple sacrifices are not merely memorial but absolutely necessary for the atonement of sins such as ceremonial uncleanness.[16]

The danger of LaHaye's literalistic approach is that "once you begin heading down that road, everything is up for grabs," including the sufficiency of Christ's atonement on the cross and his bodily resurrection. As noted in the introduction, LaHaye's literalism causes him to conclude that the Antichrist has the power to lay down his life and to take it up again, thus demonstrating that he is God. Not only does LaHaye's interpretation of Revelation 13 militate against the uniqueness of Christ's resurrection, but drawn to its logical conclusion, it erodes epistemic warrant for the resurrection and ultimately the deity of our Lord. Likewise, if temple sacrifices in the Millennium are efficacious for ceremonial uncleanness, Christ's atonement on the cross was not sufficient for all sin (see Hebrews 7:26–27; 9:12, 26, 28; 10:10–12).[17]

To avoid the dangers of hyper-literalism, one must adeptly employ the literal principle of biblical interpretation. Rather than viewing all of Scripture through the opaque lens of wooden literalism, the careful student of the Bible recognizes and accurately interprets *form*, *figurative language*, and *fantasy imagery*.

FORM

To interpret the Bible literally, we must first pay special attention to what is known as *form* or *genre*. In other words, to interpret the Bible as literature, it is crucial to consider the kind of literature we are interpreting. Just as a legal brief differs in form from a prophetic oracle, so too there is a difference in genre between Leviticus and Revelation. Recognizing the genre is particularly important when considering writings that are difficult to categorize, such as Genesis, which is largely a historical narrative interlaced with symbolism and repetitive poetic structure.

If Genesis were reduced to an allegory conveying merely abstract ideas about temptation, sin, and redemption, devoid of any correlation with actual events in history, the very foundation of Christianity would be destroyed. If the historical Adam and Eve did not eat the forbidden fruit and descend into a life of habitual sin resulting in death, there is no need for redemption. And if we consider Satan to be a slithering snake, we would not only misunderstand the nature of fallen angels, but we might also suppose that Jesus triumphed over the work of the devil by stepping on the head of a serpent (Genesis 3:15) rather than through his passion on the cross (Colossians 2:15).

A literalistic method of interpretation often does as much violence to the text as does a spiritualized interpretation that empties the text of objective meaning. A literal-at-all-costs method of interpretation is particularly troublesome when it comes to books of the Bible in which visionary imagery is the governing genre. For example, in Revelation the apostle John sees an apocalyptic vision in which an angel swinging a sharp sickle gathers grapes into "the great winepress of the wrath of God." The blood flowing out of the winepress rises as high as "the horses' bridles for a distance of 1,600 stadia" (14:19–20).

Interpreting apocalyptic imagery in a woodenly literal sense inevitably leads to absurdity. For example, the *Tim LaHaye Prophecy Study Bible* argues that the apostle John intends to convey that the blood of Christ's enemies will literally create a river of blood. Since it is difficult to imagine that the blood of Christ's enemies could create a literal river reaching as high as "the horses' bridles for a distance of 1,600 stadia," LaHaye exercises extraordinary literary license. As

21

his study Bible puts it, "Hailstones weighing 'a talent [ca. 100 pounds]' will fall from heaven (Rev. 16:21) which, with the blood of this massive army, will create a river of blood that reaches up to the horses' bridles."[18]

LaHaye's failure to consider form or genre not only leads to unbridled speculation, but ultimately misses the underlying significance of Revelation's apocalyptic imagery. Far from merely communicating that twenty-first-century Israel would be submerged in a literal river of blood, John is using the apocalyptic language of Old Testament prophets to warn his hearers of the massive judgment and destruction of the land of Israel that "must soon take place." As Isaiah and Joel used the language of sickles, winepresses, and blood to symbolize judgment against the enemies of Israel's God, so John now uses the language of the prophets to signify the impending doom of apostate Israel.

The student of Scripture immediately recognizes that the symbolic imagery used by John is multifaceted and masterful. John does not merely recapitulate the apocalyptic imagery of the prophets and apply them to the current crisis. He reconfigures and expands them to cosmic proportions as the King of Kings and Lord of Lords "treads the winepress of the fury of the wrath of God Almighty" (Revelation 19:15–16). Once he lay prostrate before his creation in the pool of his own blood, but now the blood flowing from the winepress signifies judgment for the unrepentant who cried out, "Let his blood be on us and on our children!" (Matthew 27:25).

And even then the symbolism is not exhausted. In the tapestry of Revelation's imagery, the blood-spattered robe of Christ is not only emblematic of grapes of wrath but of blood that flowed from Immanuel's veins. And still we have but scratched the surface of John's majestic imagery. As the seven heads of the

Beast point to seven hills and seven kings and as the seven lampstands symbolize seven churches,[19] so too the number sixteen hundred is pregnant with meaning. As Dr. David Chilton explains, the number sixteen hundred is a number that uniquely emphasizes Palestine. Four squared symbolizes the land and ten squared is emblematic of the largeness of the land. "Sixteen hundred stadia is slightly more than the length of Palestine: the whole Land of Israel is thus represented as overflowing with blood in the coming nationwide judgment. . . . Old Israel has become apostate and unclean, her horses swimming in blood."[20]

The point here is to underline in red the need to seriously consider form or genre in order to rightly interpret the Revelation of Jesus Christ. In the words of Dr. Dennis Johnson, "the literal meaning of a piece of language depends on what type of language it is, its genre. The literal meaning of symbolic language is the symbolic correspondence between the imagery of the language and the referent that it describes."[21] Johnson goes on to emphasize that "a literal-where-possible hermeneutic" is not particularly helpful when "visionary symbolism is the dominant feature of a book's genre."[22]

FIGURATIVE LANGUAGE

Furthermore, it is crucial to recognize that Scripture—particularly apocalyptic portions of Scripture—is replete with figurative language. Such language differs from literal language, in which words mean exactly what they say. Figurative language requires readers to use their imagination to comprehend what the author is driving at. Such imaginative leaps are the rule rather than the exception in that virtually every genre of literature contains metaphorical language.

Dr. Gene Edward Veith uses the following statement to underscore this seminal truth:

> Many people have *bouts of depression*, but when they learn to *reach out* to others they find that life looks *brighter* [emphasis added] . . . .[While] the term *depression* literally means a low point in the ground; it has become a metaphor for a mental condition, of feeling "low" (another metaphor). *Bout* refers to a round of fighting. The gesture of "reaching out" and the optical image of something becoming "brighter" are more obvious metaphors. The point is (notice the metaphor involved in that phrase), dull prose (another metaphor) is actually alive with unconscious metaphors.[23]

Scripture certainly is not the exception to Veith's observations about metaphorical language. In fact, we might well say that figurative language is the principle means by which God communicates spiritual realities to his children. In other words, God communicates spiritual realities through means of earthly, empirically perceptible events, persons, or objects—what might best be described as living metaphors.

There are a wide variety of ways in which the inspired authors of the biblical text employ figurative language. Three of the most basic literary terms used to classify these figures of speech are metaphor, simile, and hyperbole.

Metaphor

A metaphor is an implied comparison that identifies a word or phrase with something that it does not literally represent. Far from minimizing biblical truth, metaphors serve as a magnifying glass that identifies truth we might otherwise miss. This identification creates a meaning that lies beyond a woodenly literal interpretation and thus requires an imaginative leap to grasp what is meant. For example, when Jesus said, "I am the bread of life" (John 6:48), he was obviously not saying that he was literally the "staff of life" (i.e., physical bread). Rather, he was metaphorically communicating that he is the "stuff of life" (i.e., the essence of true life).

Biblical metaphors are never to be regarded as vacuous occasions for subjective flights of fantasy. On the contrary, biblical metaphors are always objectively meaningful, authoritative, and true. As Dr. N. T. Wright so poignantly puts it, apocalyptic language may never be dismissed as " 'merely metaphorical.' Metaphors have teeth" and "the complex metaphors available to first-century Jews had particularly sharp ones."[24]

A classic case in point involves Christ's reply to Caiaphas on the eve of his crucifixion. "Tell us if you are the Christ, the Son of God" Caiaphas demanded. " 'Yes, it is as you say,' Jesus replied. 'But I say to all of you: In the future you will see the Son of Man sitting at the right hand of the Mighty One and *coming on the clouds of heaven'* " (Matthew 26:63–64). A biblically illiterate person might well have missed the import of Jesus's words. Caiaphas and the Sanhedrin, however, did not. If ever there was a razor-sharp metaphor, this was it. It cut Caiaphas and the court condemning Christ to the quick.

First, they understood that in saying he was "the Son of Man" who would come "on the clouds of heaven," Jesus was making an overt reference to his coronation as the Son of Man in Daniel's vision (Daniel 7:13–14). In doing so, he was not only claiming to be the preexistent Sovereign of the universe, but prophesying that he would vindicate his claim before the very court that was now condemning him to death. It is crucial to note that in Daniel's prophecy the Son of Man is not *descending* to earth at the end of history but rather *ascending* to heaven. Moreover, by combining Daniel's prophecy with David's proclamation in Psalm 110, Jesus was claiming that he would ascend to the throne of Israel's God and share God's very glory. To students of the Old Testament, this was the height of blasphemy, thus "they all condemned him as worthy of death" (Mark 14:63–64).[25]

Further, as Caiaphas and the Sanhedrin well knew, "clouds" were a common Old Testament symbol pointing to God as the sovereign Judge of the nations. In the words of Ezekiel, "the day of the LORD is near—a day of *clouds*, a time of doom for the nations" (Ezekiel 30:3). Similarly, Joel writes, "The day of the LORD is coming. It is close at hand—a day of darkness and gloom, a day of *clouds* and blackness" (Joel 2:1–2). Isaiah is even more specific in relating the metaphor "coming on clouds" to the motif of judgment: "See, the LORD rides on a swift *cloud* and is *coming* to Egypt. The idols of Egypt tremble before him, and the hearts of the Egyptians melt within them" (Isaiah 19:1).

Like the Old Testament prophets, Jesus employs the symbolism of clouds to warn his hearers that as judgment fell on Egypt, so too, judgment would soon befall Jerusalem. Using final consummation language to characterize a near-future event, the Master of Metaphor declares, "At that time the sign of the Son of Man will appear in the sky, and all the nations of the earth will mourn. They will see the Son of Man coming on the clouds of the sky, with power and great glory" (Matthew 24:30). Gary DeMar rightly notes that "Jesus was not telling them to look for Himself in the sky. He told them that they

26

would see a *sign* that proved He was in heaven, sitting at His Father's right hand (Acts 2:30–36). Those who had witnessed Jerusalem's destruction would see the sign of Jesus's enthronement when they saw Jerusalem's destruction."[26]

Finally, the "coming on clouds" judgment metaphor was clearly not directed to a twenty-first-century audience as LaHaye presumes. Rather, it was intended for Caiaphas and the first-century crowd that condemned Christ to death. In the words of our Lord, "I say to all of *you*: In the future *you* will *see* the Son of Man sitting at the right hand of the Mighty One and coming on the clouds of heaven" (Matthew 26:64). The generation that crucified Christ would *see* the day that he was exalted and enthroned at "the right hand of the Mighty One" (another metaphor).

John makes this point explicit in Revelation 1:7: "Look, he is *coming with the clouds*, and *every eye will see him* [yet another metaphor], *even those who pierced him*; and all the peoples of the earth will mourn because of him. So shall it be! Amen" (emphasis added). As Chilton explains, "The crucifiers would see Him coming in judgment—that is, they would *experience* and *understand* that His Coming would mean wrath on the Land. . . . In the destruction of their city, their civilization, their Temple, their entire world-order, they would understand that Christ had ascended to His Throne as Lord of heaven and earth."[27] Seeing is commonly used as a metaphor for intellectual insight, while blindness is used for intellectual incomprehension.

Simile

Like a metaphor, a simile draws a comparison between two things, but whereas the comparison is *implicit* in a metaphor, it is *explicit* in a simile. Similes employ words such as "like" or "as" in making the comparison. Note for example, the similes the apostle John uses in his description of Jesus.

> Among the lampstands was someone *"like* a son of man," dressed in a robe reaching down to his feet and with a golden sash around his chest. His head and hair were white *like* wool, as white *as* snow and his eyes were *like* blazing fire. His feet were *like* bronze glowing in a furnace and his voice was *like* the sound of rushing waters. In his right hand he held seven stars, and out of his mouth came a sharp double-edged sword. His face was *like* the sun shining in all its brilliance. (Revelation 1:13–16)

Comparisons such as parables or allegories beginning with the word *like* are simply extended similes. A classic case in point is the parable of the mustard seed in which Jesus asks, "What shall we say the kingdom of God is *like*, or what parable shall we use to describe it? It is *like* a mustard seed, which is the smallest seed you plant in the ground. Yet when planted, it grows and becomes the largest of all garden plants, with such big branches that the birds of the air can perch in its shade" (Mark 4:30–32).

As with metaphors, the danger is to interpret similes in a woodenly literal fashion. The kingdom of God is obviously not like a mustard seed in every way. Nor does Jesus intend to make his parables "walk on all fours." A kingdom does not look like a mustard seed, nor is a mustard seed the smallest seed in the kingdom. Rather the kingdom of God is like a mustard seed in the sense that it begins small and becomes large.

While a hyperliteral reading is dangerous, it is also deflective to read more than what is warranted into an extended

28

simile. Jesus's parable is not intended to give us a lesson on plant development and growth. Nor did Jesus mistakenly think that a black mustard seed was smaller than an orchid seed. Instead, he was using the smallest of seeds familiar to Palestinian farmers to illustrate that while the kingdom of God began in obscurity in the end it would "fill the earth" and "endure forever" (Daniel 2:31–45).

Even Augustine "who favored restricting theology to the literal sense, nevertheless often speculated wildly."[28]

C. H. Dodd quotes as a cautionary example Augustine's allegorization of the Good Samaritan, in which the man [who fell into the hands of robbers] is Adam, Jerusalem the heavenly city, Jericho the moon—the symbol of mortality; the thieves are the devil and his angels, who strip the man of immortality by persuading him to sin and so leave him (spiritually) half dead; the priest and Levite represent the Old Testament, the Samaritan Christ, the beast his flesh which he assumed in the Incarnation; the inn is the church and the innkeeper the apostle Paul.[29]

Caird explains that such interpretive methodology spells the difference between *allegorization* and *allegory*: "An allegory is a story intended by the author to convey a hidden meaning, and it is correctly interpreted when that intended meaning is perceived. To allegorize is to impose on a story hidden meanings which the original author neither intended nor envisaged; it is to treat as allegory that which was *not* intended as allegory."[30] Caird goes on to point out that if Jesus composed similes "with more than one point of comparison, it makes little difference to our understanding of them whether we call them parables or allegories, so long as we recognize that to identify intended points is *not* to allegorize."[31]

Hyperbole

Hyperbole is another figure of speech particularly prevalent in prophetic passages. In essence, hyperbole employs exaggeration for effect or emphasis. Etymologically it is defined as exaggerated "overcasting" or extravagant "overshooting." If you step onto a scale and exclaim, "O my goodness, I weigh a ton!" you are obviously not intending to say that you literally weigh two thousand pounds. Nor is the phrase, "I was so surprised, you could have knocked me over with a feather," intended to convey that you weigh nothing at all. Similarly, when an NBA commentator looks up at the clock, sees a minute left, and says, "There's a world of time left in this game," he is using hyperbole to communicate that in the NBA a lot can happen in sixty seconds.

While hyperbole is commonly used in our culture, it is virtually ubiquitous in the Bible. This is particularly true of prophetic passages. In prophesying Jerusalem's destruction, Jesus says, "For then there will be great distress unequaled from the beginning of the world until now—and never to be equaled again" (Matthew 24:21). In doing so, he was not literally predicting that the destruction of Jerusalem would be more cataclysmic than the catastrophe caused by Noah's flood.[32] Rather, he was using apocalyptic hyperbole to underscore the distress and devastation that would be experienced when Jerusalem and its temple were judged.

Jesus goes on to predict that "immediately after the distress of those days '*the sun will be darkened, and the moon will not give its light; the stars will fall from the sky, and the heavenly bodies will be shaken'"* (Matthew 24:29). Again, Jesus is not predicting the eradication of the cosmos. Nor is he prophesying the end of civilization. If he were, there would have been no point in warning his followers to leave Judea and flee to the mountains. Rather, Jesus is employing hyperbolic language that is deeply rooted in Old Testament history.[11]

The prophet Isaiah used similar hyperbolic language when he predicted judgment on Babylon:

> See, the day of the LORD is coming
> —a cruel day, with wrath and fierce anger—
> to make the land desolate
> and destroy the sinners within it.
> *The stars of heaven and their constellations*
> *will not show their light.*
> *The rising sun will be darkened*
> *and the moon will not give its light.*
>
> (ISAIAH 13:9–10)

To those unfamiliar with biblical language, these words may well be taken to mean that the end of the world was at hand. In reality, Isaiah was prophesying that the Medes were about to put an end to the glories of the Babylonian Empire.

For evidence one need only read the preceding verses, which are packed full of prophetic hyperbole:

> Wail, for the day of the LORD is near;
> it will come like destruction from the Almighty.
> Because of this, *all hands will go limp,*
> *every man's heart will melt.*

31

Terror will seize them,
pain and anguish will grip them;
they will writhe like a woman in labor.
They will look aghast at each other,
their faces aflame.

(ISAIAH 13:6–8)

Even the most pedantic literalist intuitively recognizes that Isaiah is not literally intending to infer that all hands will literally go limp and that every heart will literally melt. Nor is he literalistically predicting that every Babylonian face will be on fire any more than John is using wooden literalism to prophesy that Revelation's two witnesses will literally emit flames of fire from their mouths (Revelation 11:5).

If the Old Testament prophet Isaiah used such apocalyptic hyperbole to predict the destruction of Babylon, we must inevitably ask ourselves whether it is indeed credible to suppose "that Jesus, the heir to the linguistic and theological riches of the prophets, and himself a greater theologian and master of imagery than them all, should ever have turned their symbols into flat and literal prose."[34]

FANTASY IMAGERY

Finally, in apocalyptic passages, it is crucial to correctly interpret fantasy imagery, such as an enormous red dragon with seven heads and ten horns;[35] locusts with human faces, women's hair, and lions' teeth;[36] and a beast that resembles a leopard with feet like a bear and a mouth like a lion.[37] What is distinct about such fantasy images is that they do not correspond to anything in the real world. As Veith explains, "A realism that confines itself to descriptions of only those things that can be seen in ordinary life necessarily excludes that which remains unseen but which nonetheless gives ordinary life its meaning, namely, truths of morality, faith, and transcendent ideals."[38] Thus, while fantasy images are unreal, they provide a realistic means by which to ponder reality.

In *How to Read the Bible for All Its Worth*, Dr. Gordon Fee provides us with an apt contrast between the fantasy imagery used in apocalyptic portions of Scripture and the figurative images used elsewhere in the Bible. As Fee explains, the non-apocalyptic prophets and Jesus "regularly used symbolic language, but most often it involved real images, for example, salt (Matt. 5:13), vultures and carcasses (Luke 17:37), silly doves (Hos. 7:11), half-baked cakes (Hos. 7:8), et al. But most of the images of apocalyptic belong to fantasy, for example, a beast with seven heads and ten horns (Rev.13:1), a woman clothed with the sun (Revelation 12:1), locusts with scorpions tails and human heads (Revelation 9:10), et al." Fee goes on to note that "the fantasy may not necessarily appear in the items themselves (we understand beasts, heads, and horns) but in their unearthly combination."[39]

Throughout the ages, Christian writers from John Bunyan to J. R. R. Tolkien and C. S. Lewis have emulated the biblical use of fantasy imagery to underscore the cardinal truths of a Christian worldview. Puritan writer William Gurnall used the otherworldly image of a man's head on a beast's shoulders to highlight the reality that righteousness without truth is abhorrent. As Gurnall put it, "An orthodox judgment coming from an unholy heart and an ungodly life is as ugly as *a man's head would be on a beast's shoulders.* The wretch who knows truth but practices evil is worse than the man who is ignorant."[40] Gurnall thus used an imaginary troll to portray an invisible truth.

Fantasy imagery, of course, is fraught with danger. That danger, however, does not lie in its use but in its abuse. In Revelation 12 the apostle John describes "an enormous red dragon with seven heads and ten horns and seven crowns on his heads. His tail swept a third of the stars out of the sky and flung them to the earth" (vv. 3–4). Interpreting such imagery in a literalistic fashion misses the point of the passage. Not only would a single star—let alone a third of the stars—obliterate earth, but dragons are the stuff of mythology not theology. The apostle John does not want us to believe that dragons are real, nor does he want us to believe that a dragon's tail could sweep a third of the stars out of the sky. Instead, he wants us to understand the reality of the devil's "cunning wisdom (seven heads), great power (ten horns), and authority to influence others (seven diadems)."[41]

A chapter later, John describes another beast he saw coming out of the sea.

> He had ten horns and seven heads, with ten crowns on his horns, and on each head a blasphemous name. The beast I saw resembled a leopard, but had feet like those of a bear and a mouth like that of a lion. The dragon gave the beast his power and his throne and great authority. One of the heads of the beast seemed to have had a fatal wound, but the fatal wound had been healed. The whole world was astonished and followed the beast. (Revelation 13:1–3)

Again the danger lies in missing the point of such fantasy imagery.

Dr. Dennis Johnson explains that "the beast is not only an image bearer of the dragon but also an imitation of the Lamb."[42] As an imitation of the Lamb, the Beast can parody the work of Christ but cannot duplicate the work of Christ. Thus, once again LaHaye is seriously misguided in supposing that the Beast, like the Lamb, has the power to lay down his life and to take it up again. Again the danger does not lie in the use of fantasy imagery, but in uncritically impregnating these images with unbiblical notions.

———

I began this chapter by noting that although Bill Maher and Tim LaHaye are polar extremes when it comes to interpreting Scripture, they do have one thing in common: they both misconstrue the literal principle of biblical interpretation. Maher supposes that all of Scripture is parabolic, while LaHaye holds that Scripture—particularly prophetic portions of Scripture—are impossible to comprehend "through symbols or confusing allegories." Both are seriously mistaken. To read the Bible for all it's worth, it is crucial to read it as literature, paying close attention to form, figurative language, and fantasy imagery. This is particularly true of the Revelation of Jesus Christ, which in part is a letter, in part is prophecy, and in part points to an impending apocalypse.

While the Scriptures must indeed be read as literature, you and I must ever be mindful that the Bible is not merely literature. Instead, the Scriptures are uniquely inspired by the Spirit. As Peter put it, "No prophecy of Scripture came about by the prophet's own interpretation. For prophecy never had its origin in the will of man, but men spoke from God as they were carried along by the Holy Spirit" (2 Peter 1:20–21). We must therefore fervently pray that the Spirit, who inspired the Scriptures, illumines our minds to what is *in* the text. With that in mind, we now turn to the illumination principle of $\boxed{e^2}$.

3

ILLUMINATION PRINCIPLE:
Faithful Illumination vs. Fertile Imagination

One of the most compelling prophetic events in the Bible is called the "rapture" of the church. It is taught clearly in 1 Thessalonians 4:13-18, where the apostle Paul provides us with most of the available details.

—TIM LaHAYE AND JERRY JENKINS,
ARE WE LIVING IN THE END TIMES?

No single verse specifically states, "Christ will come before the Tribulation." On the other hand, no single passage teaches He will not come before the Tribulation, or that He will come in the middle or at the end of the Tribulation. Any such explicit declaration would end the debate immediately.

—TIM LaHAYE, *NO FEAR OF THE STORM*
(EMPHASIS IN ORIGINAL)

CONSIDER A DOGMA VIRTUALLY UNHEARD OF BEFORE the nineteenth century. Within years it morphed from humble beginnings in the British Isles into a worldwide phenomenon. Millions extolled its virtues with unbending devotion and evangelistic fervor. By the twentieth century, its cardinal doctrines permeated bastions of education and penetrated corridors of influence and power. Masters of mass communication championed its tenets and academic institutions churned out its messengers. Despite being a misreading of data, it is so assumed that those who oppose it are shouted down as reactionaries. Its proponents consider themselves keepers of orthodoxy and react with cultlike fanaticism when their presuppositions are questioned. Though its underpinnings are racist, luminaries from politicians to playwrights laud its virtues.

The dogma to which I refer is Darwinian evolution. The intellectual revolution it initiated provided the scientific substructure for some of the most significant atrocities in human history. Hitler's genocidal mania was fueled by Darwin's racist contention that "civilized races of man will almost certainly exterminate, and replace, the savage races throughout the world."[1] In the end, Hitler's philosophy that Aryans were superhuman and Semites subhuman led to the extermination of some six million Jews. Twentieth-century physical anthropologist Sir Arthur Keith summed it up well: "The German Führer, as I have consistently maintained, is an evolutionist; he has consciously sought to make the practice of Germany conform to the theory of evolution."[2]

Like Hitler, Karl Marx, the father of communism, saw in Darwinism the scientific and sociological support for an economic experiment that eclipsed even the horrors of the Holocaust. Sigmund Freud, the founder of modern psychology, was also a faithful follower of Charles Darwin. His belief that man was merely a sophisticated animal led him to postulate that "anxiety, paranoia and other mental disorders each embody modes of behavior that were once adaptive for the human species in the stages of evolution."[3] Dr. John L. Down labeled Down syndrome "'Mongoloid idiocy' because he thought it represented a 'throwback' to the 'Mongolian stage' in human evolution."[4]

"Throwbacks," of course, are undesirable. For evolution to progress, it is as crucial that the unfit die as that the fittest survive. Marvin Lubenow aptly portrays the ghastly consequences of this notion in his book *Bones of Contention*: "If the unfit survived indefinitely, they would continue to 'infect' the fit with their less fit genes. The result is that the more fit genes would be diluted and compromised by the less fit genes, and evolution could not take place."[5]

Nowhere were the far-reaching consequences of such cosmogenic mythology more evident than in the pseudo-science of eugenics.[6] Eugenics hypothesized that the gene pool was being corrupted by the less fit genes of inferior people. As Michael Crichton has pointed out, the theory of eugenics postulated that "the best human beings were not breeding as rapidly as the inferior ones—the foreigners, immigrants, Jews, degenerates, the unfit, and the 'feeble-minded.' . . . The plan was to identify individuals who were feeble-minded—Jews were agreed to be largely feeble-minded, but so were many foreigners, as well as blacks—and stop them from breeding by isolation in institutions or by sterilization."[7]

The logical progression from evolution to eugenics was hardly a surprise. What is breathtaking, however, is the vast rapidity with which this baseless theory was embraced by the cultural elite. Crichton notes that its supporters ranged from President Theodore Roosevelt to Planned Parenthood founder Margaret Sanger. Eugenics research was funded through philanthropies such as the Carnegie and Rockefeller foundations and carried out at prestigious universities such as Stanford, Harvard, Yale, and Princeton.

Legislation to address the "problem" posed by eugenics was passed in blue states ranging from New York to California. Eugenics was even backed by the National Academy of Sciences and the American Medical Association. Those who resisted eugenics were considered backward and ignorant. Conversely, German scientists who gassed the "feeble-minded" were considered forward thinking and progressive and were rewarded with grants from such institutions as the Rockefeller Foundation right up to the onset of World War II.

It wasn't until the ghastly reality of eugenics reached full bloom in the genocidal mania of German death camps that it quietly vanished into the night. Indeed, after World War II, few institutions or individuals would even own up to their insidious belief in eugenics. Nor did the cultural elite ever acknowledge the obvious connection between eugenics and evolution.

Eugenics has faded into the shadowy recesses of history. The tragic consequences of the evolutionary dogma that birthed it, however, are yet with us today.

On the Road to Armageddon

In 1831—the same year that Charles Darwin left England and sailed into evolutionary infamy aboard the HMS *Beagle*—another nineteenth-century dogma with profound consequences for the history of humanity was birthed in the British Isles. That year John Nelson Darby, a disillusioned priest, left the Church of England and joined a separatist millenarian group called the Plymouth Brethren in the English city of Plymouth.

In general, Darby accepted the premillennial perspective

of the Brethren movement. Like Darwin, however, Darby was a trendsetter. In much the same way that Darwin imposed a speculative spin on the scientific data he encountered along the South American coasts of Patagonia, Darby imposed a subjective spin on the scriptural data he encountered in the city of Plymouth.

Darby contended that God had two distinct people with two distinct plans and two distinct destinies. Only one of those peoples—the Jews—would suffer tribulation. The other—the church—would be removed from the world in a secret coming seven years prior to the second coming of Christ. Darby's distinctive twist on Scripture would shortly come to be known as *dispensational eschatology.*

Beginning with Darby, dispensationalists held that due to the murder of their Messiah, Jews were in for a time of unprecedented suffering variously referred to as the time of "Jacob's Trouble" or the "Great Tribulation."[8] Early dispensationalists such as Arthur W. Pink and Arno C. Gaebelein underscored the contention that Jews were under a "national blood-guiltiness" for "the murder of Christ."[9]

In *Conflict of the Ages*, Gaebelein described Jews as "infidels" and "a menace" and contended, "The greater part of Jewry has become reformed, or as we call it, 'deformed.'"[10] Historian Dr. Timothy Weber notes that despite such unguarded remarks, Gaebelein's *The Conflict of the Ages* received rave reviews in dispensational oracles such as Moody Bible Institute's *Moody Monthly* and Dallas Seminary's *Bibliotheca Sacra*.[11]

In his seminal volume, *On the Road to Armageddon*, Weber chronicles a formidable list of dispensational luminaries who were on the vanguard of promoting baseless, anti-Semitic conspiracy theories. Some hailed *The Protocols of the Elders of*

Zion as proof positive that Jews were masterminding a global conspiracy to destroy Christian civilization.[12]

James M. Gray of Moody Bible Institute called the *Protocols* "a clinching argument for premillennialism."[13] And Arno Gaebelein praised Serge Nilus, who first published the *Protocols*, writing that he "was a believer in the Word of God, in prophecy, and must have been a true Christian."[14] Even after it became painfully obvious, Gaebelein remained unwilling to acknowledge the *Protocols* as an outright forgery and continued to advertise *The Conflict of the Ages* until his death in 1945.[15]

Charles C. Cook of the Bible Institute of Los Angeles likewise pronounced the *Protocols* authentic and stereotypically described the "accompanying traits" of Jews as "pride, overbearing arrogance, inordinate love for material things, trickery, rudeness and an egotism that taxes the superlatives of any language." In the institute's magazine, *King's Business*, Cook opined that the reason Jewish people were "*persona non grata* at resorts and in the best society" is that "the unregenerated Jew usually has a very unattractive personality."[16]

Such remarks impelled the venerable Harry A. Ironside to say that it grieved him "to find that the *Protocols* are being used not only by godless Gentiles, but even by some fundamentalist Christians to stir up suspicion and hatred against the Jewish people as a whole."[17] Despite the embarrassment, dispensationalists (including Ironside) persisted in predicting a future period of unprecedented tribulation for Jews.

In their view, history hinged on herding Jews back into Palestine where two-thirds of them will die in an apocalyptic Armageddon. As dispensational luminary Dr. John Walvoord explains, "Israel is destined to have a particular time of suffering which will eclipse anything that it has known in the past."

Walvoord underscored this reality by adding that Jews returning to Palestine were "placing themselves within the vortex of
this future whirlwind which will destroy the *majority* of those
living in the land of Palestine."[18]

In keeping with Walvoord's ominous prediction, Hal
Lindsey told Christian devotees that not long after their glorious rapture "a numberless multitude" of Jews would be
slaughtered in a bloodbath that would exceed the horrors of
the Holocaust. Lindsey went on to predict that the brutality of
the Beast would make the Nazi butchers "look like Girl Scouts
weaving a daisy chain."[19]

For his part, Tim LaHaye uses biblical monikers such as
"The Day of Israel's Calamity" to codify what he eerily described
as Antichrist's "final solution" to the "Jewish problem."[20] Like
Lindsey, he is convinced that this time of national suffering for
Jews will "be far worse than the Spanish Inquisition of the six-
teenth century or even the Holocaust of Adolph Hitler in the
twentieth century."[21] According to LaHaye, the time of Jewish
Tribulation will be a nightmarish reality beyond imagination:
"Take the horror of every war since time began, throw in every
natural disaster in recorded history, and cast off all restraints so
that the unspeakable cruelty and hatred and injustice of man
toward his fellow men can fully mature, and compress all that
into a period of seven years. Even if you could imagine such a
horror, it wouldn't approach the mind-boggling terror and turmoil of the Tribulation."[22]

The Heart of Dispensationalism

Like his contemporary Charles Darwin, who upon leaving
England aboard the HMS *Beagle* said, "I did not then in the
least doubt the strict and literal truth of every word in the

Bible,"[23] J. N. Darby had become increasingly embarrassed by his religious background and theological traditions. As various historians have duly noted, the premillenarianism of the early nineteenth century was fast becoming known as the religious obscurantism of "the socially disinherited, psychologically disturbed, and theologically naïve."[24]

The early 1800s found a broad range of premillennialists naively seeking to time the approaching terror and turmoil of the Tribulation with the Second Coming by correlating current events with biblical prophecy.[25] On the cultic fringe, Mormon founder Joseph Smith was propagating the notion that his generation was living in the very shadow of Christ's return. Smith alleged that God had told him the return of Christ would take place before he was eighty-five years of age, prompting historians such as Ernest Sandeen to characterize Joseph and his contemporaries as being metaphorically drunk on the millennium.[26]

In more mainstream premillennial circles, the gifted Baptist orator William Miller was also circulating the conclusion that his generation was living on the very edge of the Millennium. In 1831 he publicly identified the year of Christ's return as 1843. Using millennial mathematics, Miller calculated a day in prophetic parlance as equivalent to a year in prophetic history. He reckoned that according to Daniel 8:14, exactly 2,300 "days" after Artaxerxes' decree (457 BC), the millennium would commence.

Nineteenth-century historic premillennialists used millennial mathematics not only to date the time of Christ's descent, but also to determine such details as the time of the Antichrist's demise. They began by supposing that the Roman pontiff was the Antichrist depicted in Revelation 13. Furthermore, they speculated that according to Revelation 11, precisely 1,260 "days" after the rise of the Roman papacy (AD 538), the reign of the Beast would come to an abrupt end. Thus, the exile of the Roman pontiff by the French in 1798 was hailed as validation of their date-setting prowess.

In 1831—the year Miller announced that he had discovered the time of Christ's return—Darby added a unique twist to the dating game by introducing the concept of a secret coming seven years prior to the second coming of Christ. Thus one could only determine the time of Christ's second coming after the time of Christ's secret coming. Initially this proved a damper to the dating game. Later dispensationalists like LaHaye, however, found a variety of new rules to ensure that the dating game could continue to be played. LaHaye demonstrated an unusually fertile imagination by forwarding the notion that the generation who heard the Austrian declaration of World War I in 1914 would not pass away before Christ's second coming.[27]

While dispensationalism has evolved into the poster child for biblical literalism, the Plymouth Brethren initially exposed to Darby's unique twist on the text considered it exegetically indefensible. Thus, Darby's system of dividing the Bible divided the Brethren.[28] The Brethren scholar Samuel P. Tregelles, recognized for his historical analysis of the Greek text of the New Testament, dismissed Darby's eschatological musings as speculative nonsense. In his considered opinion, the sophistry of a secret return of Christ, seven years before the second coming of Christ, had its origin in an ecstatic utterance in the London congregation of Edward Irving, not in biblical exegesis. As Tregelles put it, "It was from that supposed revelation that the modern doctrine and the modern phraseology respecting it arose. It came not from Holy Scripture, but from that which falsely pretended to be the Spirit of God."[29]

According to Darby himself, however, his dispensational doctrines originated neither from an ecstatic utterance in Edward Irving's London congregation nor from the vision of a Scottish lassie named Margaret MacDonald. Rather, they evolved from the hypothesis that Scripture is replete with two distinct stories concerning two distinct people for whom God had two distinct plans.[30] Thus, to Darby, reading the Bible for all it is worth meant deciding in advance which Scriptures applied uniquely to Israel and which Scriptures applied unequivocally to the church.

Premillennialist luminary George Eldon Ladd explained that "this principle has frequently been called 'Rightly dividing the Word of Truth.' It is the method of deciding in advance which Scriptures deal with the Church and which Scriptures have to do with Israel, and then to interpret the passages concerned in the light of this 'division' of the Word."[31] B. W. Newton, "one of the earliest and most learned of the Brethren," however, dubbed Darby's method the "height of speculative nonsense."[32] C. I. Scofield, who followed Darby as dispensationalism's quintessential authority for biblical interpretation, thought otherwise. In 1888 Scofield published *Rightly Dividing the Word of Truth*, which became a primary defense of Darby's two people of God theory.[33]

In our generation, LaHaye is on the forefront of defending and disseminating Darby's "two people" dogma. In fiction and nonfiction, on radio and television, and in churches and schools, he underscores the nonnegotiable necessity of dispensationalism's distinctive doctrine. In his words, "The distinction between Israel and the church is important because the church's present distinctiveness in the plan of God provides the theological basis for the pretribulation Rapture."[34]

While LaHaye's prowess in marketing Darby's dogma is breathtaking, we must ultimately ask whether it is biblical. Indeed, we must determine whether dispensationalists beginning with Darby have rightly illumined the Word of Truth through faithful exegesis or whether they have wrongly divided the Word of Truth through faulty eisegesis. For nineteen hundred years of church history, no one—including historical luminaries such as Ephraim, Augustine, Calvin, Luther, Knox, Zwingli, and Wesley—had any concept of the pretribulational rapture that LaHaye claims is so "clearly taught" in Scripture. Were they all biblically blind? Or is it LaHaye and company who cannot see?

This is not the stuff of ivory-tower debates. Ideas have consequences! And the consequences of the Darbian dogma play out in the caldron of real life. As Darwin's subjective spin on science led to the nightmare of eugenics, Darby's subjective spin on Scripture leads inexorably toward a nightmarish ending. If LaHaye is right, the time of Jewish Tribulation will indeed be a nightmarish reality beyond imagination.

In previous generations, dispensationalists were content to be mere spectators to unfolding events. Today's brand, however, is bent on ensuring that the horrors of Armageddon become a self-fulfilling prophecy. As Timothy Weber has well said:

[Dispensationalists once] sat high in the bleachers on history's fifty-yard line, watching as various teams took their positions on the playing field below and explaining to everyone who would listen how the game was going to end. For the first one hundred years of their movement, then, they were observers, not shapers, of events. But all that changed after Israel reclaimed its place in Palestine and expanded its borders. For the first time, dispensationalists believed that it was necessary to leave the bleachers and get onto the playing field to make sure the game ended according to the divine script.[35]

If the evangelical death march toward the endgame of Armageddon is to be subverted, it will be because believers recommit themselves to *faithful illumination*. Put another way, it will be because believers recommit themselves to *faithful exegesis*—to mining what the Spirit has breathed into the Scriptures as opposed to reading our own predilections into the text. Sudden flashes of intuition or inspiration are poor substitutes for the scrupulous study of Scripture. We must pray that the Holy Spirit gives us clear minds and open hearts as we dig into his Word. That means a willingness to sacrifice treasured traditions on the altar of biblical fidelity. It means learning to read the Bible for all it is worth. Ultimately, it means turning away from fruitless eisegesis and marching undeterred toward the endgame of faithful exegesis.

TWO DISTINCT PEOPLE

We begin by turning our attention to the heart of the dispensational dogma, namely, that God has two distinct peoples—one of whom must be raptured before God can continue his plan with the other. Does the illumination of Scripture reveal that God has two categories of people, or does Scripture reveal only one chosen people who form one covenant community, beautifully symbolized by one cultivated olive tree?

First, far from communicating that God has two distinct peoples, the Scriptures from beginning to end reveal only *one chosen people* purchased "from every tribe and tongue and language and nation" (Revelation 5:9). As Paul explains, the "mystery is that through the gospel the Gentiles are heirs together with Israel, members together of *one* body, and sharers together in the promise in Christ Jesus" (Ephesians 3:6).

Indeed, the precise terminology used to describe the children of Israel in the Old Testament is ascribed to the church in the New Testament. Peter calls them *"a chosen people,* a royal priesthood, a holy nation, a people belonging to God, that you may declare the praises of him who called you out of darkness into his wonderful light" (1 Peter 2:9). Ultimately, they are the one chosen people of God, not by virtue of their genealogical relationship to Abraham, but by virtue of their genuine relationship to "the living Stone—rejected by men but chosen by God" (1 Peter 2:4). The true church is true Israel, and true Israel is truly the church.

Further, just as the Old and New Testaments reveal only one chosen people, so too, they reveal only *one covenant community.* While that one covenant community is physically rooted in the offspring of Abraham—whose number would be like that of "the stars" of heaven (Genesis 15:5) or "the dust of the earth" (Genesis 13:16)[36]—it is spiritually grounded in one singular Seed. Paul makes this explicit in his letter to the Galatians: "The promises were spoken to Abraham and to his *seed.* The Scripture does not say 'and to *seeds,*' meaning many people, but 'and to your seed' meaning one person, who is Christ" (Galatians 3:16). As Paul goes on to explain, "If you belong to Christ, then you are Abraham's seed, and heirs according to the promise" (v. 29).

To suggest that Israel must "fulfill her national destiny as a separate entity after the Rapture and Tribulation and during the Millennium"[37] is an affront to the One Seed in whom all the promises made to Abraham have reached their climax. As Keith Mathison has well said, "The promises made to literal, physical Israelites were fulfilled by a literal, physical Israelite, Jesus the Messiah. He is *the* Seed of Abraham."[38] The faithful remnant of Old Testament Israel and New Testament Christianity are together the one genuine seed of Abraham and thus heirs according to the promise. This remnant is not chosen on the basis of religion or race but rather on the basis of relationship to the resurrected Redeemer. Clothed with Christ, men, women, and children in every age and from "every tongue and tribe and nation"[39] form one and only one covenant community.

Finally, the one chosen people, who form one covenant community, are beautifully symbolized in the book of Romans as one cultivated olive tree (see Romans 11:11–24). The tree symbolizes national Israel, its branches symbolize those who believe, and its root symbolizes Jesus—"the Root and the Offspring of David" (Revelation 22:16). Natural branches broken off represent Jews who reject Jesus. Wild branches grafted in represent Gentiles who receive Jesus. Thus, says Paul, "Not all who are descended from Israel are Israel. Nor because they are his descendants are they all Abraham's children. . . . In other words, it is not the natural children who are God's children, but it is the children of the promise who are regarded as Abraham's offspring" (Romans 9:6–8).

Jesus is the one genuine seed of Abraham! And all clothed in Christ constitute *one* congruent chosen covenant community connected by the cross. "There is neither Jew nor Greek [Arab or Armenian, American or African, Australian or Asian, etc.], slave nor free, male nor female, for you are all one in Christ Jesus. If you belong to Christ, then you are Abraham's seed, and heirs according to the promise" (Galatians 3:28–29).

In the end, there simply is no biblical warrant for the dispensational notion that God has two distinct people. And if God has always had only one people, the dispensational dogma that God has two distinct plans for these two distinct peoples collapses under the weight of Scripture.

TWO DISTINCT PLANS

Just as there is one chosen people who form one covenant community characterized in Scripture by one cultivated olive tree, so too there is only *one distinct plan* for what Ephesians 2:15 characterizes as "the one true humanity" of God. The pretext that God postponed the original plan for Israel and initiated a parenthetical plan for the church that abruptly ends with a pretribulational rapture entirely misses the point.

First, far from the dispensational *postponement* of God's original plan *for* Israel, Scripture reveals the distinct *progression* of the divine plan to establish *through* Israel a new humanity (Ephesians 2:15) in a new homeland (Romans 4:13; Hebrews 12:18, 22). Exegetical Eschatology illumines this progressive plan commencing in Paradise lost and culminating in Paradise restored.

The biblical picture is poignant and profound. Adam falls into a life of perpetual sin and is banished from Paradise. He is relegated to restlessness and wandering separated from intimacy and fellowship with his Creator. The very chapter that references the Fall, however, also records the divine plan for the restoration of fellowship (Genesis 3:15). The plan takes on definition with God's promise to make Abram a great nation through which "all peoples on earth will be blessed" (Genesis 12:3). Abram's call, therefore, constitutes the divine antidote to Adam's fall.

God's promise that Abram's children would inherit the Promised Land was a preliminary step in a progressive plan through which Abram and his heirs would inherit "a better country—a heavenly one" (Hebrews 11:16). The plan comes into sharper focus when we see Moses leading Abram's descendants out of their four-hundred-year bondage in Egypt. For forty years of wilderness wandering, God tabernacled with his people and prepared them for the Land of Promise. Like Abram, however, Moses saw the promise only from afar.

God's plan becomes a tangible reality when Joshua leads the children of Israel into Palestine. The wanderings of Adam, Abram, and Moses finally give way to "rest on every side" (Joshua 21:43). As Joshua exudes, "Not one of all the good promises the LORD your God gave you has failed. Every promise has been fulfilled; not one has failed" (Joshua 23:14).

As Adam had fallen in Paradise, Abram's descendants would fall in Palestine. Thus, Joshua's words in his final farewell take on an ominous reality: "Just as every good promise of the LORD your God has come true, so the LORD will bring on you all the evil he has threatened, until he has destroyed you from this good land he has given you. If you violate the covenant of the LORD your God, which he has commanded you . . . you will quickly perish from the good land he has given you" (Joshua 23:15–16).

Though the land promises reached their zenith under Solomon—whose rule encompassed all of the land from the Euphrates River in the north to the River of Egypt in the south (1 Kings 4:20–21; cf. Genesis 15:18)—the land vomited out the children of the promise just as it had vomited out the Canaanites before them. During the Assyrian and Babylonian exiles, the wanderings experienced by Adam were again experienced by the descendants of Abram.

God's promises to Abraham, however, were far from exhausted. For Palestine was but a preliminary phase in the patriarchal promise. God would make Abram not just the father of *a* nation, but *Abram* would become *Abraham*—"a father of *many* nations" (Genesis 17:5). Abraham "would be heir of the world" (Romans 4:13). The climax of the promise would not be Palestine regained but Paradise restored.

As God had promised Abraham real estate, he had also promised him a royal seed. Joshua led the children of Israel into the regions of Palestine; Jesus will one day lead his children into the restoration of Paradise. There they will forever experience rest. From Adam's rebellion to Abraham's Royal Seed, the Scriptures chronicle God's one unfolding plan for the redemption of humanity. Far from a postponement in God's plans because the Jews crucified Jesus, Scripture reveals the fulfillment of God's plans in the crucifixion. For only through faith in Christ's death and his subsequent resurrection can God's one covenant community find rest from their wanderings (Hebrews 4:1–11). In Christ—"the last Adam" (1 Corinthians 15:45)—God's promises find ultimate fulfillment. As Paul so elegantly put it, "If you belong to Christ, then you are Abraham's seed, and heirs according to the promise" (Galatians 3:29).

Further, as there is no dispensational *postponement* in the plan of God, so too there is no *parenthesis* in the purposes of God. The pretext for a parenthesis during which there is a postponement in God's plans for Israel and the commencement of a plan for a church age is the product of a peculiar reading of prophecy. The main focus of the dogma is Daniel. As LaHaye exudes, "It is impossible to understand Bible prophecy without understanding the book of Daniel. Much of the information about the key players and the time sequence of the last days is given in Daniel."[40] Of particular note is Daniel's "seventy weeks" (Daniel 9:24–27).

To expound on the "key players" and "time sequence," LaHaye reads a number of presuppositions into Daniel's seventy weeks. First, he infers a gap of two thousand years between Daniel's sixty-ninth and seventieth weeks. Furthermore, he injects a "parenthetical period" of two thousand years into the gap and calls it the "Church Age."[41] Finally, he imagines that "the church was an unrevealed mystery in the Old Testament (Romans 16:25–26; Ephesians 3:2–10; Colossians 1:25–27)" and that "Israel, *and not the church*, will fulfill her national destiny as a separate entity after the Rapture and Tribulation and during the Millennium."[42]

As should be self-evident, this invention is not the product of the faithful illumination of the text, but is the by-product of a fertile imagination. The very notion that the Old Testament prophets did not see "The Valley of the Church,"[43] which "did not exist before its birth at Pentecost" and "will come to an abrupt end at the Rapture,"[44] is flatly false. The Old Testament prophets not only saw the "Valley of the Church," they *announced* it! Peter—speaking after the birth of the church at Pentecost—could not have said it any more plainly: "*All the prophets* from Samuel on, as many as have spoken, have *foretold* these days" (Acts 3:24). What is neither seen nor announced by the prophets is the notion that the New Testament church that was birthed at Pentecost would "come to an abrupt end at the Rapture." Plainly put, the notion that the church is merely a parenthesis in the plan of God has no biblical backbone.

Finally, as there is no postponement or parenthesis in the plan of God, so too there is no *pretribulational rapture*. For nineteen hundred years, the idea of a pretribulational rapture was completely foreign to mainstream Christianity. Prior to Darby, the Plymouth Brethren believed that the rapture and the return of Christ were simultaneous events. Darby's innovative invention gave birth to the notion of a pretribulational rapture. As historian Timothy Weber explains, "Before Darby, *all* premillennialists, futurists included, believed that the rapture would occur at the end of the Tribulation, at Christ's second advent. But Darby understood the rapture and the second coming as two separate events. At the rapture, Christ will come *for* his saints, and at the second coming, he will come *with* his saints. Between these two events the great tribulation would occur."[45]

Not until Darby had such a notion even been countenanced within the body of Christ. Harry Ironside—himself a pretribulational rapturist—challenged those who doubt this assertion to "search, as the writer has in measure done, the remarks of the so-called Fathers, both pre- and post-Nicene; the theological treatises of the scholastic divines; Roman Catholic writers of all shades of thought; the literature of the Reformation; the sermons and expositions of the Puritans; and the general theological works of the day. He will find the 'mystery' conspicuous by its absence."[46] Ironside—who LaHaye dubbed "one of my preacher heroes"—would frequently add the following warning as well: "Whenever you hear something *new, examine it carefully* because it may not be *true*."[47]

Heeding his hero, LaHaye has gone to great lengths to demonstrate that the pretribulational rapture is not new. In evidence he cites Grant Jeffrey's "electrifying discovery of a statement in an apocalyptic sermon from the fourth century" designated "Pseudo-Ephraim."[48] Jeffrey confides that it took him "a decade of searching" to make this discovery but that it was well worth the effort. In his words, "Ephraem's text revealed a clear statement about the pretribulational return of Christ to take His elect saints home to heaven to escape the coming Tribulation."[49]

Like LaHaye, philosopher and theologian Dr. Norman Geisler took stock in Grant Jeffrey's electrifying discovery. He references Jeffrey as the basis for his belief that "the early Ephraem manuscript . . . reveals the pretrib view was held as early as the 300s AD."[50] In his considered judgment, early church fathers "like Ephraem the Syrian, were explicitly pre-tribulationists."[51] Thus, like LaHaye, Geisler takes strong exception to the contention that belief in the pretribulational rapture originated in the nineteenth century. In his view, those who hold this notion have not only committed "the fallacy of 'Chronological Snobbery,'" but are making an assertion that is "plainly and simply false."[52] Geisler's statements in this regard are now widely circulated as the final authority. In keeping with Dr. Ironside's admonition, however, we would do well to "carefully examine" Ephraem's sermon to see if after a full decade of searching, dispensationalists have indeed come up with a pre-nineteenth-century historical precedent for the pretribulational rapture.

To begin with, it is instructive to note that while Dr. Geisler ascribes the sermon in question to "Ephraem the Syrian" writing in "the 300s AD," LaHaye now concedes that this sermon may well be ascribed to "*Pseudo*-Ephraim" and "may not have been written until AD 565–627."[53] Regardless of who wrote it or when it was written, we can say with certainty that no pretribulational rapture tradition developed around it. More important, as historians and theologians well know, a survey of Ephraem's writings demonstrate conclusively that Ephraem was posttribulational not pretribulational. Not only oo, but tho oormon in queotion plainly utilizes the posttribula-tional rapture tradition of true Ephraem.

It is difficult to imagine anyone reading this sermon in context and concluding that Ephraem is espousing a secret rapture prior to the Tribulation—particularly in light of the fact that in this very sermon, Ephraem emphasizes that Christians would indeed experience the Great Tribulation. It is far more likely that what is at issue is pretribulational regeneration rather than pretribulational rapture.[54]

While the "electrifying discovery" of Ephraim's fourth-century apocalyptic sermon makes for great rhetoric, in the end it is of little consequence. At issue is not pseudo-Ephraim but proper exegesis. Thus, rather than exegete pseudo-Ephraim, we would be better served to examine the pages of Scripture. An appropriate place to begin is Paul's first letter to the Thessalonians. For it is in this passage that dispensationalists claim to find indisputable proof for Darby's pretribulational rapture theory. Says LaHaye, "One of the most compelling prophetic events in the Bible is called the "rapture" of the church. It is taught *clearly* in 1 Thessalonians 4:13-18, where the apostle Paul provides us with most of the available details."[55]

As with Ephraim's sermon, even a cursory exegesis of 1 Thessalonians 4 reveals that Paul does not have pretribulational rapturism in mind. Far from unveiling a new teaching concerning a secret coming during which Christ will rapture the church, Paul's message is focused on the great and glorious hope of resurrection. As Bible scholars have duly noted, Paul's teaching in 1 Thessalonians 4 runs directly parallel to his teachings in 1 Corinthians 15. Together they communicate the blessed hope that at Christ's coming the end will come. He will hand the kingdom over to God the Father after he has destroyed all dominion, authority, and power. When the trumpet sounds, the dead in Christ will be changed—in a flash in the twinkling of an eye. And so we will be with the Lord *forever*.[56]

Nowhere does the text say that when Christ comes down from heaven "with a loud command, with the voice of the archangel and with the trumpet call of God" (1 Thessalonians 4:16) that Christ will hover with us in midair, suddenly change directions, and escort us to mansions in heaven while all hell breaks out on earth. Nor would the Thessalonians have understood Paul this way. As Dr. N. T. Wright has aptly noted, "Paul conjures up images of an emperor visiting a colony or province. The citizens go out to meet him in open country and then escort him into the city. Paul's image of the people 'meeting the Lord in the air' should be read with the assumption that the people will immediately turn around and lead the Lord back to the newly remade world."[57]

Moreover, there is no warrant for supposing that the pretribulational rapture theory is supported by a "similarity" between Christ's teaching in John 14:1–3 and Paul's teaching in 1 Thessalonians 4:13–18. To put it bluntly, LaHaye is off base to take the precious words of our Savior—"Let not your heart be troubled: ye believe in God, believe also in me. In my Father's house are many mansions: if it were not so, I would have told you. I go to prepare a place for you. And if I go and prepare a place for you, I will come again, and receive you unto myself; that where I am, there ye may be also" (John 14:1–3 KJV)—and pretend they represent the first teaching on the pretribulational rapture of the church in Scripture.[58]

To read into 1 Thessalonians 4 or John 14 a paradigm in which two-thirds of the Jewish people will shortly be eradicated in a holocaust massacre while Jesus's people relax in heavenly mansions is a frightful imposition on the integrity of our Savior and the Scriptures. Neither Paul's portrait of paradise nor the Master's mansion metaphor is intended to convey a temporary safe haven in heaven away from a seven-year holocaust on earth. Rather, they represent a glorious picture of "a new heaven and a new earth" in which "the dwelling of God is with men, and he will live with them. They will be his people, and God himself will be with them and be their God. He will wipe every tear from their eyes. There will be no more death or mourning or crying or pain, for the old order of things has passed away. He who was seated on the throne said, "I am making everything new!" (Revelation 21:1–5).

TWO DISTINCT PHASES

Like the presupposition that God has two distinct people for whom he has two distinct plans, the pretext that there are two distinct phases in the second coming of Christ is little more than the product of a fertile imagination. Indeed, the faithful illumination of Scripture reveals neither a secret coming of Christ followed by a seven-year Tribulation, nor a second chance for sin and salvation following the second coming of Christ. To the contrary, when Christ appears a second time, the kingdom that was inaugurated at his first appearing will be consummated in "a new heaven and a new earth, the home of righteousness" (2 Peter 3:13).

First, the very notion of a *secret coming* is without biblical precedent. As LaHaye has acknowledged, "no single verse specifically states, 'Christ will come [secretly] before the Tribulation'" to rapture the church.[59] Nor is there a collection of verses that can be construed to communicate a secret coming prior to the second coming of Christ. Instead, the notion of a secret coming, as pretribulational rapturists readily admit, is "a deduction from one's overall system of theology."[60]

LaHaye's deduction is that there is a secret coming during which *only* the church will be raptured. Conversely, as our Lord declares, "a time is coming when *all* who are in their graves will hear his voice and come out—those who have done good will rise to live, and those who have done evil will rise to be condemned" (John 5:28–29; cf. Matthew 25:31–46; Luke 12:35–48). LaHaye's theology therefore stands in stark contrast to Jesus's teachings. The plain and literal sense of our Lord's words suggests a moment in the future when both the righteous and the unrighteous will be resurrected and judged together. The notion that believers will be raptured during a secret coming of our Lord 1007 years prior to the resurrection of unbelievers is thus an imposition on the text.

Even given pretribulational presuppositions, the literal sense of the parable of the weeds suggests that the wicked will be judged prior to the wheat being gathered, not the other way round (Matthew 13:24–30). Likewise, in the Olivet Discourse, the unjust are "taken" in judgment while the righteous are left behind, not vice versa (Matthew 24:36–41). During his earthly sojourn, our Lord fervently petitioned his heavenly Father not to rapture his bride out of the world, but to protect them from the evil one while they were in the world (John 17:15).[61]

Furthermore, search as you may, you will not find a *seven-year Tribulation* in the biblical text. In fact, the future seven-year Tribulation trumpeted by LaHaye is conspicuous by its absence in the whole of Scripture. LaHaye avows that "there is little doubt as to when this Tribulation occurs or how long it will last."[62] He provides, however, precious little by way of evidence. He pretends a single pretext from the prophecy of Daniel,[63] and from Revelation he produces no proof text at all. Instead, he simply pontificates that John's revelation divides the Great Tribulation into "two periods of three and one-half years each or 1,260 days each, a total of seven years. During the first three and one-half years more than one-half the world's population dies. During the second half, conditions get even worse after Satan is cast out of heaven and indwells the Antichrist's body and demands the world worship him."[64]

It is foolhardy at best to subtract from, add to, or divide "the revelation of Jesus Christ, which God gave him to show his servants what must soon take place" (Revelation 1:1). Nowhere does the revelation of Jesus divide the Tribulation into "two periods of three and one-half years each or 1,260 days each." And if one were to add together John's references to three and a half years, forty-two months, or 1,260 days, they would greatly exceed the number seven. From the perspective of history, there was a three-and-a-half-year period of tribulation during the Jewish War beginning in the spring of AD 67 and ending in the fall of AD 70; however, there is no biblical precedent for doubling that time frame and driving it into the twenty-first century. Moreover, the biblically astute are well aware of the rich biblical symbolism invested in the number seven—and in its half.[65]

LaHaye would also do well to recognize that when Jesus spoke of a tribulation "unequaled from the beginning of the world until now—and never to be equaled again" (Matthew 24:21), he was clearly using prophetic hyperbole.[66] If this literary reality is not comprehended, Scripture collapses in hopeless contradiction. Worse yet, to embrace LaHaye's interpretation is to rob our Lord of deity. Daniel said, "Under the whole heaven nothing has ever been done like what has been done to Jerusalem" (Daniel 9:12). Likewise, God the Father said, "I will do to you what I have *never* done before and will *never* do again" (Ezekiel 5:9, cf. Exodus 11:6; Joel 2:2). If Israel faced its greatest tribulation in the past, Christ would be gravely mistaken to predict a greater tribulation in the future—moreover, one can scarcely imagine a greater tribulation in the future than the tribulation of the Flood in the past.

Despite evidence to the contrary, LaHaye persists in dragging the seven-year tribulation into the twenty-first century and describing it as the time of Jacob's Trouble or the time of Jewish Tribulation.[67] What he fails to disclose is the seminal fact that neither Jeremiah's reference to "a time of trouble for Jacob" (Jeremiah 30:7) nor Jesus's reference to a time of "great distress, unequaled from the beginning of the world until now—and never to be equaled again" (Matthew 24:21) refer to a holocaust in the twenty-first century that was precipitated by a Jewish rebellion against Jehovah in the sixth century BC or a Jewish rejection of Jesus in the first century AD. Both references incontrovertibly point to times past in which the very temple that gave Israel its theological and sociological identity was decimated.

Jeremiah explicitly communicates that "Jacob's trouble"

takes place during the Babylonian exile—some six centuries before Jesus is even born! And Jesus emphatically places the time of "Jewish tribulation" in the first century. In much the same manner that Ezekiel uses hyperbolic language to communicate that the horrors surrounding the destruction of the temple by the Babylonians would be unequaled in history, Jesus uses prophetic hyperbole to communicate that the horrors surrounding the destruction of the temple by the Romans would be unparalleled.

Pressing such statements into a literal mold inevitably leads to the conclusion that the Bible contradicts itself. If the destruction in Jeremiah's day is never to be equaled again, how could the destruction in Jesus's day possibly exceed it? Pressing hyperbolic language into a hyperliteral labyrinth necessitates either the fallibility of Jeremiah or the fallibility of Jesus. In either case, the consequences for Christianity and the biblical canon are catastrophic. In the end, there simply is no biblical warrant for a fatalistic preoccupation with a future seven-year tribulation.

Finally, as there is no biblical warrant for a secret coming and a seven-year tribulation, so too there is no biblical basis for believing in a *second chance for salvation after the second coming of Christ*. Christ is clear: "all" given to him by the Father will be raised up on the last day (John 6:37–40). In sharp distinction to such faithful illumination, LaHaye presents a fictitious interpretation in which people are saved after both the secret and second comings of Christ. The implications of his theology are as bizarre as they are blasphemous. If Christ and the church are married between the secret and second comings, "the bride of Christ" must continue to "grow to include other redeemed people in the days of the kingdom."[68] If, on the other hand, God has both a bride (church) and a wife

(Israel), those who are saved after the second coming must be added to "the wife of God" rather than "the bride of Christ." Both scenarios are unthinkable. It is bizarre to suggest that the bride whom Christ married during the Tribulation is incomplete and thus imperfect. Moreover, it is blasphemous to hold that the *one* God revealed in three persons has both a bride and a wife.[69]

Paul points out that the liberation of creation goes hand in hand with the redemption of our bodies (Romans 8:18–25). Thus we can be certain that no one will be saved during a mythological semi-golden age following the second coming of Christ. The notion that our bodies are redeemed at the rapture and the earth is liberated from its bondage to decay approximately 1007 years later is without biblical precedent. At the second coming, the bride of Christ—the church universal—is complete. No one else can be saved. The eschaton has come.

The End of the Matter Is This . . .

While LaHaye boldly asserts that the rapture is "one of the most compelling prophetic events in the Bible" and that it is clearly taught "in 1 Thessalonians where Paul provides us with most of the available details," in truth the rapture is the ripened fruit of a fertile imagination rather than the reasoned fruition of faithful illumination.

The details to which LaHaye alludes emanate from the Left Behind series, not the life-giving Scriptures. It is there, not in 1 Thessalonians, that Christ comes back secretly and silently to rapture the church some seven years prior to his second coming. After meeting somewhere in the air, Jesus allegedly reverses direction and ushers the church into mansions on high. There the church is joined with Christ in holy matrimony. Says

LaHaye, "The church ('the bride of Christ') and our Lord Jesus Christ will be officially married in heaven."[70]

Thus, "while the earth is suffering through the last throes of the Tribulation, the church will enjoy a heavenly wedding. And then a feast!"[71] Guests at the festivities are "faithful Old Testament saints" and "those who died or were martyred in the Tribulation."[72] LaHaye identifies one of the guests as John the Baptist.[73] Though beheaded on earth, and not yet in his immortal body, the disembodied Baptist enjoys the feast and festivities in heaven along with a bridegroom and a bride already in flesh.

Meanwhile, down on earth, the Jews who have gone to bed with the Beast experience a holocaust of mythic proportions. In short order, two-thirds are reduced to bloody corpses. Concurrent with the carnage, a "soul harvest" emerges—partly due to a video left behind by the now raptured T. D. Jakes[74] and partly due to the proselytizing prowess of 144,000 Jewish virgins who "did not defile themselves with women."

As festivities continue in heaven, the world is struck by "an earthquake so massive that 'every mountain and island was moved out of its place.'"[75] The sun becomes "black as sackcloth of hair, and the moon became like blood." All the while, crashing "meteorites" and "huge mushroom clouds of undetermined origin" ravage the planet.[76]

And that's just the beginning! The trumpet judgments of the first twenty-one months of tribulation represent merely the work of the Antichrist. Next, the wrath of the Almighty is unleashed. "In the first period of the Tribulation the earth has known the wrath of the Antichrist; now it will begin to feel the wrath of God Almighty."[77] The opening salvo includes ice, "fire rain," and blood that fall from heaven, creating "an ecological disaster without parallel to this point *in the history of mankind.*"⁷⁸ The previous earthquake that moved every mountain and every island out of its former place on the planet and the meteorites slamming into the earth and the mushroom clouds are insignificant compared to this ecological disaster. Not even Noah's flood, which wiped out all but eight people, approaches the carnage of this catastrophe.

In short order, another enormous meteorite strikes the earth and turns a third of the sea into blood. Yet another turns a third of the rivers and springs bitter and poisonous. Then the Almighty reduces "by a third the amount of radiant energy reaching the earth from the sun and all other celestial bodies"⁷⁹ and releases locusts with "scorpion-like power to sting and torment unbelievers."⁸⁰ After the locusts, come 200 million horsemen—or as LaHaye prefers—horse*demons!*⁸¹ (LaHaye chastises "prophecy preachers" who take the text literally, because, as he puts it, "the logistics of moving an army of 200 million from the Orient across the Euphrates and the Arabian Desert to the little land of Israel seems impossible."⁸² Evidently, moving every mountain and island out of its former place is eminently more feasible than moving an army from the Orient to Israel.) The horsedemons physically "kill one-third of the world's population," fatally stinging some with their mouths and tails and scaring others to death.⁸³

Says LaHaye, "In the first half of the Tribulation, vicious plagues sweep the earth, flaming meteorites poison a third of its water, warring armies kill millions, demonic beings torture the unredeemed, darkness swallows a third of the sun, and half the world's post-Rapture population dies horribly. *And then it gets worse.*"⁸⁴

The cultural elite move from New York, London, and Brussels to villas in the Beast's new headquarters in Babylon,⁸⁵ which, despite the ongoing carnage on earth, has been restored to greatness by none other than the late Saddam Hussein.[86] There they make the "irreversible decision" to take the "mark of the beast."[87] Before long Antichrist has control of the legions left behind. "International Big Brother—the number of his name is 666!"[88]—along with the "Trilateral Commission, CFR, and other secret and semisecret organizations" finally realize their dream of an "interdependent world economy" and a "cashless society."[89]

The Beast is now in position to break his "covenant" with Israel. As he initiates the "final solution" to the "Jewish problem," God begins to afflict those who have received the mark of the Beast with "foul and loathsome sores."[90] Then "He commands that the entire sea become 'blood as of a dead man'—that is corrupt, decaying, stinking, putrid" and turns all the rivers and springs to blood. ("If Jesus could turn water into wine at the marriage feast of Cana," exudes LaHaye, "surely He would have no problem turning water into blood.")[91]

After the earth is deprived of drinking water, God causes the sun to "scorch" it with "great heat."[92] Even this, however, is but the prelude to the grand finale. And "What a finish it is! The most severe earthquake the world has ever known 'since men were on earth' shakes the planet to its foundations."[93] "And that is not all," says LaHaye. "Enormous hailstones weighing about 135 pounds each rain out of the sky, striking men all over the planet." Finally, the stage has been set for "the most famous battle in history."[94]

Jesus returns with his bride dressed in wedding white. He touches down on the Mount of Olives and splits the mountain (which presumably along with every other mountain has been moved out of its place) wide open.[95] He slays every last person who resists him,[96] binds Satan, and initiates "a time of peace that men and women of goodwill have yearned for throughout the centuries."[97]

One might think that after the secret coming of Christ, seven years of carnage, and the second coming of Christ, the problem of Satan and sin would be fully and finally resolved. But alas, in Left Behind theology there is a second chance for salvation during the millennial reign of Christ. Men, women, and children have another thousand years during which to accept or reject the Savior.[98] While multiplied millions are saved, millions more fall under Satan's spell. Their numbers, says LaHaye, are as "the sand of the sea." Thus, after a time of peace and prosperity, once again the planet is plunged into a time of "massive destruction." "And that's it—" says LaHaye, "in a ball of celestial flame" that emanates from heaven, "human rebellion will have been wiped out of existence."[99]

Like Darwinian evolution, this dispensational eschatology continues to morph from its humble beginnings in the British Isles—with the Left Behind series leading the charge. The two people, two plans, and two phases dogma of Darby is now the norm, not the abnormality. Dispensational doctrines are propagated through major educational institutions and have penetrated the highest realms of influence and power. Billion-dollar television conglomerates, such as the Trinity Broadcasting Network (TBN), daily churn out the prophetic speculations of dispensationalism.

Those who dare question the notion of a pretribulational rapture followed by a Holy Land holocaust in which the vast majority of Jews perish are shouted down as peddlers of godless heresy. The ultimate pejorative phrase has even been coined for those who deny the heart of dispensational eschatology. They are dubbed "Replacement theologians" and are said to be guilty of spreading "the message of anti-Semitism."[100] Popular dispensationalists, such as John Hagee, are blunt in their denunciations: "Replacement theologians are now carrying Hitler's anointing and his message."[101]

One can only pray for the courage to stand in the face of vilification and to do all that is permissible to see that this pseudoeschatology—like the pseudoscience of eugenics—will one day fade into the shadowy recesses of history.

4

—◆◆◆—

GRAMMATICAL PRINCIPLE:
"It depends on the meaning of the word is*"*

We believe "this generation" refers to those alive in 1948.
> —TIM LaHAYE AND JERRY JENKINS
> *ARE WE LIVING IN THE END TIMES?*

I have not had sex with her as I defined it.
> —WILLIAM JEFFERSON CLINTON,
> FORMER U.S. PRESIDENT

ASKED UNDER OATH TO VERIFY HIS LAWYER'S declaration, "There is absolutely no sex of any kind" between the president of the United States of America and White House intern, Monica Lewinsky, William Jefferson Clinton responded, "It depends on what the meaning of the word 'is' is." Asked if he had ever been alone with Lewinsky, Clinton responded, "It depends on how you define 'alone.'" Asked to justify his testimony that they had never had a sexual relationship, Clinton answered, "I have not had sex with her as I defined it."[1]

As a Yale Law School graduate, Rhodes Scholar, and university professor, Clinton was uniquely qualified to understand the grammatical intent of the questions he was being asked. Thus, it is highly unlikely that he thought that the word *is* was intended to convey the notion that there might have been sex in the past but there *is* no sex in the present. Likewise, it is unlikely that Clinton misunderstood the definition of the word *alone*, as in his secretary, Betty Currie's, slick prevarication, "The President, for all intents and purposes, is never alone."[2] Equally unbelievable is the notion that Clinton was confused about the meaning of the word *sex*—or for that matter that anyone else was confused.

The moment Clinton commenced his grammatical gyrations, baloney detectors worldwide began blinking furiously. Anyone paying attention knew that Clinton was feigning an ignorance of context and abusing the plain meaning of words in order to avoid perjuring himself. Even someone with a grammar school education could have properly interpreted the intended meaning of the words *is*, *alone*, and *sex* by the context in which the words were used.

As the father of nine children, I can testify firsthand to what scientific research has only recently begun to validate—humans are hardwired for language from birth. From infancy onward, speech patterns are unconsciously absorbed and then modified in accord with unspoken rules of grammar. Even at age three, children display grammatical genius that enables them to master complex speech constructions and internalize sophisticated laws of language.[3] Before children formally learn the laws of language in grade school, they are already able to apply them in their own speech and can readily recognize their abuse in the speech patterns of nonnative speakers—as in the sentence "Me wants on swing to play."

In time even complex grammatical constructions and multiple word meanings become second nature. It shouldn't surprise us, then, that the basic principles of language that we unconsciously absorb in early childhood and consciously internalize from grade school onward are foundational to the grammatical principle of biblical interpretation: We interpret the Bible in accordance with the basic rules of language.[4] Suppose I told my children, "I don't want *you* to touch *this gingerbread cake*, because we are going to have dinner *soon*!" They wouldn't need an advanced degree in English from Yale to understand that by "this" I meant *this* gingerbread cake—not *that* gingerbread cake, as in a gingerbread cake that would be baked for their twenty-first birthday. Nor are they the least bit confused about the meaning of "you," which in context refers to them, not to children of a future generation. "Soon" is equally unambiguous. To say we are going to have dinner "soon" could not possibly mean dinner in the distant future.

When it comes to interpreting Scripture, we should not suppose that the rules of grammar mysteriously change. When Jesus says, "I tell you the truth, *this* generation will certainly not pass away until all these things have happened," "this" means "this."

The meaning of the pronoun *you* in the context of Christ's Olivet Discourse is just as clear. When Jesus says, "*You* will hear of wars and rumors of wars. . . . Then *you* will be handed over to be persecuted and put to death, and *you* will be hated by all nations because of me. . . . When *you* see standing in the holy place "the abomination that causes desolation,". . . Pray that *your* flight will not take place in winter or on the Sabbath. . . . So if anyone tells *you*, "There he is, out in the desert," do not go out. . . . when *you* see all these things, *you* know that it is near, right at the door,"[5] it should be obvious that he is referencing a first-century, not a twenty-first-century, generation.

Likewise, the meaning of the word *soon* in the context of the Revelation Jesus gave to the apostle John is equally self-evident. Tim LaHaye nonetheless intimates that when Jesus speaks of things that "must *soon* take place," he is really speaking of things that will take place in a distant millennium; and when Jesus says that "the time is *near*," he is really intending to say that the time is far off.[6] While this should immediately thrust our baloney detectors into overdrive, I suspect that the reason this often doesn't happen is that it is hard for us to imagine that a prophecy expert who is intimately acquainted with the grammatical principle of biblical interpretation could possibly be mistaken about something so basic. Just as we are reticent to question a president's ability to comprehend the grammatical intent of words such as *is*, *alone*, or *sex*, so too we are loath to question a prophecy expert's understanding of such words as *this*, *you*, and *soon*.

THIS GENERATION

Jesus began his famous Olivet Discourse by walking away from the very house that afforded the Jewish people their theological and sociological significance. He had pronounced seven woes on the Pharisees and then uttered the unthinkable: "*Your* house is left to you desolate" (Matthew 23:38). When Jesus drove the moneychangers out of the temple and overturned their tables, he designated it "*my* house" (Matthew 21:13). Now it was relegated to being "*your* house." What was once the dwelling of God was now a mere house of men.

God's warning regarding Solomon's temple echoed back ominously through the corridor of time: "I will cut off Israel from the land I have given them and *will reject this temple* I have consecrated for my Name. Israel will then become a byword and an object of ridicule among all peoples. And though this temple is now imposing, all who pass by will be appalled and will scoff and say, 'Why has the LORD done such a thing to this land and to this temple?'" (1 Kings 9:7–8). As Solomon's temple had been destroyed, so Herod's temple would become "a byword and an object of ridicule."

The shekinah glory of God had departed the stone temple and resided in the temple not built by human hands. As Jesus declared, "One greater than the temple is here" (Matthew 12:6). The glory that once had tabernacled among the Israelites in the wilderness now physically made his abode among men (John 1:1, 14, 18). Christ, "the light of the world" (John 8:12; 9:5), caused even the gigantic candelabra in Herod's temple to pale by comparison. Christ, the Passover Lamb (1 Corinthians 5:7), rendered temple sacrifices irrelevant. Indeed, he was the living Temple toward which their house and its sacrificial system pointed.[7]

The teachers of the law nonetheless loved their traditions more than the Teacher in whom those traditions were realized. As Jesus made plain, the living Temple was now in their midst—thus, those who worshiped God in spirit and in truth must no longer worship in a Samaritan temple on Mount Gerizim or a Jewish temple in Jerusalem (John 4:21–24). When the disciples called the Master's attention to the magnificence of the temple and its surroundings, he replied, "I tell you the truth, not one stone here will be left on another; every one will be thrown down" (Matthew 24:2).

Filled with apocalyptic awe and anxiety, the disciples asked, "*When* will this happen, and *what* will be the sign of your coming and of the end of the age?" (Matthew 24:3). In sober response, Jesus predicted that first the "gospel of the kingdom will be preached in the whole world as a testimony to all nations, and then the end will come" (v. 14). His prophetic pronouncements continue with such words as, "The sun will be darkened, and the moon will not give its light; the stars will fall from the sky, and the heavenly bodies will be shaken" (v. 29). He even pointed out that the disciples themselves would "see standing in the holy place the abomination that causes desolation, spoken of through the prophet Daniel" (v. 15). "At that time" said Jesus, "the sign of the Son of Man will appear in the sky, and all the nations of the earth will mourn. They will see the Son of Man coming on the clouds of the sky, with power and great glory" (v. 30). So as to leave no doubt regarding the time of his coming, Jesus said, "I tell you the truth, *this generation* will certainly not pass away until all these things have happened. Heaven and earth will pass away, but my words will never pass away" (vv. 34–35).

Skeptics have been quick to point out that by these very words, Jesus disqualified himself as deity and demonstrated beyond peradventure of doubt that he was a false prophet. World-class philosopher and leading intellectual Bertrand Russell summarizes such sentiments in an essay titled "Why I Am Not a Christian":

[Jesus] certainly thought that His second coming would occur in clouds of glory before the death of all the people who were living at that time. . . . It is quite clear that He believed that His second coming would happen during the lifetime of many then living. That was the belief of His earlier followers, and it was the basis of a good deal of His moral teaching. When

He said, "Take no thought for the morrow," and things of that sort, it was very largely because He thought that the second coming was going to be very soon, and that all ordinary mundane affairs did not count.[8]

Like Russell, the great missionary physician and New Testament scholar Albert Schweitzer believed that Jesus was a false prophet because he testified that his second coming would occur within the lifetime of his disciples. As Schweitzer explains in his autobiography, "The bare text compelled me to assume that Jesus really announced persecutions for the disciples and, as a sequel to them, the immediate appearance of the celestial Son of Man, and that His announcement was shown by subsequent events to be wrong."[9]

Unbelieving Jews routinely discredit Christ and Christianity on precisely the same basis. On the Web site Jews for Judaism, Gerald Sigal writes:

There is no need to interpret the verse, "*Truly I say to you this generation will not pass away until all these things take place*" otherwise than that Jesus was speaking here of his contemporary generation. The expression "this generation" appears fourteen times in the Gospels and *always* applies to Jesus's contemporaries. That generation passed away without Jesus returning. Therefore, we are confronted by another unfulfilled promise by Jesus.[10]

Sigal sums up this sentiment, saying, "No amount of Christian theological acrobatics will ever solve the problems engendered by the historical reality that a promised imminent fulfillment made two thousand years ago did *not* occur as expected by the New Testament. Simply stated, Jesus is never coming back, not then, not now, not ever."[11]

Although quite clever, Tim LaHaye's rebuttal, "We believe 'this generation' refers to those alive in 1948" is about as believable to a discerning skeptic as Clinton's quip, "It depends on what the meaning of the word 'is' is." In fact, the moment dispensationalists such as LaHaye utter such statements, our baloney detectors must surely flash, "Warning! Grammatical gyrations ahead!!!" As the skeptic Gerald Sigal has well said, "This generation" appears fourteen times in the Gospels and *always* applies to Jesus's contemporaries."

Allow me to state the obvious. Our Lord is not grammatically challenged in the least! Had he wanted to draw the attention of his disciples to a generation nineteen hundred years hence, he would not have confused them with the adjective *this*.[12] As Dr. Kenneth Gentry has aptly noted, "this generation," in the context of the Olivet Discourse, is "a nonapocalyptic, nonpoetic, unambiguous, didactic assertion."[13] Thus, there is no mysterious esoteric meaning locked up in the grammar. When Jesus said, "When *you* see standing in the holy place 'the abomination that causes desolation' spoken of through the prophet Daniel" (Matthew 24:15), his disciples did not for a moment think he was referencing a far future generation.

As noted, "this generation" appears with surprising regularity in the Gospels, and it always applies to Jesus's contemporaries. In Matthew 11, Jesus asks, "To what can I compare *this generation*" (v. 16). Here as in every other usage of this phrase, the generation in view is the very generation that rejected the incarnate Christ who performed miracles in their midst. Jesus therefore denounced "the cities in which most of his miracles had been performed, because *they* did not repent"

77

(v. 20). It was clearly the cities in which the miracles were performed, not future cities, that Jesus had in mind. So as to leave no doubt, Jesus said, "Woe to you, Korazin! Woe to You, Bethsaida! If the miracles that were performed in you had been performed in Tyre and Sidon, they would have repented long ago in sackcloth and ashes" (v. 21).

And who can forget the seminal words of Christ recorded in Matthew 12? When the Pharisees and teachers of the law asked him for a miraculous sign, Jesus answered them, saying, "A wicked and adulterous *generation* asks for a miraculous sign! But none will be given it except the sign of the prophet Jonah. For as Jonah was three days and three nights in the belly of a huge fish, so the Son of Man will be three days and three nights in the heart of the earth" (Matthew 12:39–40). Not even LaHaye has the temerity to suggest that Jesus here is alluding to anything other than his death, burial, and resurrection in the first century.

Jesus went on to declare, "The men of Nineveh will stand up at the judgment with *this generation* and condemn it; for they repented at the preaching of Jonah, and now one greater than Jonah is here (Matthew 12:41). It would be a grammatical blunder of gargantuan proportions to interpret Jesus here as referencing any generation other than the one to whom he was speaking. Jesus left no doubt that he was speaking of particularly those present as he continued his rebuke of the Pharisees and teachers of the law. "The Queen of the South will rise at the judgment with *this generation* and condemn it; for she came from the ends of the earth to listen to Solomon's wisdom, and now one greater than Solomon is here" (Matthew 12:42). Jesus concluded his condemnation, saying, "That is how it will be with *this* wicked *generation*" (Matthew 12:45).

Just as it is grammatically implausible for Jesus to have meant anything other than the generation to whom he was speaking in this context, so too it is grammatically impossible for him to have been referencing anything other than the generation present during his delivery of the Olivet Discourse—as "this" means "this" and not "that" here, so "this" means "this" and not "that" there.

One final example should suffice. In the "seven woes" preceding the Olivet Discourse, Jesus warned the Pharisees and the teachers of the law of the judgment *they* would experience for rejecting the Messiah in their midst. While anti-Semites have delighted in assigning the judgments of Jesus to Jews in their contemporary generations, Jesus left no room for such misguided interpretations. Instead, he directly and specifically addressed his contemporaries, saying, "I tell you the truth, all this will come upon *this generation*" (Matthew 23:36). Without exception, the phrase "this generation" refers to the then present generation, not to a generation that is "alive in 1948."

In the interest of fairness, I should point out that the "this is that" argument is not the only argument in the dispensationalist arsenal. As former President Clinton offered an alternate meaning for the word *sex* (to those who would not buy the "It depends on what the meaning of the word 'is' is" rhetoric), so prophecy experts offer an alternate meaning for the word *generation*. Legendary dispensationalist Dr. C. I. Scofield suggested that *generation* did not mean "generation"—it meant "race."[14] Thus, in answer to the question, "When will this happen?" Jesus really meant to say, "I tell you the truth, *this race* will certainly not pass away until all these things have happened. Heaven and earth will pass away, but my words will never pass away."

Scofield went so far as to say that, as "all lexicons" reflect, the Jewish "race . . . will be preserved . . . a promise wonderfully fulfilled to this day."[15] One might presume that because this premise is postulated in a popular reference Bible, it is true. In reality, however, it is not. As noted by Gary DeMar, a perusal of popular lexicons reveals that the word "generation" in the context of Matthew's gospel references an interval of time, not an ethnic race of people. For example, Thayer's *Greek-English Lexicon of the New Testament* defines the Greek word *genea* as "*the whole multitude of men living at the same time*. Mt. xxiv.34; Mk. Xiii. 30; Luke i.48.' Thayer cites Matthew 24:34 and Mark 13:30 in support of translating *genea* as 'generation.' Thayer does not apply the 'race' translation to Matthew 24:34. A check of other lexicons and theological dictionaries will show that *genea* in Matthew 24:34 is translated 'generation'—'those living at the same time'—not 'race.'"[16]

DeMar goes on to explain that "the Greek word *genos* rather than *genea* is best translated 'race' (see Mark 7:26; Acts 4:36; 7:19; 13:26; 17:28; 18:24; 2 Cor. 11:26; Gal 1:14; Phil. 3:5; 1 Peter 2:9)."[17] This reality is reflected in modern Bible translations such as the New King James Version, New American Standard Bible, and New International Version. Scofield's superstar status, however, has ensured that his equivocation on the word *generation* persists in the present as a pragmatic method of saving Jesus from the charge of making false prophecies.

This ploy, however, is seldom satisfying to those who doubt the credibility of the Gospels. Common sense dictates that in answering the question, "When will these things happen?" Jesus does not respond by saying, "I tell you the truth, this race of people will certainly not pass away until all these things have happened. Heaven and earth will pass away, but my words will never pass away." Rather, our Lord is delineating the very signs that would precede the judgment of Jerusalem and the end of the age of sacrifice.

To contend that Jesus merely meant to say that the Jewish race would continue on into the twenty-first century is to suggest that his prediction was virtually meaningless. It would be like prophesying, "I tell you the truth, the Egyptian race will certainly not pass away until all these things have happened. Heaven and earth will pass away, but my words will never pass away." Or, "I tell you the truth, there will still be Greeks running around on the planet when all these things come to pass." Like it or not, Jesus gave his disciples specific verifiable signs that would identify him as either deity or deceiver (cf. Matthew 16:28; Mark 9:1; Luke 9:26–27).

THE PRONOUN *YOU*

Suppose I say to my children, "I tell you the truth, this day will certainly not pass away until I have taken *you* all to Disney World." Do you suppose they might scratch their heads and wonder whether I had a future generation of children in mind? Of course not! If I did not take them to Disney World that very day, I could not vindicate myself by explaining that I was really talking about my great-grandchildren.

In like fashion, Jesus's use of the pronoun *you* cannot possibly be taken to mean anything other than a reference to the generation that cried out, "Crucify him! . . . Crucify him! . . . Let his blood be on us and on our children!" (Matthew 27:22–25). They were the generation that had experienced the incarnate Christ in their midst yet had begged to have the notorious Barabbas released in his stead. Thus, said Jesus: "Upon *you* will come all the righteous blood that has been shed on earth, from the blood of righteous Abel to the blood of Zechariah son of Berekiah, whom you murdered between the temple and the altar" (Matthew 23:35).

As context makes clear, Jesus is not addressing a past generation, for he denounces as hypocrites the present generation of teachers of the law and Pharisees who say about themselves, *"If we had lived in the days of our forefathers*, we would not have taken part with them in shedding the blood of the prophets. So *you* testify against *yourselves* that *you* are the descendants of those who murdered the prophets. Fill up, then, the measure of the sins of *your* forefathers!" (Matthew 23:30–32). Nor is Jesus referencing a future generation, for he specifically says, "I tell *you* the truth, all this will come upon *this generation* (v. 36).[18]

In answer to the questions, "When will this happen, and what will be the sign of your coming and of the end of the age?" Jesus gave his disciples both the time of the signs and signs of the time. As Dr. Luke makes clear, the disciples essentially asked two questions *"When* will these things happen? And *what* will be the sign that they are about to take place?" (Luke 21:7)

In response, Jesus prophesied both the time of his coming and predicted the signs that would signal the end of the age. Skeptics and infidels have seized upon Christ's words to designate him a false prophet. Recall Bertrand Russell who said it was quite clear that Jesus believed his second coming would happen during the lifetime of his disciples. Or Albert Schweitzer who said that Christ's announcement regarding his second coming was shown by subsequent events to be wrong because the disciples of Christ died prior to his coming. As Jewish skeptic Gerald Sigal put it, "No amount of Christian theological acrobatics will ever solve the problems engendered by the historical reality that a promised imminent fulfillment made two thousand years ago did *not* occur as expected by the New Testament."

Had these men understood the language of the Bible, they may not have been as quick to wag their fingers at the Master. While they were correct in dismissing such grammatical gyrations as *"this* means *that"* they were incorrect in assuming that Jesus was predicting the time of his second coming. When Jesus said, "They will see the Son of Man *coming* on the clouds of the sky, with power and great glory" (Matthew 24:30), he was using language that anyone familiar with the Old Testament would readily grasp.

Recall the familiar Old Testament passage in which Daniel sees a vision of "one like a son of man, *coming* with the clouds of heaven. He approached the ancient of Days and was led into his presence" (Daniel 7:13). Here Christ is clearly not *descending* to earth in his second coming but rather *ascending* to the throne of the Almighty in vindication and exaltation.

As the student of Scripture well knows, "clouds" are a common Old Testament symbol pointing to God as the sovereign Judge of the nations. In the words of Ezekiel, "The day of the LORD is near—a day of *clouds*, a time of doom for the nations" (Ezekiel 30:3). Or as the prophet Joel put it, "The day of the LORD is coming. It is close at hand—a day of darkness and gloom, a day of *clouds* and blackness" (Joel 2:1–2).

No doubt at this very moment a host of similar passages are flooding through the minds of readers familiar with the Scriptures. Many can readily recall the epic language used regarding the judgment of Egypt: "See, the LORD rides on a swift cloud and is *coming* to Egypt. The idols of Egypt tremble before him, and the hearts of the Egyptians melt within them" (Isaiah 19:1). Certainly no one is so benighted as to think that coming on clouds in this context is anything other than language that denotes judgment. Why then should anyone suggest that Christ's coming on clouds in the context of the Olivet Discourse would refer to anything other than the judgment Jerusalem would experience within a generation just as Jesus had prophesied? As previously noted, we must inevitably ask ourselves whether it is indeed credible to suppose that Jesus, "the heir to the linguistic and theological riches of the prophets, and himself a greater theologian and master of imagery than them all, should ever have turned their symbols into flat and literal prose."[19]

Like Daniel, Isaiah, Ezekiel, and a host of prophets before him, Jesus employed the language of "clouds" to warn his disciples of judgment that would befall Jerusalem within a generation. Using final consummation language to characterize a near-future event, the Master prophesied, "At that time the sign of the Son of Man will appear in the sky, and all the nations of the earth will mourn. They will see the Son of Man coming on the clouds of the sky, with power and great glory" (Matthew 24:30). Far from predicting his second coming, however, Jesus was telling his disciples that those who witnessed Jerusalem's destruction would likewise see his vindication and exaltation as Israel's rightful king.

Similarly, when the disciples asked Jesus about "the end of the age," they were not asking Jesus about the end of the world (*kosmos*). They were rather asking Jesus about the end of the current corrupt age (*aion*) in the context of his chilling prediction of the destruction of the temple and its buildings. With the destruction of the temple would come the end of the

old covenant age of sacrifices that pointed forward to the ultimate sacrificial Lamb in whom the symbols would be fully and
completely satisfied.[20]

This is precisely what John the Baptist had in mind when
he called Jesus "the Lamb of God, who takes away the sin of
the world" (John 1:29). Jesus was "the guarantee of a better
covenant" (Hebrews 7:22). "Unlike the other high priests, he
does not need to offer sacrifices day after day, first for his own
sins, and then for the sins of the people. He sacrificed for their
sins once for all when he offered himself" (v. 27). "The ministry Jesus has received is as superior to theirs as the covenant
of which he is mediator is superior to the old one" (Hebrews
8:6). "By calling this covenant 'new,' he has made the first one
obsolete; and what is obsolete and aging will soon disappear"
(v. 13). "Christ was sacrificed once to take away the sins of
many people; and he will *appear a second time*, not to bear sin,
but to bring salvation to those who are waiting for him"
(Hebrews 9:28). Thus, the end of the age of sacrifice is found
in a Temple not built by human hands.

Common sense alone should be sufficient to convince the
unbiased that redefining "coming" to mean "second coming"
and "end of the age" to mean "end of the world" is at best misguided. As N. T. Wright artfully explains, the disciples

> had come to Jerusalem expecting Jesus to be enthroned
> as the rightful king. This would necessarily involve
> Jesus taking over the authority which the Temple sym-
> bolized. They were now confronted with the startling
> news that this taking over of authority would mean the
> demolition, literal and metaphorical, of the Temple,
> whose demise Jesus had in fact constantly predicted,

and which he had already symbolically overthrown in his dramatic (but apparently inconsequential) action in the Temple itself. The disciples now "heard" his prophetic announcement of the destruction of the Temple as the announcement, also, of his own vindication; in other words, of his own "coming"—not floating around on a cloud, of course, but of his "coming" *to Jerusalem as the vindicated, rightful king.*[21]

In the end it is safe to maintain that when Jesus said, "I tell *you* the truth, *this generation* will certainly not pass away until *all these things* have happened" his disciples did not for a moment think he was speaking of his second coming or of the end of the cosmos. As conflicted as they may have been about the character of Christ's kingdom or the scope of his rule, they were not in the least confused about whom he was addressing.

Little wonder then that all who read Christ's Olivet Discourse—whether skeptic or seeker—immediately presume that when Jesus uses the pronoun *you,* he is directly and obviously addressing a first-century audience. When someone attempts to convince them otherwise, their baloney detectors should immediately register full. The result of such grammatical gyrations is that many who may otherwise be drawn to the claims of Christ become galvanized in unbelief. Far better that those who love God and his Word learn to reach out to the lost by explaining the context in which such words as "coming" and "age" were used by Christ.

As Jesus was addressing a first-century audience when he spoke of the destruction of the temple, so too he was addressing his contemporaries when he said:

So when *you* see standing in the holy place '*the abomination that causes desolation*,' spoken of by the prophet Daniel—let the reader understand—then let those who are in Judea flee to the mountains. Let no one on the roof of his house go down to take anything out of the house. Let no one in the field go back to get his cloak. How dreadful it will be in those days for pregnant women and nursing mothers! Pray that *your* flight will not take place in winter or on the Sabbath. For then there will be great distress unequaled from the beginning of the world until now—and never to be equaled again. (Matthew 24:15–21)

"The abomination of desolation" spoken of by Jesus, had been prophesied six centuries earlier by Daniel, who wrote, "His armed forces will rise up to desecrate the temple fortress and will abolish the daily sacrifice. Then they will set up the abomination that causes desolation. With flattery he will corrupt those who have violated the covenant, but the people who know their God will firmly resist him" (Daniel 11:31–32). In 167 BC Daniel's prophecy became an unforgettable reality when Antiochus IV Epiphanes took Jerusalem by force, abolished temple sacrifices, erected an abominable altar to Zeus Olympus, and violated the Jewish covenant by outlawing Sabbath observance.

Therefore, when Jesus referenced the desolation spoken of by the prophet Daniel, everyone in his audience knew precisely what he was talking about. The annual Hanukkah celebration ensured that they would ever remember the Syrian antichrist who desecrated the temple fortress, the pig's blood splattered on the altar, and the statue of a Greek god in the Holy of Holies. Had God not supernaturally intervened

87

through the agency of Judas Maccabaeus, the epicenter of their theological and sociological identity would have been destroyed, not just desecrated.

In the Olivet Discourse, Jesus had taken the quintessential Jewish nightmare and extended it to cosmic proportions. In the fullness of time, what Jesus declared desolate was desolated by Roman infidels. They destroyed the temple fortress and ended the daily sacrifice. This time the blood that desolated the sacred altar did not flow from the carcasses of unclean pigs, but from the corpses of unbelieving Pharisees. This time the Holy of Holies was not merely desecrated by the defiling statue of a pagan god, but was manifestly destroyed by the pathetic greed of despoiling soldiers. This time no Judas Maccabaeus intervened. Within a generation, the temple was not just desecrated, it was destroyed! "Not one stone here," said Jesus, "will be left on another; every one will be thrown down" (Matthew 24:2). A generation later, when the disciples saw "Jerusalem being surrounded by armies" they *knew* "its desolation" was near (Luke 21:20). Thus, as Jesus had instructed, they *fled to the mountains* (Matthew 24:16; Luke 21:21).

The Jews who had failed to heed Christ's warning were savagely slaughtered. Some one million fell by the sword; myriad others were taken prisoner. When they saw Jerusalem "surrounded by armies," they should have known "that its desolation was near." However, though they knew the pronoun *you* specifically referenced their generation, they failed to heed the warning because of unbelief. So what Jesus had envisioned when he wept over Jerusalem became their worst nightmare: "The days will come upon *you* when *your* enemies will build an embankment against *you* and encircle *you* and hem *you* in on every side. They will dash *you* to the ground,

GRAMMATICAL PRINCIPLE

you and the children within *your* walls. They will not leave one stone on another, because *you* did not recognize the time of God's *coming* to *you*" (Luke 19:43–44).

One thing should be crystal clear to all those who read Christ's Olivet Discourse through biblical eyes. Our Lord's use of the pronoun *you* throughout, directly and specifically references a first-century, not a twenty-first-century, audience. Indeed, our Lord's words are directly in keeping with the Old Testament prophets. When he says, "The sun will be darkened, and the moon will not give its light; the stars will fall from the sky, and the heavenly bodies will be shaken" (Matthew 24:29; cf. Mark 13:24–25; Luke 21:25), fiery images of the Old Testament prophets should flash before our eyes.

Recall, for example, the vivid images used by Isaiah with regard to the judgment of Babylon in 539 BC:

> See, the day of the LORD is coming
> —a cruel day, with wrath and fierce anger—
> to make the land desolate
> and destroy sinners within it.
> *The stars* of heaven and their constellations
> will not show their light.
> The rising *sun will be darkened*
> and *the moon will not give its light.*
>
> (ISAIAH 13:9–10)

Surely no one supposes that the stars went into supernova in the days of Isaiah.

Rather, as Isaiah used the sun, moon, and stars as judgment metaphors against Babylon, so our Lord used them as judgment images against Jerusalem. In the end, it does not

89

depend on "what the meaning of the word 'is' is," but on whether "you 'is' or you 'isn't'" going to interpret Scripture in light of Scripture rather than Scripture in light of the *Daily Star*! No amount of grammatical gyrations should ever convince anyone otherwise.

THE ADVERB *SOON*

Ironically, the quintessential example of not reading the Bible literally (in the sense in which it is intended) is found in LaHaye's interpretation of the very first sentence of "the revelation of Jesus Christ, which God gave him to show his servants what must *soon* take place" (Revelation 1:1). According to LaHaye, our Lord's "emphasis" here "is on future events."[22] In other words, by using the word "soon," Jesus intends to emphasize that which will happen "to those alive in 1948."[23]

Again, such grammatical gyrations should cause our baloney detectors to go into red alert. It is one thing to suppose that a former president is confused about the meaning of the word *sex*; it is quite another to imagine that a prophecy expert who has studied prophecy for more than fifty years is confused about the meaning of the adverb *soon*. Though LaHaye spiritualizes the meaning of "soon" in the first verse of Revelation, there is no reason for anyone else to take it any way other than in its plain and natural sense.

First, allow me to restate the obvious. Neither Jesus nor John is grammatically challenged in the least. Had Jesus and John merely intended to emphasize imminence with respect to a generation that would come into being in the far-distant future, they would have had no difficulty whatsoever in doing so.

Furthermore, while it is one thing to misunderstand

grammatical constructions in apocalyptic or prophetic portions of the book of Revelation, it is quite another to misconstrue Jesus or John in the letter's introduction. The natural reading of such phrases as "what must soon take place" or "the time is near" is that the events that follow are *fore* future and not *far* future. To suppose that Jesus was actually intending to show his servants that which would take place "quickly" when it does take place, even if it is a very long way off, is a sure misunderstanding of the plain and literal sense of the language.[24]

Finally, as the whole of Revelation makes clear, Jesus used the adverb *soon* to solemnly testify to that which was near. For example, Jesus was obviously speaking of a fore-future event when he encouraged the church in Smyrna with the words, "Do not be afraid of what *you* are *about* to suffer. I tell *you*, the devil will put some of *you* in prison to test *you*, and *you* will suffer persecution for ten days. Be faithful, even to the point of death, and I will give *you* the crown of life" (Revelation 2:10). To suggest that our Lord's intent here is to address a "reformed church" in the pre-enlightenment era[25] is not only an affront to the faithful believers in the church of Smyrna, but is just plain silly. The faithful in Smyrna would not have taken our Lord to be addressing anyone other than themselves, and neither should we. Make no mistake: while our Lord's words apply to us, they were written to a first-century church about to face the mother of all tribulations.

As with the church at Smyrna, Jesus says to the church of Philadelphia, "I will also keep you from the hour of trial that is going to come upon the whole world to test those who live on the earth" (Revelation 3:10). It is incredible to suppose that Jesus is telling this first-century church that he is going to protect them from an hour of trial that is going to take place sometime between the eighteenth and twentieth centuries. Yet this is precisely what LaHaye would have us believe.[26]

Or who can forget the words of the angel who said to John, "Do not seal up the words of the prophecy of this book, because the time is near" (Revelation 22:10)? Are we really to suppose that the angel was referencing a time more than two thousand years hence? Of course not! When we read that the angel told Daniel to seal up his prophecy "until the time of the end" (Daniel 12:4), we do not suppose that the prophecy would be fulfilled in the fore future. Likewise, when we read that the angel told John not to seal up his prophecy, we do not suppose that the prophecy will be fulfilled in the far future.

Just as the angel in Daniel provides us with a perspective on time, so the angel in Revelation answers the question "How long?" with phrases like "There will be no more delay!" and words such as "soon" (see Revelation 1:1, 3; 2:16; 3:11; 10:6; 11:14; 22:6, 7, 10, 12, 20).[27] Says Richard Bauckham:

> Just as Daniel 12:7 answers the question, 'How long?' (12:6), so the angel in Revelation implicitly responds to the question 'How long?' which has been in the reader's mind since it was raised by the martyrs in 6:10. The answer is that there is now to be no more delay before the final period which will bring in the Kingdom, the Danielic "time, times and half a time". . . . the final period is about to begin in the immediate future.[28]

Of course, the fact that the book of Revelation is predominantly focused on fore-future events should not lead anyone to suppose that Revelation is exhausted in the holocaust of AD 70. As with the unfolding revelation in the whole of Scripture, the book of Revelation points forward to the restoration of all things—a time in which Jesus will appear a second time, the problem of sin will be fully and finally resolved, and Paradise lost will become Paradise restored. Jesus not only predicts that the Old Jerusalem will be destroyed; he promises that a New Jerusalem will descend. Thus, in Revelation 21 we read of a new heaven and a new earth.

> The first heaven and the first earth had passed away, and there was no longer any sea. I saw the Holy City, the new Jerusalem, coming down out of heaven from God, prepared as a bride beautifully dressed for her husband. And I heard a loud voice from the throne saying, "Now the dwelling of God is with men, and he will live with them. They will be his people, and God himself will be with them and be their God. He will wipe every tear from their eyes. There will be no more death or mourning or crying or pain, for the old order of things has passed away."
>
> He who was seated on the throne said, "I am making everything new!". . .
>
> I did not see a temple in the city, because the Lord God Almighty and the Lamb are its temple. The city does not need the sun or the moon to shine on it, for the glory of God gives it light, and the Lamb is its lamp. The nations will walk by its light, and the kings of the earth will bring their splendor into it. On no day will its gates ever be shut, for there will be no night there. The glory and honor of the nations will be brought into it. Nothing impure will ever enter it, nor will anyone who does what is shameful or deceitful,

but only those whose names are written in the Lamb's book of life. (vv. 1–5, 22–27)

In the end knowing the truth depends on whether we interpret Scripture in light of pet traditions or in keeping with the grammatical principle of biblical interpretation. To interpret Scripture Clintonian style is to turn Scripture into a wax nose capable of being twisted any way the interpreter likes. When Jesus said "this generation," he did not mean *that*; when he used the pronoun *you*, his hearers knew precisely who he was talking about; and when he said "soon," his servants did not suppose he was referencing a time twenty-one centuries future in which two-thirds of the Jews in Palestine would perish for the sins of their forefathers.

5

HISTORICAL PRINCIPLE:
Historical Realities vs. Historical Revisionism

Revelation was written by John in A.D. 95, which means the book of Revelation describes yet future events of the last days just before Jesus comes back to this earth.

—TIM LAHAYE, *THE END TIMES CONTROVERSY*

I tell you the truth, this generation will certainly not pass away until all these things have happened.

—JESUS CHRIST

AS I BEGIN THIS CHAPTER, IT IS THE EASTER season of 2006, and the Gospel of Judas is front and center in the news. On Good Friday, *USA Today* ran a Cover Story titled "Long-Lost Gospel of Judas Casts 'Traitor' in New Light."[1] And on Palm Sunday, the National Geographic channel featured a two-hour made-for-television special on thirteen papyrus pages that promised to challenge our deepest spiritual convictions and produce a genuine crisis of faith.[2] Indeed, according to a vast majority of scholars chronicled in newspapers such as *USA Today* and consulted on television broadcasts such as those on National Geographic, the greatest story ever "told" might well be the greatest story ever "sold."

Thus, on Easter 2006, as Christians worldwide celebrate the bodily resurrection of Christ, the historical veracity of the sacred text on which their faith is founded has been called into question. A majority of scholars chronicled in the Good Friday newspaper article and the Palm Sunday television special lent credibility to the notion that Judas was likely Christ's ultimate benefactor rather than his unseemly betrayer. According to Michael White, director of the Institute for the Study of Antiquity and Christian Origins at the University of Texas–Austin, "Scripture, like history, was codified by the winners, by those who emerged with the greatest numbers at the end of three centuries of Christianity."[3] Manuscripts such as the Gospel of Judas did not make it into the Bible because they were out of line with the direction "winners" wanted to take their newly minted religious notions. As a result, dozens of credible gospels simply lost out.

Princeton University religious scholar Elaine Pagels called the Gospel of Judas "an astonishing discovery that along with dozens of similar texts have in recent years transformed our understanding of early Christianity."[4] Although pronounced heretical by the hierarchy of the early Christian church, the Gospel of Judas was purportedly loved and revered by early followers of Christ. Bart Ehrman, who chairs the department of Religious Studies at the University of North Carolina–Chapel Hill is so enamored with the Gospel of Judas that in his view, had we embraced its perspective on Judas, we might well have avoided the Holocaust.[5] This from a man who was converted to faith in Jesus through Youth for Christ, received a diploma in Bible from Moody Bible Institute, and took his undergraduate degree from Wheaton College before studying under the esteemed Bruce Metzger at Princeton.[6]

Likewise, Coptic expert Marvin Meyer, who received his MDiv at Calvin Theological Seminary and his PhD from Claremont and now cochairs the Department of Religious Studies at Chapman University, holds that embracing a new view of Judas might well quell the flames of anti-Semitism.[7] In short, a new generation of scholars is disseminating the notion that the Bible is merely the product of historical winners who preferred the dark anti-Semitic overtones of manuscripts such as the Gospel of John over more racially sensitive gospels such as the Gospel of Judas.

The predilections of White, Pagels, Ehrman, Meyer, and others are not only being disseminated through newspapers and television specials, but by authors such as Dan Brown (*The Da Vinci Code*), Michael Baigent (*Holy Blood, Holy Grail*), and William Klassen (*Judas: Betrayer or Friend of Jesus?*). Dan Brown lends credence to the notion that more than eighty gospels were considered for the New Testament canon, but only four were chosen—Matthew, Mark, Luke, and John edged out gospels such as Judas because history is codified by triumphal winners rather than trustworthy witnesses.[8] Michael Baigent dismisses the canonical gospels as legendary and characterizes Christ's crucifixion as an elaborate hoax.[9] And Klassen pulls the race card by suggesting that John wanted "to vilify Judas"; thus his gospel gets "caught up in anti-Jewish propaganda."[10]

Jesus Seminar founder Robert Funk took it one step further when he suggested that Judas might well have been invented as an anti-Semitic slur. Said Funk, the story of Judas's betrayal of Jesus was "probably a fiction because Judas looks to many of us like the representation of Judaism or the Jews as responsible for His death. If it is a fiction it was one of the most cruel fictions

97

that was ever invented . . . because of the untold hostility that has persisted between Christians and Jews all down through the centuries."[11] As his Jesus Seminar cofounder, John Dominic Crossan, affirms, these scholars view Judas as the "typical quintessential Jew" because " 'Judas' meant 'Jew.' "[12]

Is it true that history was codified by triumphant "winners" who preferred the dark anti-Semitic overtones of manuscripts such as the Gospel of John over more racially sensitive texts such as the Gospel of Judas? Is the crucifixion of Christ and his subsequent resurrection a cruel hoax rather than credible history? Are the canonical gospels legendary, not legitimate? Or did the gospel writers faithfully record what they knew to be true?

To answer such questions requires familiarity with the historical principle of e^2, which is to say that in order to properly evaluate ancient manuscripts, we must take into account their historical legacy. Indeed, the acronym LEGACY is an apt way of remembering factors historians consider in determining the historical viability and meaning of ancient manuscripts.

Location. To begin with, the historian wants to know the *where* of an ancient manuscript. The location that a text was written as well as the locations that are referenced in the text provide crucial clues to meaning and historical trustworthiness. In the case of the Gospel of John, myriad internal details demonstrate that it was written by someone intimately acquainted with the topography of ancient Palestine.[13] John references a pool of Bethesda surrounded by five covered colonnades (5:2) as well as a pool of Siloam used by those who were infirm (9:7). Archaeology has verified the descriptions and locations of both of these pools. John also correctly notes changes in elevation between Cana in Galilee, Capernaum, and Jerusalem (2:11–13). Other examples include the two Bethanys—one less than two miles from Jerusalem on the road to Jericho where Mary, Martha, and Lazarus lived (11:18); the other beyond the Jordan River, which only an ancient Palestinian could have identified (1:28).

In the case of the Gnostic Gospel of Judas, there is no evidence that it was written by someone familiar with the geographical setting that existed in Palestine prior to the holocaust of AD 70. The very fact that Judas is a late Coptic manuscript discovered in Upper Egypt may well explain its complete lack of locational qualities.[14]

Essence. As with location, it is helpful to comprehend the essence of a manuscript. For example, the apostle John communicates the essence of love by describing Jesus as the sacrificial Lamb who atones for the sins of fallen humanity (1:29), defines life as knowing the only true God (17:3), and portrays Jesus as the "light of the world" (1:4, 5, 9; 3:19; 8:12; 9:5; 12:46). "This is the verdict," says John, "Light has come into the world, but men loved darkness instead of light because their deeds were evil" (3:19). The central themes of love, life, and light permeate John's gospel, providing a distinctive cohesiveness and context.

As narratives recorded in close proximity to the historical events they chronicle, the canonical gospels are eminently understandable. Conversely, the Gnostic gospels written long after the fact are esoteric, and therefore it is often difficult to decipher their meaning. If there is a common thread, it is the Gnostic notion that matter is inherently evil. While early Christians embraced the goodness of the physical world

(Genesis 1), the Gnostics shunned physicality. And that is precisely why Judas is characterized as a benefactor: he purportedly participates in a plan that will set the spirit of Jesus free from the prison house of his body.[15] Thus, the amount of time between the historical events and the recording of the events greatly influences its content.

Genre. Grasping genre—or form—is crucial in understanding what a text means by what it says. Where visionary imagery is the governing genre, it is foolhardy to interpret literalistically. Conversely, where historical narrative is preeminent, it is imperative not to overspiritualize. Even historical narratives, however, can employ richly symbolic imagery, metaphors, and wordplays. In fact, the biblical writers frequently use historical objects or events to teach spiritual realities. Consider, for example, our Lord's words in John's gospel: "Destroy this temple, and I will raise it again in three days" (2:19). The Jews interpreted Jesus literalistically. They, therefore, misunderstood Jesus's words to refer specifically to the destruction of their physical temple, which had "taken forty-six years to build" (v. 20). Jesus, however, purposely equivocated on the word "temple" to show the Jews that their covenant God would no longer meet with them through the mediation of an earthly temple built with human hands. Rather, Yahweh now tabernacled among them in flesh. As the apostle John explained, "The temple he had spoken of was his body" (v. 21).[16]

Author. Knowing who wrote a text is helpful in establishing historical reliability. While we do not know who wrote the Gospel of Judas, we do know that it was written pseudonymously.[17]

Pseudonymity was largely practiced by writers who lacked credibility.[18] Thus they borrowed the monikers of authentic eyewitnesses to the life and times of Christ to create an air of credibility. In sharp contrast, canonical gospels such as John provide ample internal evidence that they were written by Jews who were intimately acquainted with locations and events they recorded.[19] John, for example, was a Palestinian Jew and an eyewitness to the events recorded in his gospel. Thus, he had firsthand knowledge of the motivations, meditations, and movements of our Lord and his apostles.

Context. Understanding the historical milieu within which a manuscript was written provides further insight into its relia-bility and meaning. Though parasitic with respect to the canonical gospels, the Gnostic gospels were largely written to refute them.[20] Gnostics contrasted secret *gnosis* (knowledge) received directly from the Supreme Father with what they believed to be the inferior faith of Christians, and held that the physical world was the work of an inferior creator and was inherently evil. For example, while Christianity regards the proper use of sex as one of the greatest gifts God has given to humanity, Gnostics regarded sex as an evil practice. And whereas early Christianity defied the culture by placing women on the exact same footing as men, Gnosticism denigrated women in patriarchal fashion. Further, unlike the canonical gospels, the Gnostic gospels ascribe patently ignorant and politically incorrect statements to Jesus. The Gospel of Thomas records the following conversation between Peter and Jesus: "Simon Peter said to them, 'Make Mary leave us, for females don't deserve life.' Jesus said, 'Look, I will guide her to make her male, so that she too may become a living spirit resembling you males. For every female who makes herself male will enter the domain of Heaven."[21]

Years. Finally, of paramount significance to the historical principle of Exegetical Eschatology is when a text was recorded. While the esoteric nature of the text lends credence to the notion that the Gospel of Judas came into existence in an era in which Gnosticism was in full bloom, the thirteen papyrus pages offer no evidence that they were written by someone who would have been intimately acquainted with the landmarks and topography that existed prior to the holocaust of AD 70. If a gospel is written hundreds of years after the events it records, it is far less reliable than if it is written early. Thus, Judas, carbon dated to around AD 280,[22] is far less credible than John, which was most certainly written prior to the Jerusalem holocaust in AD 70.[23]

What can be said with respect to the dating of John can likewise be said of Matthew, Mark, and Luke. Dr. Luke, who recorded the Acts of the Apostles as well as his gospel narrative, concluded his two-part series with the apostle Paul still under house arrest in Rome. Since Paul was martyred under Nero in the early to midsixties,[24] Acts must have been written prior to that.[25] And since Acts is the second book in Luke's two-part account (see Acts 1:1), the Gospel of Luke is dated even earlier. Moreover, a majority of New Testament scholars hold that Luke and Matthew each rely in part on Mark, whose gospel is dated even earlier.[26]

The historical principle of Exegetical Eschatology not only affirms that the canonical gospel writers faithfully recorded what they knew to be true, but underscores the early dating and absolute reliability of the rest of the New Testament Scriptures as well. For example, a consensus of both liberal and conservative scholars dates the apostle Paul's first letter to the Corinthian Christians to the AD 50s,[27] no more than twenty-five years after Jesus's death. But it gets even better. In his first letter to the Corinthian Christians, the apostle Paul recites a creedal statement that can be traced all the way back to the formative stages of the early Christian church.[28] Incredibly, scholars of all stripes agree that this creed (1 Corinthians 15:3–7) can be dated to within three to eight years of the crucifixion event itself.[29] The short time span between Christ's crucifixion and the composition of this early Christian creed precludes the possibility of legendary corruption.[30]

In sum, faithful application of the historical principle of e^2, as codified in the LEGACY acronym, provides ample evidence that the Gospels are not lamentably biased by anti-Semitic sentiments and slurs. Instead, the presuppositions of fundamentalist scholars on the left are largely based in antihistorical sophistry.

Anti-Semitic Slur or Antihistorical Sophistry

Had Ehrman, Klassen, Jesus Seminar fellows, and the like heeded the historical principle encapsulated in the LEGACY acronym, they would not have fallen for their own antihistorical sophistry. Anti-Semitism had nothing to do with the canonization of Matthew, Mark, Luke, and John. Early dating, eyewitness attestation, and extrabiblical corroboration did! Even a cursory reading of the Gospel of Judas is enough to convince an unbiased reader that it was deeply influenced by Gnostic concepts that came into vogue long after the New Testament era. Conversely, the canonical gospels were recorded within a generation of the events they document.

The sentiments of such scholars clearly represent little more than vindictive prejudice. Even Crossan sees the flaw: "The trouble is, of course, that that was not the way people in the first century would have heard it, because [Judas] was an ordinary name. There's a lot of evidence that somebody—I'm deliberately putting this very vaguely—somebody close to Jesus betrayed Him."[31] As acknowledged by Crossan, Judas was a rather common name. There are several men named Judas in the Gospels, one of whom was a truly devoted disciple of Christ (Luke 6:16), while another wrote the New Testament epistle Jude (see Matthew 13:55; Jude 1). First-century gospel readers would hardly have taken the name Judas to signify Judaism.

Moreover, New Testament writers clearly proclaimed that salvation through the Jewish Messiah was given first to the Jewish people and then to the rest of the world (Matthew 15:24; Romans 1:16). Additionally, Peter's vision followed by Cornelius's receiving the Holy Spirit (Acts 10) and the subsequent Jerusalem council (Acts 15) clearly demonstrate both the inclusive nature of the church as well as the initial Jewish Christian resistance to gentile inclusion (see also Galatians 2:11–14). While the early Christians were certainly not anti-Semitic, at least some initially manifested the opposite prejudice! Far from being anti-Semitic, the New Testament simply records the outworking of redemptive history as foretold by the Jewish prophets who prophesied that one of Christ's companions would betray him (Psalm 41:9; John 13:18). There is nothing subtle about the crucifixion narrative. The Jewish gospel writers explicitly state that it was their leaders who condemned Christ of blasphemy. There would be no motive to fabricate a fictional Judas to represent the quintessential Jew.

As is obvious to any unbiased person from scholar to schoolchild, the New Testament is anything but anti-Semitic.

Jesus, the twelve apostles, and the apostle Paul were all Jewish! In fact, Christians proudly refer to their heritage as the Judeo-Christian tradition. In the book of Hebrews, Christians are reminded of Jews from David to Daniel who are members of the faith hall of fame. In fact, Christian children grow up with Jews as their heroes! From their mothers' knees to Sunday school classes, they are treated to Old Testament stories of great Jewish men and women of faith, from Moses to Mary and from Ezekiel to Esther.

The Bible goes to great lengths to underscore the fact that when it comes to faith in Christ, there is no distinction between Jew and Gentile (Galatians 3:28) and that Jewish people throughout the generations are no more responsible for Christ's death than anyone else. As Ezekiel put it, "The son will not share the guilt of the father, nor will the father share the guilt of the son" (Ezekiel 18:20). The "cruel fiction" referred to by Funk is not Judas, but the notion that Christianity is anti-Semitic. Truly, such scholars owe the world an apology for an idiosyncratic brand of fundamentalism that foments bigotry and hatred by entertaining the absurd notion that the biblical accounts of Judas were fabricated because "Judas meant Jew."

Apocalypse Now!

Even when fundamentalists on the left are forced to concede the historical reliability of New Testament accounts, they are prone to misinterpreting their historical meanings. Professor Ehrman not only ascribes anti-Semitic motives to the apostle John, but attributes apocalyptic sophistry to Jesus. Ehrman holds that the historical Jesus was an apocalyptic prophet who was not only mistaken but misguided in predicting that his generation would experience the end of the world.

105

Why? Because according to Ehrman, the apocalyptic Jesus "urged his followers to abandon their homes and forsake families for the sake of the Kingdom that was soon to arrive. He didn't encourage people to pursue fulfilling careers, make a good living, and work for a just society for the long haul; for him, there wasn't going to *be* a long haul. The end of the world as we know it was already at hand."[32]

In fact, Jesus did not predict the end of the world! Rather, Jesus was predicting an apocalypse now—within a generation the Jews would experience the destruction of their city and its temple. As previously demonstrated, when Jesus told followers that within a "generation" they would see him "coming on the clouds of heaven," he was using an Old Testament judgment metaphor. While Ehrman seems oblivious to the import of Jesus's words, Caiaphas and the council that condemned Christ were not! Far from saying that the end of the world was at hand, Jesus employed the Old Testament symbolism of clouds to warn the council that just as judgment had fallen on Egypt, so too, judgment would fall on Jerusalem (see Matthew 24:34; 26:64; cf Isaiah 19:1).[33]

Historical context should have been sufficient to ascertain that Jesus was not giving Caiaphas a dissertation on the end of the space-time continuum. Rather, Jesus was prophesying that those who would not bow the knee before the living Temple in their midst would experience the demolition of a physical temple that had become the object of their idolatry. Caiaphas and the Jewish ruling council would see Christ coming with the clouds as Judge of earth and sky (cf. Revelation 1:7). Christ was not saying Caiaphas would *see* him riding a cloud-chariot of sorts, but that he would *understand* that Jesus was indeed who he claimed to be. With the destruction of Jerusalem and the temple, they would understand that Jesus had indeed ascended to the right hand of power as the Judge of heaven and earth. Thus, "seeing" is an obvious metaphor for comprehension and understanding.

Misunderstanding figures of speech not only causes Ehrman to misconstrue the meaning of Jesus's words before Caiaphas, but elsewhere as well. Ironically, one of the reasons he cites for transitioning from fundamentalist Christian to fundamentalist atheist is the biblical claim that "a mustard seed is the smallest of all seeds." As he opines in his best-seller, *Misquoting Jesus*, "Maybe, when Jesus says later in Mark 4 that the mustard seed is 'the smallest of all seeds on the earth,' maybe I don't need to come up with a fancy explanation for how the mustard seed is the smallest of all seeds when I know full well it isn't. And maybe these 'mistakes' apply to bigger issues."[34]

The problem with Ehrman's misinterpretation is that like such fundamentalists on the left as Bill Maher he attempts to make the language of Scripture "walk on all fours." As noted previously, the kingdom of God is obviously not like a mustard seed in every way. A kingdom does not look like a mustard seed, nor is a mustard seed the smallest seed in the kingdom. Rather the kingdom of God is like a mustard seed in the sense that it begins small and becomes large (cf. Daniel 2:31–45).

As with the Savior's seed simile, Ehrman's error is to interpret Christ's "cloud" metaphor in a literalistic fashion. Like Caiaphas—who was conversant with Old Testament history— Ehrman should have immediately recognized Christ's words as an overt reference to his ascension to the right hand (another metaphor) of the "Ancient of Days" (see Daniel 7:13–14; cf. Acts 1:9). Unfortunately, error begets error. Thus, Ehrman's error with respect to the clouds metaphor leads to the further error that Luke (who in his view was writing after the death of Caiaphas and the destruction of the temple in AD 70) modifies the words of Christ to absolve him of a false prophesy.[35] In place of the clouds metaphor, Luke writes, "from now on the Son of Man will be seated at the right hand of the power of God" (Luke 22:69).[36] Had Ehrman taken seriously the historical meaning of the metaphor, he would have recognized that Luke—writing to a predominantly gentile audience—was simply communicating the phrase "coming on clouds" in the common vernacular of his day.[37]

Apocalypse Later

As we have seen, Ehrman correctly understands Jesus to be speaking about an apocalypse now—an apocalypse in *this* generation! However, he incorrectly charges Jesus with making a false prophecy by applying his prophecy to "the end of the world." Ehrman's solution of choice is to write Jesus off as a false prophet and retreat into the philosophically implausible world of atheism.

Tim LaHaye makes an equal and opposite error. He agrees with Ehrman that Jesus is speaking about the end of the world but absolves Christ of false prophecy by suggesting that "this generation" does not really mean "this generation"—"this" means "that," and "generation" means "race."[38] Similarly, when Jesus in the book of Revelation shows his servants "what must soon take place" (Revelation 1:1), LaHaye says our Lord's "emphasis" is on "future events."[39] When Revelation declares, "Look, he is coming with the clouds, and every eye will see him, even those who pierced him" (Revelation 1:7), LaHaye (much like Ehrman) contends that John intends to communicate that "all men will see the Lord Jesus Christ at His coming—those in

108

heaven, those on earth, and evidently, even those under the earth 'who pierced Him.' Again, this cannot refer to anything short of a physical, literal *second coming*."[40]

For LaHaye, everything hinges on proving that the book of Revelation was written long after the destruction of the temple in AD 70. If, like the rest of Scripture, Revelation was written prior to AD 70, his entire Left Behind juggernaut is compromised. Thus LaHaye is dogmatic in declaring that "Revelation was written by John in AD 95, which means the book of Revelation describes yet future events of the last days before Jesus comes back to this earth."[41] He goes on to assert that the Beast of Revelation is a twenty-first-century character. For LaHaye the notion that Revelation was written early and that Nero is the Beast is "historically ridiculous."[42] "Such an idea" says LaHaye, "is fraught will all kinds of distortions of history; it contradicts the known statements of Irenaeus and other early church fathers that it was written by John during the reign of Domitian and even ignores internal scriptural evidence to the contrary." LaHaye is so certain of his late date that he dismisses the early dating of Revelation as "impossible" and "preposterous"[43]

But is it really? The answer once again lies in the historical principle of Exegetical Eschatology. As the LEGACY acronym revealed the sophistry of scholars who assign an anti-Semitic bias to Matthew, Mark, Luke, and John, so too it may well reveal the utter falsity of the assertion that Jews right now are living in the shadow of the mother of all holocausts—a holocaust that will wipe out two-thirds of them. Not just two-thirds of the Jewish population in the Middle East, mind you, but two-thirds of the Jewish population on Mother Earth![44] Perhaps the notion that Revelation, like the gospel narratives, was written prior to the destruction of Jerusalem in AD 70 is *historically reasonable* rather than *historically ridiculous*. Maybe the first-century Nero Caesar rather than a twenty-first-century Nicolae Carpathia was the Beast of Revelation. Let's take a closer look.

LOCATION

First, we should note that Revelation is identified as a letter sent from John "to the seven churches in the province of Asia" (Revelation 1:4). The fact that the number seven is biblically imbued with a sense of completeness or wholeness should immediately alert us to the reality that Revelation is relevant to the whole church throughout the whole of history.[45] While seven is used symbolically throughout the whole of Scripture, there is no warrant for the mythology forwarded by the *Scofield Study Bible* that the seven churches in the province of Asia are symbolic of "seven phases of the *spiritual* history of the church from, say, AD 96 to the end . . . and in this precise order."[46]

Nowhere in Revelation is there any indication that John has two thousand years of church history in mind. Rather, as John makes clear in the prologue, his letter concerns things that "must *soon* take place" (Revelation 1:1). Indeed, says John, "the time is *near*" (Revelation 1:3). To suggest, as Scofield does, that "Thyatira is the Papacy" and "Sardis is the Protestant Reformation"[47] is an unwarranted allegorical imposition.

As it is wrongheaded to suggest that Revelation symbolizes seven consecutive historical eras, from the apostolic church in Ephesus to the apostate church in Laodicea, so too it is foolhardy to suggest that Revelation is principally a book describing what will take place in the twenty-first century. If this were so, Revelation would be largely irrelevant to its original hearers. We must ever be mindful that though Revelation, like the rest of Scripture, was written *for* us and is thus "useful for teaching, rebuking, correcting, and training in righteousness" (2 Timothy 3:16), it is not addressed *to* us. While Revelation is as relevant as Romans to redeemed readers throughout the whole of history, in the end it is addressed to seven historical churches in the province of Asia about to face the full fury of an ancient Roman beast.

The churches to which the Revelation of Jesus Christ was addressed were located in Asia Minor—the center of the Caesar cult.[48] From Jupiter Julius,[49] the father of the Roman Empire who was voted by the senate into the hierarchy of gods as "divine Julius," to Nero Claudius Caesar who was worshiped as "Almighty God" and "Savior," the Caesars deified themselves as gods. Octavius, successor to Julius Caesar, took on the moniker Augustus meaning "worthy of reverence and worship." A two-headed coin bearing the image of Julius on one side and Augustus on the other rendered Octavius "The divine Caesar—and the Son of God." Upon the death of Tiberius—the third Roman Caesar—the city of Smyrna was awarded the privilege of erecting a temple in which to worship him as god. Caligula, who succeeded Tiberius, was so convinced of his own divinity that he purposed to have a colossal image of himself erected in the Jewish temple in Jerusalem. Only death prevented his perverted ambition to be enshrined as god in the holy of holies. For Claudius, the fifth Caesar, the spiritual supremacy of the state was paramount. His philosophy was summed up in the phrase "Caesar is Lord."

The pretense that Caesar was Lord was customary for both Caesars and citizens. One need only think back to the jeers of the Jews in Jerusalem when Pilate presented Jesus to them as "King of the Jews." In one voice they shouted, "Anyone who claims to be a king opposes Caesar!" Again, when Pilate asked, "Shall I crucify your king?" They roared back, "We have no king but Caesar."[50] Indeed a generation later, when Nero succeeded Claudius, he was worshiped as both Savior and Lord.

It is in this milieu that John admonishes the seven churches in the province of Asia to stand firm in the conviction that Christ, not Caesar, is both Savior and Lord. They, as the bride of the Lamb, would face the lion's gory mane, the tyrant's brandished steel, and the fires of a thousand deaths.[51] But in the end, though they suffered persecution for *ten days* (Revelation 2:10), those who did not worship the Beast or his image and did not receive his mark on their foreheads or their hands would reign with Christ a *thousand years* (Revelation 20:4).

Furthermore, John tells us that the historical location on which Revelation was recorded was Patmos:

I, John, your brother and companion in the suffering and kingdom and patient endurance that are ours in Jesus, was on *the island of Patmos* because of the word of God and the testimony of Jesus. On the Lord's Day I was in the Spirit, and I heard behind me a loud voice like a trumpet, which said: "Write on a scroll what you see and send it to the seven churches: to Ephesus, Smyrna, Pergamum, Thyatira, Sardis, Philadelphia and Laodicea." (Revelation 1:9–10)

Patmos is a Sporades island in the Aegean Sea located off the coast of Asia Minor on which enemies of imperial Rome were often exiled. It is not uncommon for commentators to describe Patmos as a rocky penal colony—an Alcatraz of sorts.[52] This, however, is far from true.[53] Due to an inviting harbor that bisected the island, Patmos was a place of commerce and convenience for subjects of the empire traveling from Rome—capital of the empire, to Ephesus—epicenter of Caesar worship. Archaeological evidence documents that even centuries prior to the birth of Christ, Patmos boasted a civic center or gymnasium that doubled as a training center for athletes and a forum for intellectual pursuits. Not only so, but Patmos featured major temples to such gods as Apollo and Artemis, son and daughter of Zeus, as well as a statue to Hermes, herald of the Olympian gods. In reality, the prevailing notion that Patmos was a barren Alcatraz may well be little more than the imposition of twentieth-century anachronistic prejudices on first-century realities. While John was banished to Patmos by authorities in Asia Minor, he was likely not imprisoned. In fact, he may well have had access to the entire thirty-mile circumference of a well-developed island during the entirety of his exile, and he may have "stood on the shore" while seeing the vision of a beast "coming out of the sea" (Revelation 13:1).

Finally, John describes the historical location of the looming apocalypse as the domain of the first-century Roman Empire—not a ten-nation confederacy in the twenty-first century: "The seven heads are seven hills on which the woman sits. They are also seven kings. Five have fallen, *one is*, the other has not yet come; but when he does come, he must remain for a little while" (Revelation 17:9–10).[54] As the student of history well knows, Rome is historically depicted as the city of seven hills—Capitoline, Palatine, Esquiline, Aventine, Caelian, Viminal, and Quirinal. Thus, there is little doubt that John had the ancient Roman Empire in mind.

Likewise, the seven kings are seven Roman Caesars. The first five—Julius[55], Augustus, Tiberius, Caligula and Claudius— had fallen, Nero was presently on the throne, and Galba the seventh king had not yet come; But when he did he only remained on the throne for seven months—or as John put it— "a little while."[56] Internal evidence points to the fact that when John recorded the Revelation of Jesus Christ, the sixth king— Nero Caesar—ruled the Imperial Roman Empire. Only when we grasp the reality that Revelation was addressed to seven historical churches located in the epicenter of Caesar worship and written by John, who was exiled on Patmos during the Neronian persecution, will we fully appreciate the great tribulation chronicled within its pages.

We must ever be mindful of the fact that the ghastly terrors of Revelation are designed the "Great Tribulation" not just because Jerusalem and its temple were destroyed, or because of the massive loss of life, but because the Beast of Revelation purposed to destroy the very apostles and prophets who formed the foundation of the Christian church of which Christ himself was the chief cornerstone. The Great Tribulation instigated by Nero is thus the archetype for every type and tribulation that follows before we experience the reality of our own resurrection at the second appearing of Christ.

Let us be done with the patronizing nonsense of historical revisionists—like LaHaye—who characterize Nero as "a poor excuse for an Antichrist" and "a wimpy emperor who preferred to act on the stage of his day and recite poetry."[57] As the historically literate well know, the Beast of Revelation, who determined to slaughter the bride of the Lamb, was a maniacal megalomaniac who built a statue to himself more than a hundred feet tall and enshrined it in the Roman temple of

Mars, demanded to be worshiped as "Almighty God and Savior," castrated a young boy named Sporus and married him with pomp and ceremony, delighted in homosexual rape and sodomy, kicked his pregnant wife Poppaea to death, and exhausted the imperial treasury for his personal pleasures.[58]

And that is but a glimpse into the personification of evil. Tacitus amplifies Nero's nefarious nature in his *Annals*. Nero falsely accused early Christians as the cause of the great fire of Rome and subjected them to "the most exquisite tortures." He had them "covered with the skins of beasts," "torn by dogs," "nailed to crosses," and "burned to serve as a nightly illumination."[59]

Apollonius of Tyana described Nero as a beast more evil than any he had ever encountered in the wild. Like Lactantius, Sulpicius Severus, and the *Sibylline Oracles*, he described Nero as a destructive and noxious beast: "Of wild beasts you cannot say that they were ever known to eat their own mother, but Nero has gorged himself on this diet."[60] Says Suetonius, "He so prostituted his own chastity that after defiling almost every part of his body, he at last devised a kind of game, in which, covered with the skin of some wild animal, he was let loose from a cage and attacked the private parts of men and women, who were bound to stakes."[61]

ESSENCE

The essence of Revelation is the unveiling of a bride. It is a wedding covenant from beginning to end—from first to last—from Alpha to Omega. It begins with seven love letters to a *persecuted bride*—true Israel. It continues with the noxious vision of a *prostituted bride*—apostate Israel. In graphic Old

Testament pictures, we see the judgment of God written on a seven-sealed scroll, announced by seven angels with seven trumpets, and depicted through the seven plagues that befall a prostitute in bed with a beast. It concludes with the unveiling of a *purified bride*—true Israel. She is carried by the bridegroom over the threshold of Jordan into a New Jerusalem that "comes down out of heaven from God" (Revelation 21:10). First, Revelation unveils the *persecuted bride*. True Israel represented by the faithful in seven churches in the province of Asia face the full fury of a ferocious beast bent on her obliteration. Thus the Bridegroom exhorts and encourages his bride to be faithful and fearless. Those who do not forsake their "first love" (2:4) may "suffer persecution for ten days" (2:10), but in the end they will "reign with Christ a thousand years" (20:4). Like Antipas, who was put to death in Pergamum (2:13), they will partake of "hidden manna" (2:17), receive a "new name" (3:12) and "be dressed in white" (3:4, 5).

The purpose of the seven letters to the persecuted bride was to proclaim Christ as Lord in a historical milieu in which Caesar was hailed as Lord. The content of the letters is distinctly relevant to a first-century bride persecuted by a first-century beast. Those today who narcissistically insist that the seven letters are addressed to them are bound to miss their meaning. Tim LaHaye wrenches Christ's letter to the church at Philadelphia out of its historical context by supposing that it is replete with the "specific guarantee" that those who heed its warnings will not experience a twenty-first-century tribulation. Instead, they will be raptured in typical Left Behind fashion while all hell breaks loose on earth.[62] This despite the fact that there is nary a mention of a pretribulational rapture in the letter to Christ's persecuted bride in Philadelphia.

Would Christ have derided his first-century bride by saying, "I will also keep *you* from the hour of trial," when the "you" he had in mind was LaHaye and his twenty-first-century Left Behind audience? Is it credible to suppose that our Lord was informing a suffering first-century church that a twenty-first-century church of the future would be spared persecution by means of a pretribulational rapture? Is it conceivable that our Lord would befuddle his persecuted first-century bride with riddles concerning the far-distant future? Of course not!

Revelation is not a mere book of riddles originating from a shallow post-Christian mind; it is a book of symbols deeply rooted in Old Testament history. We mistake their meanings when we fail to hear the background music of the Old Testament.[63] The *tree of life* referred to in Jesus's letter to the church in Ephesus first appears in Genesis; the *ten days of testing* in Smyrna find their referent in Daniel; the heavenly *manna* promised to the church of Pergamum first fell from heaven in Exodus; the *Jezebel* who promoted sexual immorality in Thyatira is the mirror image of the idolatrous Jezebel in Kings; the *seven spirits* of the letter to the church in Sardis hark back to the Spirit as described by Zechariah; the *key of David* referenced in the letter to Philadelphia echoes the words of Isaiah; and Christ's rebuke to the church in Laodicea alludes to the words of Proverbs, "My son, do not despise the LORD's discipline and do not resent his rebuke" (3:11). Furthermore, as the letters of Christ to his *persecuted bride* utilize images deeply embedded in language of the Bible, so too the judgment of Christ against a *prostituted bride*—written on a seven-sealed scroll, announced with seven trumpets, and depicted by seven plagues—find their referent in the history of the Old Testament Scriptures. The pattern of sevenfold judgment against unfaithfulness on the part of Israel is spelled out in dreadful detail in Leviticus. Four times God tells his covenant people, "I will punish you for your sins seven times over."[64] In like fashion, the imagery of sevenfold judgment against apostate Israel is unveiled on four occasions in Revelation. The pronouncement of judgment for unfaithfulness in the seven churches is followed by the judgments of the seven seals, seven trumpets, and seven bowls.

Following on the heels of the judgment of the seven bowls is the judgment of the prostituted bride. She is described as "the great prostitute who sits on many waters. With her the kings of the earth committed adultery" (Revelation 17:1). In verses 3–5, John gives more detail:

> I saw a woman sitting on a scarlet beast that was covered with blasphemous names and had seven heads and ten horns. The woman was dressed in purple and scarlet, and was glittering with gold, precious stones and pearls. She held a golden cup in her hand, filled with abominable things and the filth of her adulteries. This title was written on her forehead:
>
> MYSTERY
> BABYLON THE GREAT
> THE MOTHER OF PROSTITUTES
> AND OF THE ABOMINATIONS OF THE EARTH.

The Great Prostitute

What has puzzled me over the years is not the identity of "the great prostitute," but how so many could mistake her historical identity. Tim LaHaye, who has studied biblical prophecy for more than fifty years, is absolutely certain that the mother of prostitutes and the abominations of the earth covered with blasphemous names is none other than the Roman Catholic Church of the twenty-first century. "Today" says LaHaye, "the Church of Rome is doctrinally a mixture of Babylonian paganism and Christianity . . . a far cry from the faith once for all entrusted to the saints." And he is just hitting his stride. In page after page he incriminates the Roman Catholic Church in the most pejorative of terms—"pseudo-Christian," "false religion," "mother of idolatry a lá [*sic*] Nimrod." In his view, "Rome is not the only form of *Babylonian mysticism*, but merely the one that has *infiltrated Christianity*. And after the Rapture, their leaders that remain will bring all the *Babylonian-based religions* together with one *global idolatrous religion*."[65] Not even Brown's *The Da Vinci Code* approaches the invective launched by LaHaye against this already vulnerable target.

Like LaHaye, hundreds of prophecy experts misidentify the great prostitute as the contemporary Roman Catholic Church. On the flip side of the coin, hundreds of commentators identify ancient (or revived) imperial Rome as the great harlot. The InterVarsity Press New Testament Commentary Series posits this as self-evident truth. The point is made with such force that anyone missing "the clarity of the identification" is left to wonder how he or she could possibly have been mistaken on something so painfully obvious.[66] Like New Testament scholar Richard Bauckham, hundreds confidently identify the great harlot who rides the beast as "Roman civilization," which "as a corrupting influence, rides on the back of Roman military power."[67]

The application of the historical principle of e^2, however, demonstrates that this is a clear case of mistaken identity. In biblical history only one nation is inextricably linked to the moniker "harlot."[68] *And that nation is Israel!* Anyone who has read the Bible even once has flashbacks to the graphic images of apostate Israel when they first encounter the great prostitute of Revelation. From the Pentateuch to the Prophets, the image is repeated endlessly. Perhaps the most gut-wrenching portrayal of Israel as prostitute is found in Hosea.

Hosea's marriage to the prostitute Gomer is a poignant parallel to God's wedding covenant with Israel. Though Gomer repeatedly whores after other lovers, Hosea doggedly pursues reconciliation and relationship with his bride. Hosea's love for Gomer is emblematic of God's love for his prostituted bride. Verse by verse, the painful picture of a people who prostitute themselves with pagan deities emerges. It culminates in Hosea's lament over a people who "love the wages of a prostitute at every threshing floor" (Hosea 9:1). The image is pregnant with meaning. Not only was the threshing floor a place of intimacy in which the kinsman redeemer spread the corner of his garment over Ruth, but the very temple itself was built on the threshing floor (2 Chronicles 3:1–2).[69] Unlike Ruth, however, the prostituted bride had little interest in seeking intimacy with God in his temple. Instead, she craved intimacy with foreign gods on the threshing floors of perverse temples.

As with Hosea, apostate Israel plays the part of a prostitute in Jeremiah. Once again the language is chilling and explicit.

> "Indeed, on every high hill
>   and under every spreading tree
>   you lay down as a prostitute. . . .
> You are a swift she-camel
>   running here and there,
> a wild donkey accustomed to the desert,
>   sniffing the wind in her craving—
>   in her heat who can restrain her?

Any males that pursue her need not tire themselves;
at mating time they will find her."

(2:20–24)

Jeremiah continues:

"You have defiled the land
with your prostitution and wickedness.
Therefore the showers have been withheld,
and no spring rains have fallen.
Yet you have the brazen look of a prostitute;
and refuse to blush with shame."

(3:2–3)

The portrayal of Jerusalem as a prostitute is even more brazen in Ezekiel. Indeed, says Ezekiel, the prostitution of Jerusalem made that of her sisters, Samaria and Sodom, look insignificant by comparison. Jerusalem "saw men portrayed on a wall, figures of Chaldeans portrayed in red, with belts around their waists and flowing turbans on their heads; all of them looked like Babylonian chariot officers, natives of Chaldea. As soon as she saw them, she lusted after them" (23:14–16). Thus says the Lord, "I turned away from her in disgust, just as I had turned away from her sister. Yet she became more and more promiscuous as she recalled the days of her youth, when she was a prostitute in Egypt. There she lusted after her lovers, whose genitals were like those of donkeys and whose emission was like that of horses" (vv. 18–20; see vv. 9–20).

Ezekiel's depiction of apostate Israel as an insatiable prostitute is particularly significant in light of the self-evident parallels to Revelation. Indeed, Revelation is a virtual recapitulation of

121

Ezekiel, from the four living creatures (Ezekiel 1//Revelation 4) to the mark on the foreheads of the saints (Ezekiel 9//Revelation 7); from the eating of the scroll (Ezekiel 3//Revelation 10) to the measuring of the temple (Ezekiel 40//Revelation 11); from Gog and Magog (Ezekiel 38//Revelation 20) to the river of the water of life (Ezekiel 47//Revelation 22). And even that but scratches the surface. A Sunday school child with Bible in hand can find a hundred or more parallels on a quiet Sunday afternoon. Nowhere are the parallels more poignant than in Ezekiel 16 and Revelation 17—sequentially linked and memorable.

In Ezekiel 16 we encounter Jerusalem as a discarded baby kicking about in her nakedness and blood. Had the Kinsman Redeemer not passed by and cared for her, she most surely would have died. Instead, like Ruth, she became the object of the Lord's affection. And, like Boaz, when the Lord saw that she had grown "old enough for love," the Kinsman Redeemer spread the corner of his garment over her, covering her nakedness, thus entering into a covenant of faithfulness with her (v.8). He bathed her with water, dressed her in glittering gold and precious stones—and made her his bride. In return she sacrificed her children to idols and prostituted her beauty to entice the kings of the earth to commit adultery with her. She engaged in prostitution with the Egyptians. Even the Philistines were shocked by her lewd conduct. She engaged in prostitution with the Assyrians, too, because she was insatiable. Then she increased her promiscuity to include Babylonia, a land of merchants, but even with this she was not satisfied (vv. 15–29).

The similarities are striking! In both Ezekiel and Revelation, the prostitute commits adultery with the kings of the earth; she is dressed in splendor and glitters with gold and precious jewels; and she is drunk with the blood of the righteous. And that's just a glimpse of her unveiling. Throughout the Old Testament, the harlot prostitutes herself with imperial rulers—with kings of Egypt, Assyria, and Babylon. Likewise, in Revelation she is in bed with imperial Rome. When the ultimate Kinsman Redeemer seeks to cover her with the corner of his robe of righteousness, she cries out, "We have no king but Caesar" (John 19:15). "Intoxicated with the wine of her adulteries," they fail to recognize the Messiah in their midst. Tragically, Israel, called to be a light to those in darkness, aligns herself with Caesar in piercing Christ and persecuting Christians. The golden cup in her hand is filled with "the blood of prophets and of the saints and of all who have been killed on the earth" (Revelation 18:24). Shrouded in mystery, she was glorious—like "the most beautiful of jewels" (Ezekiel 16:7). Unveiled as apostate Israel, she is grotesque.

Now the sixty-four-million-dollar question! If the unveiling of the prostitute of Revelation as the very prostitute identified by the Pentateuch and the Prophets is so self-evident, why do so many prophecy experts misidentify her? The answer once again lies in the maxim "Error begets error." Just as the error of misdating John's gospel has led scholars on the left to misidentify Judas as Christ's ultimate benefactor rather than his unseemly betrayer, so the error of misdating John's revelation has led scholars on the right—and seemingly everyone in-between—to misidentify the prostitute as either Rome or the Roman Catholic Church.

If Revelation was written in the midnineties during the reign of Domitian, apostate Israel would already have been destroyed. If, on the other hand, Revelation was written in the midsixties, the quintessential case of mistaken identity could

not possibly have taken place. The biblical link between
Ezekiel 16 and Revelation 17 in itself would have been enough
to preclude the misidentification. Had LaHaye taken seriously
the historical principle of e^2, the Roman Catholic Church
would not have suffered yet another gratuitous broadside.
Bearing false witness is a serious matter.

Finally, Revelation is the unveiling of the purified bride,
dressed in fine linen bright and clean. Though she suffers for
ten days, she will reign with Christ for a thousand years. The
contrast between the purified bride and the prostituted bride
could not be starker. While the prostituted bride bears the
mark "MYSTERY BABYLON THE GREAT THE MOTHER OF PROS-
TITUTES AND OF THE ABOMINATIONS OF THE EARTH" (17:5),
the purified bride bears the moniker of the Lord and the Lamb
on her forehead. Unlike "the synagogue of Satan"(2:9)—those
who claim to be Jews though they are not—she need not fear
the judgment about to befall Jerusalem, for she has been sealed
by "the Lamb that was slain from the creation of the world"
(13:8). In fact, before apostate Israel is judged, true Israel must
be sealed. Says John: "[An angel] called out in a loud voice. . . :
'Do not harm the land or the sea or the trees until we put a seal
on the foreheads of the servants of our God.' Then I heard the
number of those who were sealed: *144,000 from all the tribes of
Israel*" (Revelation 7:3–4).

The 144,000

Among the numbers of Revelation none is more misunderstood than the number of the purified bride. Jehovah's Witnesses
teach that 144,000 represent the total number of Jehovah's
Witnesses who will make it to heaven. The rest of the faithful
will live apart from Christ on earth. Thus in Watchtower lore

there is a "little flock" of 144,000 who get to go to heaven and a "great crowd" of others who are relegated to earth. Unlike the earthly class, the heavenly class are born again, receive the baptism of the Holy Spirit, and partake of communion.[70]

Like Watchtower founder Charles Taze Russell, Tim LaHaye believes that God has two distinct people with two distinct plans and two distinct destinies. Unlike the Watchtower, however, he holds that the 144,000 are Jewish witnesses, not Jehovah's Witnesses. There is not a Gentile among them. Nor for that matter are there any women. In fact, according to LaHaye, 144,000 is a number representing *exactly* 144,000 Jewish males who have not "defiled themselves with women." They must have a visible mark on their foreheads and they must be virgins.[71]

In truth, the number 144,000 excludes neither non-Jewish men nor women. Far from fixated on race and gender, the number 144,000 is focused on relationship. It represents true Israel—not by nationality but by spirituality, not by circumcision of the flesh but by circumcision of the heart. Indeed, the 144,000 are "*a great multitude* that no one can count, from every nation, tribe, people and language, standing before the throne and in front of the Lamb. They were wearing white robes and were holding palm branches in their hands. And they cried out in a loud voice: 'Salvation belongs to our God, who sits on the throne and to the Lamb'" (Revelation 7:9–10).

Contra Jehovah's Witnesses and LaHaye, the 144,000 and the great multitude are not two different peoples, but two different ways of describing the same purified bride. Literarily, the 144,000 and the great multitude are comparable to the Lion and the Lamb. Just as John is *told* about a

Lion and turns to *see* a Lamb (Revelation 5:5–6), so he is *told* about the 144,000 and turns to *see* a great multitude (Revelation 7). Thus, the 144,000 are to the great multitude what the Lion is to the Lamb, namely, the same entity seen from two different vantage points. From one vantage point, the purified bride is numbered; from another, she is innumerable—a great multitude that no one can count.

To suggest as LaHaye does that "12,000" from each of the twelve tribes means exactly 12,000—not 11,999 or 12,001— must surely stretch the credulity of even the most ardent literalist beyond the breaking point. To begin with, ten of the twelve tribes lost their national identity almost three thousand years ago in the Assyrian exile. The other two, Judah and Benjamin, were largely decimated two thousand years ago by Roman hordes. Furthermore, God's priority is not race but relationship. Christians are portrayed in Scripture as true Israel as a result of their relationship to Jesus, who is described as the Lion of the tribe of Judah. Finally, the pattern of Scripture is to refer to the community of faith, whether Jew or gentile, with Jewish designations. New Jerusalem itself is figuratively built on the foundation of the twelve apostles and is entered through twelve gates inscribed with the names of the twelve tribes of Israel. Not only so, but its walls are twelve times twelve, or 144, cubits thick (Revelation 21:12–17).

It is far more likely that 144,000 is a number that represents the twelve apostles of the Lamb multiplied by the twelve tribes of Israel, times one thousand. The figurative use of the number twelve and its multiples is well established in biblical history. For example, the tree of life in Paradise restored is said to bear twelve crops of fruit, yielding its fruit every month

(Revelation 22:2), and the great presbytery in heaven is surrounded by twenty-four elders (Revelation 4:4). Likewise, the figurative use of the whole number one thousand is virtually ubiquitous in Old Testament usage. For example, God increased the number of the Israelites a thousand times (Deuteronomy 1:11); God keeps his covenant to a thousand generations (Deuteronomy 7:9); God owns the cattle on a thousand hills (Psalm 50:10); the least of Zion will become a thousand and the smallest a mighty nation (Isaiah 60:22); a day in God's sight is better than a thousand elsewhere (Psalm 84:10); God shows love to a thousand generations (Exodus 20:6). A thousand more examples (figuratively speaking) could easily be added to the list.[72]

Just as the woman who rides the beast is symbolic of apostate Israel, so the 144,000 represent true Israel as it was intended to be—in perfect symmetry and providentially sealed. Who can help but think back to Ezekiel's epic depiction of a man clothed in linen etching a mark on the foreheads of those who grieved and lamented over all the detestable things done in Jerusalem prior to its destruction by the Babylonians six centuries before Christ (Ezekiel 9:4)? Or fail to realize that those who were marked were the earnest of the 144,000 sealed prior to Jerusalem's destruction in AD 70? She is the purified bride from every nation, tribe, people, and language who will step over Jordan into the New Jerusalem prepared for her from the very foundations of the world.

In sum, Revelation is the unveiling of a bride. It commences with seven letters to a persecuted bride; continues with a sevenfold judgment against a prostituted bride, which was written on a seven-sealed scroll, announced by seven angels with seven trumpets, and depicted through seven plagues; and crescendos with the unveiling of a purified bride by a bridegroom described as having seven horns and seven eyes.

GENRE

As with location and essence, it is crucial to consider genre in establishing the historical meaning imbedded in the text of Revelation. By way of illustration, as I write, it is Father's Day and I have just finished writing letters to each of my eight living children. As with John's letter to the seven churches in the province of Asia, each letter opened with a salutation and closed with a blessing that anyone reading the letters in our day could easily understand. Not so, however, with the body of my letters. For example, I wrote to Hank Jr. about the pride I felt in watching him "turn a snowman into a tweeter on number seven" the day before. Unless you were familiar with golf lingo in general or "Hankisms" in particular, you would have little hope of comprehending my meaning. Like my letters, Revelation contains a distinct language system. One must be familiar with the epistolary, apocalyptic, and prophetic literature common to second-temple Judaism in order to grasp its meaning. Thus, the key to reading Revelation for all it is worth is to carefully consider the distinct genres it employs.

To begin with, Revelation is a letter. It starts with a salutation that identifies both the author of the letter and the audience to whom it is addressed ("John, to the seven churches in the province of Asia" [1:4]) and concludes with an ancient epistolary blessing ("The grace of the Lord Jesus be with God's people. Amen" [22:21]). Like the New Testament letters (epistles) that precede it, Revelation addresses the contemporary historical situation of Christ's bride—the church. As noted by G. K. Beale, the epistolary writers in the New Testament "appeal to the readers' present and future participation and blessings in Christ as the basis for their appeals to obedience. If the epistolary form of Revelation functions like that of the other letters in the [New Testament], then its purpose likewise is to address contemporary problems among the seven churches by appealing to the hearers' present and future share in Christ's blessings."[73]

Beale's point bears repeating. As a letter, Revelation addresses contemporary problems among the seven churches in the province of Asia. Therefore, it is crucial to have a grasp of the historical situation that the letter addresses. Again, John is writing to his contemporaries in the first century, not to the contemporary Christian church of the twenty-first. Antipas, the faithful witness, was not put to death in twenty-first century Izmir, he was put to death in first-century Smyrna! Likewise, to suggest that the hour of trial that Christ references in his letter to Philadelphia is a symbolic reference to a twenty-first-century rapture completely misses the point. Like all of the New Testament letters, Revelation is not a letter addressed *to* us but rather a letter that has application *for* us in every epoch of time.

As previously noted, one of the key reasons LaHaye thinks that aspects of the letters to the seven churches in the province of Asia relate directly to events that will take place in the twenty-first century is that he reads strained foreign connotations into straightforward communications. "Soon" does not mean "soon" and "near" does not mean "near." To suggest, as LaHaye does, that Jesus was actually intending to show his servants that which would take place "quickly" when it begins to take place in the twenty-first century should be a clear tip-off that you have just entered a spin zone. It is one thing to misunderstand what is being communicated in apocalyptic or prophetic portions of Revelation; it is quite another to misconstrue the plain sense of the introductory remarks of a letter.

Furthermore, Revelation is an apocalypse—not just in the sense of an unveiling but in the sense of what might best be described as a language system or matrix that is deeply embedded in the Old Testament canon. A classic case in point involves the two witnesses of Revelation 11. "These" says John, "are the two olive trees and the two lampstands that stand before the Lord of the earth. If anyone tries to harm them, fire comes from their mouths and devours their enemies. This is how anyone who wants to harm them must die (vv. 4–5). They "have power to shut up the sky so that it will not rain during the time that they are prophesying; and they have the power to turn the waters into blood and to strike the earth with every kind of plague as often as they want" (v. 6).

After the Beast arises from the Abyss and kills them, their bodies will lie open and exposed "in the street of the great city, which is *figuratively* called Sodom and Egypt, where also their Lord was crucified. For three and a half days men from every people, tribe, language and nation will gaze on their bodies and refuse them burial" (vv. 8–9). After three and a half days, however, a breath of life from God will enter them, and they will stand up, and terror will strike those who see them. Then they will hear a loud voice from heaven saying to them, "Come up here." And they will go up to heaven in a cloud, while their enemies look on (vv. 11–12).

The Two Witnesses

As with my letter to Hank Jr., the identity of the two witnesses of Revelation 11 cannot be comprehended apart from a familiarity with the language system employed by the text.

Only a modern-day golfer comprehends that a snowman is a metaphor for the number eight and a tweeter is a birdie (one under par on a hole)—in this case hole number seven. In like fashion, only someone with the background music of the Old Testament coursing through their minds comprehends that the two witnesses are a metaphorical reference to Moses and Elijah and reflect Old Testament jurisprudence that mandated at least two witnesses to convict of a crime (Deuteronomy 19:15).

Equally significant is the fact that the two witnesses are described as two olive trees and two lampstands. The imagery harks back to a familiar Old Testament passage in which Zechariah sees two olive trees on the right and the left of a lampstand that symbolize "the two who are anointed to serve the Lord of all the earth" (Zechariah 4:14). In Zechariah's day the two witnesses were Zerubbabel, the governor of Judah who returned to Jerusalem to lay the foundation of a second temple, and Joshua, the high priest commissioned to preside over its altar. In Revelation this imagery is invested in two witnesses who, as literary characters in the apocalyptic narrative, represent the entire line of Hebrew prophets in testifying against apostate Israel and preside over the soon-coming judgment and destruction of Jerusalem and the second temple. Like Moses, the witnesses have power to turn water into blood and to strike the earth with plagues (Exodus 7:17ff; 1 Samuel 4:8; Revelation 11:6). And like Elijah, they have power to call down fire from heaven to consume their enemies and to shut up the sky so that it will not rain for three and a half years (1 Kings 18; Luke 4:25; Revelation 11:6).

Even more to the point, like Jesus they become sacrificial lambs before the fury of a beast. Their corpses unceremoniously litter the streets of the very city in which their Lord was crucified. The city is figuratively called Sodom in that it epitomized human wickedness and heavenly wrath as well as Egypt in that it is emblematic of the slavery from which only Jesus Christ can emancipate. Their resurrection after three and a half days parallels the resurrection of Christ in much the same way that their three and a half years of ministry mirrors that of the Messiah.

Two things we must never do. One is to attempt to draw exact parallels between John's apocalyptic imagery and the scriptural referents from which they are drawn. When we first encounter the two witnesses of Revelation 11, our minds are inexorably drawn to Zechariah's vision of a solid gold lampstand replete with seven lamps and seven channels connected to two olive trees that pour out golden oil. Zechariah's imagery points inexorably to the sevenfold Spirit who fills Zerubbabel and Joshua to overflowing as they lead God's people in the rebuilding of Jerusalem and the temple—"not by might nor by power, but by my Spirit" (Zechariah 4:6). Not so in Revelation 11. Here the imagery of the lampstand and the two olive trees are reconfigured into an intricate linguistic tapestry, the threads of which are drawn from a host of Old Testament passages. In sum, they form a composite image of the Law and the Prophets, culminating in the life, death, resurrection, and ascension of a Prophet and Priest who is the earnest of all who are his witnesses and who will reign with him in a New Jerusalem wherein dwells righteousness. We must ever be mindful of the dangers inherent in seeking to unravel the linguistic matrix of Revelation without first immersing ourselves in the wellspring of Old Testament imagery.

The second thing we must never do is attempt to press the language system of Revelation into a literalistic labyrinth.

Indeed, the literal-at-all-cost methodology of people like LaHaye is interpretive suicide when it comes to apocalyptic genre. Just as little Hank did not literally turn a snowman into a tiny bird on a gigantic number seven, so too the two witnesses will not literally turn their mouths into blow torches on the streets of Jerusalem. Nor should we suppose that Moses and Elijah will be literally transported to the twenty-first century in a time machine—or for that matter, that CNN will focus their television cameras on the dead bodies of Moses and Elijah for three and a half days. Nevertheless, LaHaye writes:

> The only way in which people all over the world can see two bodies lying in the streets of a city over a three-day period of time is through the medium of television; in fact, in recent years it has been possible by the launching of television satellites for many parts of the world to view the same sight at the same time. CNN International newscasts are already beamed into more than two hundred countries of the world. In fact, ours is the first generation that can literally see the fulfillment of [Revelation] 11:9 in allowing the people of the entire world to see such an awesome spectacle.[74]

It seems LaHaye cannot conceive of himself as living at any time other than in close proximity to "the end of the age."

Finally, while revelation is cast in the form of a letter and communicated through the genre of apocalyptic judgment language, including such fantasy imagery as an enormous red dragon with seven heads and ten horns and seven crowns on his heads, it is ultimately a prophetic word to the persecuted churches in the province of Asia Minor. As prophecy, Revelation *foretells* and *forthtells*. It foretells fore-future and final-future events and forthtells in the sense of exhorting and encouraging a persecuted bride destined to be purified.

As a prophetic *foretelling*, Revelation reveals "what must *soon* take place." Lest, we be seduced into supposing that a great parenthesis of two thousand years is wedged between John's apocalyptic vision and the judgments the vision symbolizes, we should take careful note of the repetition of the words "soon" and "near." We must ever be mindful that the angel of Revelation 22 explicitly tells John, "Do not seal up the words of the prophecy of this book, because the time is near" (Revelation 22:10).

Of course, the fact that the book of Revelation is predominantly focused on fore-future events should not lead anyone to suppose that the imagery of Revelation is exhausted in the holocaust of AD 70. As with the unfolding revelation in the whole of Scripture, the book of Revelation points forward to the final future when Jesus will appear a second time, the problem of sin will be fully and finally resolved, the dead will be resurrected, and the universe will be recreated without the stain of disease, destruction, death and decay (Romans 8:21). John, like the rest of the prophets, uses final consummation language to describe near-future events.

The sun, moon, and stars of Revelation 6 are an apt example. As the Lamb opened the sixth seal, "there was a great earthquake. The sun turned black like sackcloth made of goat hair, the whole moon turned blood red, and the stars in the sky fell to earth, as late figs drop from a fig tree when shaken by a strong wind. The sky receded like a scroll, rolling up, and every mountain and island was removed from its place" (vv. 12–14).

John's words find their referent in the words spoken by Jesus as he sat on the Mount of Olives surrounded by his disciples. Using the same imagery, he described the coming judgment of Jerusalem: "Immediately after the distress of those days", said Jesus, "The sun will be darkened, and the moon will not give its light; the stars will fall from the sky, and the heavenly bodies will be shaken" (Matthew 24:29). As John's words hark back to the words of Jesus, so the words of Jesus hark back to Isaiah's epic prophecy regarding the judgment of Babylon some six centuries earlier: "See the day of the LORD is coming—a cruel day, with wrath and fierce anger—to make the land desolate and destroy the sinners within it. The stars of heaven and their constellations will not show their light. The rising sun will be darkened and the moon will not give its light (Isaiah 13:9–10).

In all three cases, the prophets use apocalyptic language pointing to final-future realities to describe judgment in their generation. While the near-future catastrophe (demolition of Babylon and destruction of Jerusalem) fulfills the cosmic language, it does not exhaust its meaning. Indeed, as Peter's apocalyptic prophecy of judgment on Jerusalem suggests, a day of ultimate judgment looms on the horizon: "The heavens will disappear with a roar; the elements will be destroyed by fire, and the earth and everything in it will be laid bare. . . . That day will bring about the destruction of the heavens by fire, and the elements will melt in the heat. But in keeping with his promise we are looking forward to a new heaven and a new earth, the home of righteousness" (2 Peter 3:10–13).[75] While Peter's prophecy was fulfilled in the destruction of Jerusalem, the events of AD 70 and the cosmic language Peter used to describe them point forward to an even greater day of judgment when the problem of sin and Satan will be fully and finally resolved! In the new heaven and the new earth, those exemplified by the purified bride will no longer have need of the sun, moon, or stars for "there will be no more night. They will not need the light of a lamp or the light of the sun, for the Lord God will give them light. And they will reign for ever and ever" (Revelation 22:5).

In sum, then, John, like Jesus and the prophets before him, uses the imagery of sun, moon, and stars to refer to the near-future judgment of Jerusalem. While the language finds ultimate fulfillment in the second coming of Christ, it is inaugurated in the Jewish holocaust of AD 70. To suppose that stars are literally going to fall from the sky is nonsense. One star alone would obliterate the earth—let alone a hundred billion stars. Likewise, to recast the stars as "meteors" that "will fall to the ground and hit as hard, unripe things,"[76] as per LaHaye, is interpretive suicide. There is no warrant for figuratively reinterpreting stars as meteors. Nor should our interpretations ever be untethered from the pillar and post of Scripture. The code of Revelation is not broken through unrestrained subjectivity, but through understanding Scripture.

We must ever be mindful that Revelation was relevant to its original readers. It not only foretells fore and final future events, but it forthtells in the sense of exhorting and encouraging first-century believers in the midst of their trials and travails. Though Roman hordes and religious hypocrites plunder and pervert Jerusalem, they are to live with the vision of a New Jerusalem emblazoned upon their minds. "Nothing impure will ever enter it [the New Jerusalem], nor will anyone who does what is shameful or deceitful, but only those whose names are written in the Lamb's book of life" (Revelation 21:27).

AUTHOR

I am presently in the process of building a home. My wife, Kathy, and I have therefore spent a good deal of time looking at houses. In the process, we have become rather adept at identifying architectural nuances. Kathy has become so good at it that she can often look at the design of a home in an architectural digest and identify the architect without even reading the copy. From cornice detail to column design, she is all over it! What is true of a building is true of a book. In much the same way that a building contains clues that unveil the identity of its architect, a book contains clues that unveil the identity of its author. In the case of Revelation, three possibilities have been put forward, but only one fits the design.

First is a notion that can be dismissed rather rapidly—namely, the idea that Revelation was written pseudonymously. As noted by G. K. Beale, this is extraordinarily unlikely. "If an unknown author were attempting to identify himself with a well-known Christian figure like the apostle John, he would probably call himself not just 'John' but 'John the apostle.' This the author does not do. Indeed, there is little information about the author other than his self-identification as a servant, a fellow believer, a witness for Christ, and one who is suffering exile for that witness (1:1, 9–10)." Beale goes on to say that the scholarly consensus is that Revelation was not written pseudonymously but is "a personal self-reference to a real John."[77]

As discussed earlier, pseudonymity was largely practiced by writers who lacked authority. Thus, they borrowed the monikers of authentic eyewitnesses to the life and times of Christ to create an air of credibility. In sharp contrast, the book of Revelation provides ample internal evidence that it was written by a Jew intimately acquainted with the historical events and locations he wrote about. Only a handful of extremists today even countenance the possibility that Revelation could have been written pseudonymously. Most noteworthy among them is the aforementioned Bart Ehrman. Even Ehrman, however, allows for the possibility *only* if one subscribes to the further notion that the apostle John actually claimed to have authored Revelation. Then, says Ehrman, "the book would probably have to be considered pseudonymous."[78]

Ehrman goes on to dogmatically assert that neither Revelation nor the Gospel of John could have been written by the apostle John. As evidence he avers that John never identifies himself as one of the apostles seated around the throne of God in Revelation 4.[79] This, however, is hardly a defensible argument. Can anyone seriously imagine an "Ehrman version" of Revelation 4:4 in which John writes: "Surrounding the throne were twenty-four elders. They were dressed in white and had crowns of gold on their heads. *And I, John, son of Zebedee, was third from the left, the apostle sitting next to James.*" Such reasoning is not just silly but represents a new low in idiosyncratic conjecture.

Furthermore, as is the case with Ehrman, it is commonly argued that Revelation was written by someone other than the apostle John. The most frequently cited alternative is John the Elder. Like pseudonymity, this contention has its feet firmly planted in midair. It would be better grounded if there were even a shred of historical certainty that John the Elder existed in the first place.

Those who forward "the Elder" theory almost universally appeal to the conjecture of Dionysius of Alexandria, a pupil of Origen. Dionysius speculated that two noteworthy John's existed alongside each other in Ephesus. As Donald Guthrie has well said,

[Dionysius's] suggestion does not inspire confidence, for his "second John" has remarkably flimsy testimony to his existence. It is strange that such a scholar as Dionysius should give credence to a traveler's tale about the two tombs of John in Ephesus without entertaining the possibility that the rival tomb may be due to some local opportunist, after the pattern of the extraordinary multiplication of relics in subsequent history.[80]

According to R. C. H. Lenski, the reason the two Johns theory caught on in the first place was not historical evidence but distaste for chiliasm (millenarianism). Says Lenski: "Eusebius (about 270 to 340) adopted the view of Dionysius and, for the same reason, dislike of the chiliasm that sought its support in Revelation. . . . Thus was launched this view about a 'presbyter John' [elder John]."[81] In short, the "traveler's report" of Dionysius is tentative at best.

It is far more likely that John the Elder is just another way of referring to John the apostle. John described himself as "the Elder," not to distinguish himself from "the apostle," but to emphasize his authority and seniority. The early church father, Papias, in fact referred to the apostles as elders.[82] In short, there is scant evidence that a distinct John the elder even existed, and there is sufficient evidence that John the elder and John the apostle are one and the same.

Finally, while there is little to commend the notion that a shadowy figure named John the Elder wrote the book of Revelation, there is ample evidence that it was written by John the apostle. The very fact that the author of the Apocalypse simply calls himself *John* is a dead giveaway that he was well-known throughout the churches in Asia Minor. As William Hendriksen explains, "There was only one John who did not need to add 'the apostle,' for the very reason that he was known as the apostle! Besides, the author does not call himself *apostle* for the simple reason that he wrote this book in the capacity of *seer*, to whom visions were revealed (cf. Jn. 15:27; Acts 1:22–23; 1 Cor. 9:1)."[83] Guthrie adds that Justin, Irenaeus, Clement, Origen, Tertullian and Hippolytus

> assume it without discussion. So strong is this evidence that it is difficult to believe that they all made a mistake in confusing the John of the Apocalypse with John the apostle. The usual treatment of this evidence by those who deny apostolic authorship is to suppose that these early Fathers were unaware of the true origin of the book and, therefore, guessed that the John must have been the well-known son of Zebedee.

Guthrie goes on to explain that this supposition is often

> based on the theory of two Ephesian Johns, who could quite easily be mixed up, or else on the theory that the only John of Ephesus was the Elder who was later mistaken for the apostle. If all this evidence is due to a mistake it would be an extraordinarily widespread case of mistaken identity. It must be conceded that taken as a whole it points very strongly to the probability that the John of the Apocalypse was, in fact, John the apostle.[84]

In fact, the fingerprints of the apostle are all over the apocalypse! One need only open their eyes and ears to apprehend the clues. For example, John, and John alone, identifies Jesus as the Word, or Logos (John 1:1, 14; Revelation 19:13). Likewise, John alone identifies Jesus as the true witness (John 5:31–47; 8:14–18; Revelation 2:13; 3:14), and it is John who most exploits the Mosaic requirement of two witnesses (John 8:12–30; Revelation 11:1–12). Other exclusive parallels between the Gospel of John and Revelation include Jesus's invitation to all who are thirsty to come to him and drink (e.g., John 7:37; Revelation 22:17) and Jesus's reference to his having received authority from his Father (e.g., John 10:18; Revelation 2:27).

Additional similarities that are not exclusive to John but are clearly parallel in the gospel and the Apocalypse include white garments symbolizing holiness (John 20:12; e.g., Revelation 3:4) and reference to Jesus as the Lamb of God (John 1:29, 36; Revelation 5:6, 8, 12, et al.). More significantly, both the Gospel of John and Revelation present an explicitly high Christology, such that Jesus is God in the flesh and worthy of worship. In fact, it is in these two books that we find perhaps the clearest passages of the divinity of Christ in all of Scripture (see, e.g., John 1:1–3, 14, 18; 20:28; Revelation 4–5).

Added to all this, there is an undeniable commonality in the symbolic use of the number seven. Says Guthrie: "The Apocalypse is constructed on this pattern and so is the Fourth Gospel (cf. for instance its seven 'signs,' its seven-day opening of the Lord's ministry, its seven-day account of the passion story). This characteristic would not be so significant were it not confined in the New Testament to the Johannine writings."[85] David Chilton likewise points out that "both books are arranged in a series of 'sevens;' both are structured in terms of the Biblical/heavenly liturgy and festive calendar; and both books use numbers in a symbolic sense that transcends their literal significance."[86]

It is also noteworthy that, like the Gospel of John, Revelation is a literary masterpiece. Says Bauckham, "The Apocalypse of John is a work of immense learning, astonishingly meticulous literary artistry, remarkable creative imagination, radical political critique, and profound theology."[87] Even John's so-called defective Greek grammar is due to literary artistry, not deficient linguistic acumen. R. H. Charles has well said that such anomalies "are not instances of mere license nor yet mere blunders, as they have been most wrongly described, but are constructions deliberately chosen"—in many cases reflecting Hebrew idioms.[88]

An apt example of a deliberately chosen grammatical construction for which John is often unjustly chided is found in the following greeting to the seven churches in the province of Asia—"Grace and peace to you *from him* who is, and who was, and who is to come" (Revelation 1:4). Though technically the phrase "from him" should be in the genitive rather than the nominative case, John uses this peculiar Greek construction to make a point about the unity and nature of God. As Dr. James Moffatt explains, this is "a quaint and deliberate violation of grammar . . . in order to preserve the immutability and absoluteness of the divine name."[89]

We must be careful not to fall for historical revisionists who, like Ehrman, would have us believe that the apostle John was illiterate. Not surprisingly, Ehrman goes so far as to opine: "Peter and John are explicitly said to be 'illiterate' in the book of Acts (4:13)."[90] This, of course, is far from true. As Dr. Craig

Blomberg explains in his review of Ehrman's book *Misquoting Jesus*, "One surprising factual error occurs when Ehrman insists that Acts 4:13 means that Peter and John were illiterate (the term *agrammatos*—'unlettered' in this context means not educated beyond the elementary education accessible to most first-century Jewish boys)."[91] Not only is it a stretch to demean the apostle John as illiterate from the standpoint of his formal education, but this criticism neglects the immediate and overall context of Acts. The "unlearned" apostles were astonishing the Jewish teachers of the Law with their knowledge and wisdom in much the same way as Jesus himself had (cf. Luke 12; Mark 1:22), though he too was without the prerequisite rabbinic training demanded by Ehrman. Acts 4:13, however, says nothing about whether John was literate! Moreover, following the resurrection of the Master Teacher, there is every indication that the apostles devoted themselves to the study and ministry of the Word of God (Acts 6:2).[92] An entire adult lifetime of such study could easily account for John's literary expertise, not to mention the role of divine inspiration in the writing of John's epistles, his Gospel, and the Apocalypse.

Identifying John as the author of the apocalypse goes a long way towards shutting the door to speculations that Revelation was a late first-century—or even a second- or third-century—pseudepigraphal gospel like the gospel of Judas. Moreover, the later the date the less the likelihood that Revelation was written by an apostle or an associate of an apostle as posited by the early Christian Church. The conclusion of the matter is this: there is no evidence that Revelation was written pseudonymously or by an imaginary *John the Elder.* The evidence convincingly points instead to John the Apostle as the author of the apocalypse. Just as the architect's fingerprints are all over our residence, so the apostle's finger-prints are all over Revelation.

CONTEXT

As with *location*, *essence*, *genre*, and *author*, comprehending the context in which Revelation was written is crucial for ascertaining its authority and making sense of its meaning. As will be further demonstrated, Revelation was recorded during the reign of the sixth Roman Emperor—Nero Claudius Caesar Augustus Germanicus—better known today for his number than his name. Twenty-first century believers, like their first-century counterparts, can be absolutely certain that 666 is the number of Nero's name and that Nero is the beast who ravaged the bride in a historical milieu that includes three-and-a-half years of persecution, a year in which the Roman Empire tottered on the precipice of extinction, and the year in which Jerusalem and the temple were destroyed.

Six Hundred Sixty Six—χξϛ

First, John identifies the Beast as number six of seven kings and identifies the number of his name as 666. He informs his readers that the seven-headed Beast represents both a kingdom and kings of that kingdom. He further makes clear that with "wisdom" and "insight," his first-century readers can "calculate the number of the beast, for it is man's number." Obviously no amount of wisdom would have enabled John's first-century audience to calculate the number of a twenty-first-century Beast.

Gematria, the practice of transforming names into numbers, was common in antiquity. The first ten letters of the alphabet corresponded to the numbers 1 through 10; the eleventh letter represented 20, the twelfth letter 30, and so on until 100. The twentieth letter was 200, and each new letter represented an additional hundred. In *Lives of the Twelve Caesars*, Roman historian Suetonius identifies Nero by a numerical designation equal to a nefarious deed. This numerical equality (isopsephism) is encapsulated in the phrase "A calculation new. Nero his mother slew."[93] In Greek the numerical value of the letters in Nero's name (Νέρων) totaled 1,005, as did the numerical value of the letters in the rest of the phrase. This clever numerical cryptogram circulated during Nero's reign and reflected the widespread knowledge that Nero had indeed killed his mother, Agrippina.[94]

Another example of the use of gematria in antiquity comes from the New Testament itself. As prologue to his gospel, Matthew retraces the lineage of Jesus. He concludes his genealogical account by explaining that "there were fourteen generations in all from Abraham to David, fourteen from David to the exile to Babylon, and fourteen from the exile to the Christ" (Matthew 1:17). Skeptics have long accused Matthew of being an amateur arithmetician for miscounting the generations. Far from requiring lessons in counting, however, Matthew, a former tax collector, displayed arithmetic genius in abridging the genealogies. He skillfully employed gematria to organize the genealogy of Jesus into three groups of fourteen, the numerical equivalent of the three Hebrew letters in King David's name (4=ד + 6=ו + 4=ד).[95] Thus, the genealogies simultaneously highlight the most significant names in the lineage of Jesus and artistically emphasize our Lord's identity as the long-awaited Messiah who would sit on the throne of David forever.

This is precisely the sort of gematrial genius displayed by John's use of the triple 6. As Chilton notes, Austin Farrer explains that 666 is a twelvefold triangle with a periphery of thirty times three and a half:

> The coincidence between this reckoning and the factors of the *666* triangle is no mere accident. St. John's reckoning of the period is artificial, devised for the sake of conformity with the factors of the 666 triangle. There neither is nor was any calendar in which 3½ years are 3½ times twelve months of thirty days each. The purpose of the artificial reckoning is to exhibit the Beast's fatally limited reign as a function of his number.[96]

F. W. Farrar conveys how the early readers of Revelation perceived the mysterious 666 (χξϛ): "The very look of it was awful. The first letter was the initial letter of the name of Christ. The last letter was the first double-letter (*st*) of the Cross (*st*auros). Between the two the Serpent stood confessed with its writhing sign and hissing sound. The whole formed a triple repetition of 6, the essential number of toil and imperfection."[97] That is the biblical significance of the number six—incompleteness and imperfection—one short of seven.

As previously noted, the number of Nero's name in a Greek isopsephism totaled 1,005. However, transliterated from the Greek—Νέρων Καῖσαρ—into Hebrew—קסר נרון—the sum total of "Nero Caesar" equals exactly 666. Proceeding from right to left, נ = 50; ר = 200; ו = 6; ן = 50; ק = 100; ס = 60; ר = 200 totaling 666. Moreover, the presence in some ancient manuscripts of a variation in which 666 is rendered 616 lends further credence to the notion that Nero is the intended referent. As

John's letter was increasingly circulated among Latin-speaking audiences, biblical scribes aided them in identifying the Beast by transliterating the Latin spelling—"Nero Caesar"—into Hebrew—נרו קסר. The sum of the letters in the Hebrew transliteration from the Latin form of his name totals 616, just as the Hebrew transliteration of the Greek (Νέρων Καῖσαρ), which includes an additional letter, renders 666. Subtract the additional letter in the Hebrew transliteration from 666, and you are left with 616—two seemingly unrelated numbers that both amazingly lead you to the same doorstep, that of a beast named Nero Caesar.[98]

Revelation records the first all-out assault of the Beast against the Bride, lasting approximately three and a half years. Prior to AD 64, the church was persecuted by the woman who rides the beast (apostate Israel), but shortly after the Great Fire of Rome, the beast unleashed its full fury against a fledgling Christian church. That Nero started the Great Fire of Rome is historically debatable.[99] That Nero used it as the catalyst for the first state assault against the emerging Christian church is not.

To quell rumors that he himself was the incendiary, the arsonist-matricide, who had ignited the Great Fire that transformed Rome into a smoldering inferno, Nero purposed to make Christians scapegoats. As Roman historian Tacitus explains in *The Annals of Imperial Rome*: "To get rid of the report, Nero fastened the guilt and inflicted the most exquisite tortures on a class hated for their abominations, called Christians by the populace."[100]

In November AD 64 the persecutions began in earnest. Dr. Paul Maier, professor of ancient history at Western Michigan University, provides gut-wrenching color commentary in a documentary novel titled *The Flames of Rome*.[101] Vast numbers of Christians were arrested, convicted, and sentenced to death. Tacitus records, "Covered with the skins of beasts, they were torn by dogs and perished, or were nailed to crosses, or were doomed to the flames and burnt, to serve as a nightly illumination, when daylight had expired. Nero offered his gardens for the spectacle, and was exhibiting a show in the circus, while he mingled with the people in the dress of a charioteer."[102]

Those who, like LaHaye, suggest that Nero "was a wimpy emperor" who "went down in history as the emperor who fiddled while Rome burned"[103] do violence against the collective memories of those who suffered valiantly in the first Roman persecution of the bride of Christ. Nowhere in the annals of credible history is there any evidence for the legend that Nero fiddled—he may have sung or swayed in maniacal madness—but he did not fiddle! In fact, to hold LaHaye to his own literalistic standards, the violin was not even invented until several hundred years after the Great Fire.[104]

Far from the wimpy Nero invented by LaHaye, the Nero of history was the very personification of wickedness. The malevolent state massacre of Christians he instituted continued unabated for some three and a half years. In the end, Peter and Paul themselves were persecuted and put to death at the hands of this Beast. Indeed, this was the only epoch in human history in which the Beast could directly assail the foundation of the Christian church of which Christ himself was the cornerstone. Only with Nero Caesar's death, June 9, AD 68, did the carnage against the bride of Christ finally cease. Not only is there a direct correspondence between the name Nero and the number of his name (666), as noted above, but the "forty-two months" he was given "to make war against the saints" (Revelation 13:5–7) is emblematic of the time period during which the Beast wreaked havoc on the Bride. If LaHaye is looking for a literalistic interpretation for his ubiquitous three and a half years, he need look no further!

Moreover, it is no mere coincidence that within a year of Nero's suicide, June 9, AD 68, the Roman Empire suffered a near-fatal wound. In a moment, in the twinkling of an eye, a dynasty that had resided in the Julio-Claudian line of Roman Caesars for a century disappeared from the face of the earth. In fact, AD 69 would go down in history as the year of the four emperors—Galba, Otho, Vitellius, and Vespasian.

Nero's death not only brought an end to the Julio-Claudian dynasty but the near extinction of imperial Rome. From the perspective of a first-century historian, it appeared certain that the death of the emperor was tantamount to the death of the empire. Civil war raged in the territories as four Caesars, beginning with Nero, were felled by the sword. Galba, who reigned but a little while (seven months), was decapitated, impaled, and paraded around with grotesque and grizzly gestures. Otho, rumored to have been one of Nero's lovers, stabbed himself to death. And Vitellius, engorged and inebriated, was butchered and dragged by hook into the Tiber.

The very symbols of Roman invincibility—shrines and sacred sites—collapsed in evidence of the empire's near extinction. Tacitus says in his *Histories* that this was

> a period rich in disasters, frightful in its wars, torn by civil strife, and even in peace full of horrors. Four emperors perished by the sword. There were three civil wars; there were more with foreign enemies; there were often wars that had both characters at once. . . . Cities in Campania's richest plains were swallowed up

and overwhelmed; Rome was wasted by conflagrations, its oldest temples consumed, and the Capitol itself fired by the hands of citizens. Sacred rites were profaned; there was profligacy in the highest ranks; the sea was crowded with exiles, and its rocks polluted with bloody deeds. In the capital there were yet worse horrors. . . . Besides the manifold vicissitudes of human affairs, there were prodigies in heaven and earth, the warning voices of the thunder, and other intimations of the future, auspicious or gloomy, doubtful or not to be mistaken. Never surely did more terrible calamities of the Roman People, or evidence more conclusive, prove that the Gods take no thought for our happiness, but only for our punishment.[105]

For three and a half years the Beast systematically ravished the persecuted bride and sought the ruin of the prostituted bride. Now the kingdom of the Caesars was itself writhing in the throes of certain death. To friend and foe alike, it appeared as though the empire had suffered a mortal wound. The imminent collapse of Rome seemed so certain that Vespasian and his son Titus lost all will to advance on Jerusalem in the Jewish Wars. Just as all seemed lost, however, an empire tottering on the edge of extinction arose from its funeral dirge with renewed malevolence. General Vespasian was proclaimed emperor, and he not only succeeded in resurrecting Roman sovereignty, but in rehabilitating the Roman senate as well. Vespasian "resurrected" the empire and ushered in a Flavian dynasty that would rule Rome until AD 96.

Finally, while Revelation was inscripturated in the shadow of three and a half years of tribulation, it encompasses the year that will forever stand in infamy. With the resurrection of the Roman beast, Vespasian and his son Titus once again set their sights on Jerusalem. By spring AD 70, Titus had besieged the city. By summertime he had surrounded it with a wall, relegating the Jews within to either starvation or surrender. Jewish historian Josephus describes the horror that ensued. Those who had failed to flee to Pella "prowled around like mad dogs, gnawing at anything; belts, shoes, and even the leather from their shields." In graphic detail he recounts stories such as that of Mary of Bethezuba. "Maddened by hunger, she seized the infant at her breast and said, 'Poor baby, why should I preserve you for war, famine, and rebellion? Come, be my food—vengeance against the rebels, and the climax of Jewish tragedy for the world.' With that, she killed her infant son, roasted his body, and devoured half of it, hiding the remainder." Josephus's words inevitably bring to mind Jesus's warning a generation earlier, "How dreadful it will be in those days for pregnant women and nursing mothers!" (Matthew 24:19).

By August the altar of the temple was littered with heaps of rotting corpses, and "streams of blood flowed down the steps of the sanctuary."[106] And on August 30 the unthinkable happened. "The very day on which the former temple had been destroyed by the king of Babylon,"[107] the second temple was set ablaze. As John had prophesied, "In one day her plagues will overtake her: death, mourning and famine. She will be consumed by fire, for mighty is the Lord God who judges her (Revelation 18:8). "While the temple was in flames, the victors stole everything they could lay their hands on, and slaughtered all who were caught. No pity was shown to age or rank, old men or children, the laity or priests—all were massacred."[108] By September 26 all Jerusalem was in flames. "The total number of prisoners taken during the war was 97,000 and those who died during the siege 1,100,000."[109]

So great was the devastation of Jerusalem and its temple "that there was left nothing to make those that came thither believe it had ever been inhabited."[110] As the starved and shackled survivors slumped out of the smoldering ruins, no doubt more than a few remembered the words of Jesus, "O Jerusalem, Jerusalem, you who kill the prophets and stone those sent to you, how often I have longed to gather your children together, as a hen gathers her chicks under her wings, but you were not willing. Look, your house is left to you desolate" (Matthew 23:37–38). Some may even have recalled the scene. As his words still hung in the air, Jesus turned his back on the place that had tabernacled the shekinah glory of the Almighty. Sensing the gravity of the moment, his disciples had called his attention to the majesty of the temple and its buildings. "Do you see all these things?" he had responded, "I tell you the truth, not one stone here will be left on another; every one will be thrown down" (Matthew 24:1–2). An improbable prophecy had become a nightmarish reality.

YEARS

Just as it is common to describe Patmos as a barren Alcatraz, misidentify the great prostitute as the Roman Catholic Church, or identify the 144,000 as exclusively Jewish male virgins, so too it is common to contend that John was imprisoned during the reign of Domitian in the midnineties rather than the reign of Nero in the midsixties. Thus, according to LaHaye, Revelation describes events that will likely take place in the twenty-first century rather than the first century. In his words, "Revelation was written by John in AD 95, which means the book of Revelation describes yet future events of the last days just before Jesus comes back to this earth."[111]

LaHaye's late dating is largely dependent on a single, and markedly ambiguous, sentence in the writings of Irenaeus, bishop of Lyons.[112] Because of the complexity of the Greek grammar, the sentence can be translated as saying that either *John* or John's *apocalyptic vision* was seen toward the end of Domitian's reign.[113] Ironically, LaHaye does not appeal to the "credibility" of Irenaeus, who in the same volume contends that Jesus was crucified when he was about fifty years old.[114] LaHaye is so certain of his late dating that he dismisses the notion that Revelation was written before AD 70 as "historically ridiculous."[115] A closer look at the evidence, however, reveals not only that LaHaye's dismissive language is palpably unwarranted but that his position is patently untenable.

First, if the apostle John were indeed writing in AD 95, it seems incredible that he would make no mention whatsoever of the most apocalyptic event in Jewish history—the demolition of Jerusalem and the destruction of the temple at the hands of Titus. In more reflective moments, this must surely give LaHaye cold shudders. Imagine writing a history of New York today and making no mention of the destruction of the twin towers of the World Trade Center at the hands of terrorists on September 11, 2001. Or, more directly, imagine writing a thesis on the future of terrorism in America and failing to mention the Manhattan Massacre.[116]

Consider another parallel. Imagine that you are reading a history concerning Jewish struggles in Nazi Germany and find no mention whatsoever of the Holocaust. Would it be "historically ridiculous," rather than "historically reasonable," to suppose this history was written prior to the outbreak of World War II? The answer is self-evident. Just as it stretches credulity to suggest that Revelation was written twenty-five years after the destruction of Jerusalem and yet makes no mention of the most apocalyptic event in Jewish history, so too it is unreasonable to think that a history of the Jews in Germany would be written in the aftermath of World War II and yet make no mention of the Holocaust. This by itself is enough to cause a reasonable person to temper his dogmatism.

Furthermore, those who hold that the book of Revelation was written in AD 95 face an even more formidable obstacle! Consider one of the most amazing prophecies in all of Scripture. Jesus is leaving the temple when his disciples call his attention to its buildings. As they gaze upon its massive stones and magnificent buildings, Jesus utters the unthinkable: "I tell you the truth, not one stone here will be left on another; every one will be thrown down" (Matthew 24:2; Mark 13:2; Luke 21:6). One generation later this prophecy, no doubt still emblazoned on the tablet of their consciousness, became a vivid and horrifying reality. As noted by Josephus, the temple was doomed August 30, AD 70, "the very day on which the former temple had been destroyed by the king of Babylon."[117]

As incredible as Christ's prophecy and its fulfillment one generation later are, it is equally incredible to suppose that the apostle John would make no mention of it. Norman Geisler—himself a committed dispensationalist—argues the point as follows:

Imagine this. You're a devout Jew in the first century. The center of your national, economic, and religious life is Jerusalem, and especially the temple. It has been that way in your nation, your family, and almost every Jew's family for a thousand years—ever since Solomon built the first temple. Most of the newest temple, constructed by King Herod, was completed when you were a child. But portions of it are still under construction and have been since 19 BC. For your entire life you have attended services and brought sacrifices there to atone for the sins you've committed against God. Why? Because you and your countrymen consider this temple the earthly dwelling place of the God of the universe, the maker of heaven and earth, the very Deity whose name is so holy you dare not utter it.

As a young man, you begin following a Jew named Jesus who claims to be the long-awaited Messiah predicted in your Scriptures. He performed miracles, teaches profound truths, and scolds and befuddles the priests in charge of the temple. Incredibly, he predicts his own death and resurrection. He also predicts that the temple itself will be destroyed before your generation passes away (Mark 13:2, 30).

This is scandalous! Jesus is convicted of blasphemy by your temple priests and is crucified on the eve of the Passover, one of your holiest holidays. He's buried in a Jewish tomb, but three days later you and his other followers see Jesus alive just as he predicted. You touch him, eat with him, and he continues to perform miracles, the last being his ascension into heaven. Forty years later, your temple is destroyed just as Jesus had predicted, along with the entire city and thousands of your countrymen.

Question: If you and your fellow-followers write

accounts of Jesus *after* the temple and city are destroyed in AD 70, aren't you going to at least mention that unprecedented national, human, economic, and religious tragedy somewhere in your writings, especially since this risen Jesus had predicted it? Of course! Well, here's the problem for those who say the New Testament was written after 70—there's absolutely no mention of the fulfillment of this predicted tragedy anywhere in the New Testament documents. This means most, if not all, of the documents must have been written prior to 70.[118]

As the student of Scripture well knows, New Testament writers were quick to highlight fulfilled prophecy. The phrase "This was to fulfill what was spoken of by the prophet" permeates the pages of Scripture and demonstrates conclusively that the Bible is divine rather than human in origin. Thus, it is inconceivable that Jesus would make an apocalyptic prophecy concerning the destruction of Jerusalem and the Jewish temple and that John would fail to mention that the prophecy was fulfilled one generation later just as Jesus had predicted it. To recapitulate the words of Dr. Geisler, "If you and your fellow-followers write accounts of Jesus *after* the temple and city are destroyed in AD 70, aren't you going to at least mention that unprecedented national, human, economic, and religious tragedy somewhere in your writings, especially since this risen Jesus had predicted it? Of course!"

Finally, let me highlight an additional piece of internal evidence that should give pause to those who are overly dogmatic about the late dating of Revelation. In Revelation 11 John says,

"I was given a reed like a measuring rod and was told, 'Go and measure the temple of God and the altar, and count the worshipers there. But exclude the outer court; do not measure it, because it has been given to the Gentiles. They will trample on the holy city for 42 months'" (vv. 1–2). In context, Jesus has sent his angel "to show his servants what must soon take place." Thus, the prophecy concerns a future event, not one that took place twenty-five years earlier. Again, Dr. Geisler—though he is a dispensationalist—recognizes the force of this argument and thus cites Revelation 11 to demonstrate that "the New Testament documents speak of Jerusalem and the temple, or activities associated with them, as if they were still intact at the time of the writings."[119]

In summary, among the reasons we can be certain that the book of Revelation was not written twenty-five years after the destruction of Jerusalem, three tower above the rest. First, just as it is unreasonable to suppose that someone writing a history of the World Trade Center in the aftermath of September 11, 2001, would fail to mention the destruction of the twin towers, so too it stretches credulity to suggest that Revelation was written in the aftermath of the devastation of Jerusalem and the Jewish temple and yet makes no mention of this apocalypse. Additionally, if John is writing in AD 95, it is incredible to suppose he would not mention the fulfillment of Christ's most improbable and apocalyptic vision. Finally, New Testament documents—including the book of Revelation—speak of Jerusalem and the Jewish temple intact at the time they were written.

If Revelation was written *before* AD 70, it is reasonable to assume that the vision given to John was meant to reveal the apocalyptic events surrounding the destruction of Jerusalem—events that were still in John's future but are in our past. This, of course, does not presuppose that *all* the prophecies in Revelation have already been fulfilled. Just as thoughtful Christians should distance themselves from the fully futurist fallacy, they should disavow a predominantly preterist perspective.

What's at Stake

As documented in this chapter, faithful application of the historical principle demonstrates beyond peradventure of doubt that the Gospel of Judas is a Gnostic pretender recorded hundreds of years after the events it chronicles. It lacks the credibility of the canonical gospels, which were clearly written prior to the Jerusalem holocaust of AD 70. The notion that the Gospel of Judas did not make it into the Bible because it was out of line with the direction "historical winners" wanted to take their newly minted religious notions is simply false.

The inflammatory suggestion that John was canonized because the early Christian church preferred its dark anti-Semitic overtones over more racially sensitive gospels such as Judas are largely based on antihistorical sophistry. Had Professor Ehrman and company heeded the historical principle as codified by the LEGACY acronym, they would not have succumbed to such vindictive prejudice. Anti-Semitism had nothing to do with the canonization of John. Early dating, eyewitness attestation, and extrabiblical corroboration did.

The aforementioned scholars not only demonstrate antihistorical sophistry with respect to *why* the Gospels were canonized, but with respect to *when* they were recorded. In their view they were written long after the destruction of Jerusalem and the temple. Likewise, in lockstep fashion they date the writing of Revelation decades after the Jewish holocaust of AD 70. Tragically they are not alone. LaHaye is so certain of this late dating that he dogmatically dismisses the notion that Revelation was written during the reign of Nero as historically ridiculous.

Nothing could be further from the truth. As the historical principle codified in the LEGACY acronym reveals the sophistry of fundamentalists on the left who assign an anti-Semitic bias to the Gospel of John, so too it unveils sensationalistic assertions of fundamentalists on the right who suppose Jews are awaiting a holocaust that will exterminate two-thirds of them. Indeed, the LEGACY acronym provides proof positive that it is historically reasonable rather than historically ridiculous to suppose that Revelation was written prior to the Jewish holocaust of the first-century AD.

If Revelation is principally a book that describes what is about to take place in the twenty-first century, it would have been largely irrelevant to first-century Christians. While Revelation is as relevant as Romans to modern-day readers, it was written to seven historical churches living in the shadow of the Neronian persecution. It is in this milieu that John admonishes the churches of Asia to stand firm in the conviction that Christ, not Caesar, is both Lord and Savior. The ghastly terrors of Revelation are not solely designated "the great tribulation" (Revelation 7:14) because the foundation of the temple was destroyed, but because the Beast of the apocalypse had purposed to decimate the foundation of the Christian church of which Christ is himself the chief cornerstone. The Great Tribulation instigated by the Roman Beast is the archetype for every type and tribulation until we experience the reality of resurrection at the second appearing of Jesus Christ.

Those who stridently insist that the seven letters to the persecuted bride are addressed to modern-day believers are bound to muddle their meaning. Christ would not have deluded first-century believers by saying, "I will also keep *you* from the hour of trial" (Revelation 3:10) when the *you* intended were twenty-first-century believers. It is inconceivable that our Lord was informing a persecuted first-century church that twenty centuries later the church would be spared persecution via a pretribulational rapture invented by nineteenth-century believers.

Lest we be seduced into adding a great parenthesis of two thousand years between John's apocalyptic vision and the judgments the vision symbolizes, we should reread Revelation with an eye toward the words "soon" and "near." We must ever be mindful that in sharp distinction to the angel in Daniel's apocalypse, the angel of Revelation explicitly warns John, "Do not seal up the words of the prophecy of this book, *because the time is near*" (22:10). In the words of Milton Terry, "When a writer says that an event will shortly and speedily come to pass, or is about to take place, it is contrary to all propriety to declare that his statements allow us to believe the event is in the far future. It is a reprehensible abuse of language to say that the words *immediately*, or *near at hand*, mean *ages hence*, or *after a long time*."[120]

Likewise, we should never suppose that the imagery of Revelation is exhausted in a first-century historical milieu. For one day, the Lord himself will come down from heaven, and the dwelling of God will forever be with men (Revelation 21:3); each person will be resurrected and "judged according to what he has done" (20:13); and the problem of sin will be fully and finally resolved (21:27).

6

———✿✿✿———

TYPOLOGY PRINCIPLE:
The Golden Key

I am a Palestinian [Christian] living under Israeli occupation. My captor daily seeks ways to make life harder for me. He encircles my people with barbed wire; he builds walls around us, and his army sets many boundaries around us. He succeeds in keeping thousands of us in camps and prisons. Yet despite all these efforts, he has not succeeded in taking my dreams from me. I have a dream that one day I will wake up and see two equal peoples living next to each other, coexisting in the land of Palestine, stretching from the Mediterranean to the Jordan.

—BETHLEHEM PASTOR MITRI RAHEB,
IN GARY M. BURGE, *WHOSE LAND? WHOSE PROMISE?*

God's Word is very clear! There will be grave consequences for the nation or nations that attempt to divide up the land of Israel. God's love for Israel is expressed in the words of Zechariah: "He who touches you [Israel] touches the apple of His eye."

—PASTOR JOHN HAGEE, CHRISTIAN ZIONIST
JERUSALEM COUNTDOWN:
A WARNING TO THE WORLD

ANTI-SEMITISM IS A HORRIFIC EVIL—ESPECIALLY when justified in the name of religion. Hitler, however, needed no such pretext. His belief that Jews were subhuman and Aryans supermen fueled a mad rush toward ethnic cleansing. As the smoke from the crematoriums wafted over steeples in the German countryside, another evil reared its ugly head. German pastors and parishioners remained strangely silent. For some it was simply a matter of self-preservation. Others sought to justify their apathy by blaming Jews for the Great War. Still others believed that Jews were fatalistically destined to face the wrath of Antichrist—and thus did nothing.

Dietrich Bonhoeffer was not among them. "If we claim to be Christians" he said, "there is no room for expediency."[1] He not only denounced a Nazi regime that had turned its führer into an idol and god, but a confessional church more concerned with survival than with the sins of anti-Semitism and slavery. "When Christ calls a man," said Bonhoeffer, "He bids him come and die."[2] On April 9, 1945, at age thirty-nine, Bonhoeffer experienced the ultimate "cost of discipleship." By special order of Reichsführer Heinrich Himmler, he was hanged at the concentration camp at Flossenberg.

On April 9, 1948, three years to the day that Bonhoeffer was martyred in the struggle against anti-Semitism, another Semitic horror unfolded on the western outskirts of Jerusalem at Deir Yassin. In a book titled *The Birth of the Palestinian Refugee Problem, 1947–1949*, Benny Morris, Jewish professor of history at Ben-Gurion University of the Negev in Be'er Sheva, describes the Zionist slaughter of Arab civilians and children by Israeli paramilitary. Before the day ended, "some 250 Arabs, mostly noncombatants, were murdered; there were also cases of mutilation and rape. The surviving inhabitants were expelled to Arab-held East Jerusalem." In clinical fashion, Morris unmasks "the Zionist murders, terrorism, and ethnic cleansing that drove 600,000–750,000 Palestinians from their homes in 1948."[3]

Morris marshals evidence from the Israel Defense Forces archives to document "Israeli acts of massacre." "To my surprise" he says, "there were also many cases of rape. In the months of April–May 1948, units of the Haganah were given operational orders that stated explicitly that they were to uproot the villagers, expel them and destroy the villages themselves." Morris recounts graphic episodes of rape and murder. "In Acre four soldiers raped a girl and murdered her and her father. In Jaffa, soldiers of the Kiryati Brigade raped one girl and tried to rape several more. At Hunin, which is in the Galilee, two girls were raped and then murdered." Morris goes on to describe the horror of four female prisoners who were raped in the village of Abu Shusha—one raped repeatedly. "Usually there were one or two Palestinian girls. In a large proportion of the cases the event ended with murder." And "they," says Morris, "are just the tip of the iceberg."[4]

While Morris condemns such acts of rape and massacre as war crimes, he expresses no moral outrage against the expulsion of hundreds of thousands of Palestinians. "There are circumstances in history that justify ethnic cleansing" he opines. "A Jewish state would not have come into existence without the uprooting of 700,000 Palestinians." Morris cites the United States as the prime example. "The great American democracy could not have been created without the annihilation of the Indians. There are cases in which the overall, final good justifies harsh and cruel acts that are committed in the course of history." According to Morris, if there was a serious historical mistake in 1948, it was that David Ben-Gurion, first and third prime minister of the state of Israel, "got cold feet" and did not complete the job of cleansing the land of Palestinian people. "He should have," concludes Morris, "done a complete job."

In *Light Force*, Brother Andrew provides graphic details on how the "job" of ethnic cleansing has continued on since 1948. He chronicles a fateful day in December 1992 when "a total of 415 Palestinians, many of them doctors, lawyers, university professors, businessmen, and other professionals, had been rounded up from the West Bank and Gaza—snatched from their homes and workplaces, plus a few from prison—transported over the border into Lebanon, and deposited on the side of a mountain."[5] While Hamas was certainly a threat to Israel's security, explains Brother Andrew, "these particular men had been accused of nothing; Israeli officials even admitted that the deportees had no complicity in the killings. They had committed no crime and faced no judge, yet they were dumped on the side of a rugged mountain in a foreign country that didn't want them, and they were left to struggle as best they could in miserable conditions."[6]

Though "the world community raised an outcry over the deportations, claiming they were a violation of the Geneva Convention" justice remained unserved—415 Palestinians were left "shivering on the side of a mountain in Lebanon."[7] When Brother Andrew prayed for these displaced Palestinians at a Christian Missions conference, several students asked for forgiveness. The thought of praying for a Palestinian had never even entered their minds. Others were outraged. "Why do you love Palestinians?" they demanded. "Don't you know that Israel belongs to the Jews?"

While Palestinians comprise the largest displaced people group in the world,[8] they are no longer a mere nameless, faceless mass of humanity. Like Brother Andrew, Gary Burge, professor of New Testament at Wheaton College and Graduate School and president of Evangelicals for Middle East Understanding, has given definition to the plight of numerous displaced Palestinians such as Nora Kort.[9] Nora and her family were "Jerusalemites" who had lived in the shadow of the famous Jaffa Gate since the 1800s. Her grandfather was a committed Palestinian Christian who used personal savings to build Saint George's Church on their forty-eight acres of land. "In 1948," writes Burge, "war erupted and some of Israel's most vicious fighters (the Stern Gang and the Haganah) charged over the hill. Fighting was fierce, and Nora's parents fled into Jerusalem's walled city." Unlike many of their friends, they survived, but their property slipped into the hands of Jewish settlers. "When Israel occupied all of Jerusalem in 1967 and the borders moved, Nora's father made his first trip home and even opened his old front door with his own key. He was met by a Jewish family from Yemen who refused him entry. . . . When he died in 1994, his last words to his daughter were: 'Nora, do not forget.'" Though Nora was born after the war, she did not visit the family estate until 1995. By then the family home had been transformed into the Zionist Confederation House. As she sat in what had once been their living room, she could hear the echo of her father's voice and desperately wanted to tell him that she had not forgotten.

When Professor Burge visited the Zionist Confederation House, he discovered an Israeli propaganda piece claiming that this house "had once been 'a base for Arab terrorists.' But, of course, it just wasn't true." He discovered something equally amazing. Unlike many of those who had lost their families and possessions, Nora had not become bitter. Instead, she counsels the downtrodden, raises money for impoverished Arab families, and counsels Palestinians who have lost all hope for justice. "God is the Father and Defender of those who are oppressed and treated unjustly," says Nora, "This is and has been my mission and my commitment." As with Corrie ten Boom's sister Betsie, who died at the Ravensbruck concentration camp, she is living proof "that there is no pit so deep that [God] is not deeper still."

While Zionists seek to dismiss such stories, they are undeniable historical realities. Israeli historians such as Benny Morris have opened Pandora's box, and the world has viewed its grisly contents. Indeed, there is an uncanny irony, says Burge, in that you can almost see the site of the Deir Yassin massacre from the Yad Vashem Memorial.

> It has always struck me as ironic that if you stand in the right place at the Jewish Holocaust Memorial in Jerusalem (Yad Vashem), you can almost see the village of Deir Yassin. Even the family home of Menachem Begin (the leader of the massacre) is just across the valley. But Deir Yassin was not an exception to the Israeli's ethnic cleansing. Countless villages received severe treatment. In the end, over 350 villages were turned to rubble. From the Palestinian view, these events were the first use of terrorism in the country.[10]

Zionism

For cultural Zionists such as Benny Morris, the ethnic cleansing of Palestinians is a defensible cruelty. In his words,

"The overall final good justifies harsh and cruel acts that are committed in the course of history." The compulsory expulsion of Palestinians is defensible on the basis of pragmatic considerations. "We must expel the Arabs and take their places" said David Ben-Gurion, "and if we have to use force—not to dispossess the Arabs of the Negev and Transjordan, but to guarantee our own right to settle in those places—then we have force at our disposal."[11] No one summed up the ramifications of ethnically cleansing the Palestinian people from the land better than did Moshe Dayan, chief of staff of the Israeli Defense Forces from 1955 to 1958. In eulogizing an Israeli killed by Arabs, he pleaded for understanding. "What do we know of their fierce hatred for us? For eight years they have been living in refugee camps in Gaza while right before their eyes we have been turning the land and the villages in which they and their forefathers lived into our own land. We should demand Roi'i's blood not from the Arabs in Gaza but from ourselves, for closing our eyes to our cruel fate and the role of our generation."[12]

In stark contrast to cultural Zionists who deem ethnic cleansing as a defensible cruelty, Christian Zionists defend ethnic cleansing as a divine command. From Darby in the past to LaHaye in the present, they militantly forward the notion that God has covenanted to give Eretz Israel—from the river of Egypt to the river Euphrates—exclusively to Jews. "The Lord will purify His land of all the wicked," wrote Darby, "from the Nile to the Euphrates."[13] John Hagee is equally explicit. "God has given Jerusalem," he says, *"only to the Jews."*[14] Supporting the displacement of Arabs in order to make room for Jews is rationalized as fulfillment of the purposes of God.

Those like Bethlehem Pastor Mitri Raheb who support a two-state solution and pray that one day Jews and Palestinians

167

will live together in peace, are said to be poking their finger into the very eye of God. In fact, when Israeli prime minister Ariel Sharon began dismantling Israeli settlements in Gaza as a step toward peace, he was savagely denounced by Christian Zionists. Pat Robertson went as far as to suggest that the establishment of a Palestinian state was a direct violation of "God's plan." His immediate reaction was to attribute the stroke Sharon suffered on January 4, 2006, as divine retribution for dividing God's land. "Woe unto any prime minister of Israel who takes a similar course to appease the United Nations or the United States of America,"[15] he warned. Robertson went on to link Sharon's stroke to the 1995 assassination of Israeli leader Yitzhak Rabin who similarly suffered the wrath of God Almighty for signing the Oslo Peace Accords granting limited self-rule to Palestinians.[16]

Leading Christian Zionist Michael Evans, who considers Palestinians "a tainted and brainwashed people"[17] is equally adamant in the belief that Palestine belongs exclusively to those who are racially and religiously Jewish. When President George W. Bush demanded that "Israel should freeze settlement construction, dismantle unauthorized outposts, end the daily humiliation of the Palestinian people, and not prejudice final negotiations with the placements of walls and fences,"[18] he declared Bush to be under a curse.[19] According to Evans, "If America divides Jerusalem, there will be no forgiveness. America will tragically end up on the ash heap of history."[20] John Hagee agrees. "Any nation, America included, that forces Israel to give up land for peace is going to experience the wrath and the judgment of God," says Hagee. "I am saying to those of you who are running this nation in Washington, D.C., if you are forcing Israel to give up land through our State Department, you stop!

You are bringing the wrath and the judgment of God to the United States of America."[21]

Such inflammatory insinuations on the part of Christian Zionists raise questions of the greatest import. Does the promise to Abraham—"To your descendants I give this land, from the river of Egypt to the great river, the Euphrates—the land of the Kenites, Kenizzites, Kadmonites, Hittites, Perizzites, Rephaites, Amorites, Canaanites, Girgashites and Jebusites" (Genesis 15:18–20)—provide a rationale for ethnic cleansing? Does the Bible mandate Jerusalem as the eternal capital of the Jewish people? Is there truly a need to rebuild a temple and inflame the fires of Armageddon in the twenty-first century in light of our Messiah's first-century reminder that the time had come when true worshipers would no longer worship on a mountain in Samaria or in a temple in Jerusalem (John 4:21–22)? The quintessential question is this: Was the land the focus of our Lord or is the Lord the locus of the land?

These and a host of attendant questions are sufficiently answered when we come to grips with the biblical principle of typology.

Typology

A *type* (from the Greek word *typos*) is a person, event, or institution in the redemptive history of the Old Testament that prefigures a corresponding but greater reality in the New Testament. It literally refers to a mark or scar. John uses the term "type" in recounting Thomas's doubt concerning the reality of the resurrection: "Unless I see the nail marks [*typos*] in his hands and put my finger where the nails were, and put my hand into his side, I will not believe it" (John 20:25). A type is thus a copy, a pattern, or a model (e.g., the scars on

Christ's hands) that signifies an even greater reality (e.g., the actual nails that pierced Christ's hands).

The greater reality to which a type points and in which it finds its fulfillment is referred to as an *antitype* (from the Greek word *antitypos*). The writer of Hebrews specifically employs the word *antitype* to refer to the greatness of the heavenly sanctuary of which the Holy Land, the Holy City, and the holy temple are merely types or shadows: "Christ did not enter a man-made sanctuary that was only a copy of the true one [antitype]; he entered heaven itself, now to appear for us in God's presence" (Hebrews 9:23–24). The antitype of the land is found in the Lord, the antitype of Jerusalem is found in Jesus, and the antitype of the majestic temple is found in the Master Teacher.

In Hebrews, as in the rest of the New Testament, the Old Testament history of Israel is interpreted as a succession of types that find ultimate fulfillment in the life, death, and resurrection of our Lord. Far from being peripheral, typology is central to the proper interpretation of the infallible Word of God. One cannot fully grasp the meaning of the New Testament apart from familiarity with the redemptive history and literary forms of the Old Testament. Likewise, the New Testament shines its light on the Old Testament and reveals the more complete significance of God's redemptive work in and through the nation of Israel. This relationship between the Testaments is in essence typological.[22] Thus, as eschatology is the thread that weaves Scripture into a glorious tapestry; typology is the material out of which that thread is spun.

The New Testament writers' typological interpretation of the Old Testament, though often implicit in allusions to the Hebrew Scriptures, is made explicit in Paul's epistles. The apostle explains to the Corinthian church that the experiences of Israel prefigured the experiences of the believers under the new covenant as "examples [types] and were written down as warnings for us, on whom the fulfillment of the ages has come" (1 Corinthians 10:11; cf. v. 6). In his letter to the Romans, Paul refers to Adam as a "pattern" (literally, type) of Jesus Christ (Romans 5:14). Similarly, the writer of Hebrews explains that the earthly temple is merely "a copy and shadow of what is in heaven" (8:5), and "the law is only a shadow of the good things that are coming—not the realities themselves" (10:1). Paul, likewise, taught the believers at Colossae that the dietary laws, religious festivals, and Sabbath of the old covenant were "a shadow of the things that were to come; the reality, however, is found in Christ" (Colossians 2:17).

The interpretive principle of typology is equally pervasive in the Gospels. Jesus's successful resistance of temptation in the desert after forty days of fasting is a direct typological contrast with the disobedience of the Israelites that resulted in their forty years of wilderness wanderings (see Matthew 4:1–11; Mark 1:12–13; Luke 4:1–13). In remaining faithful to his Father, Jesus did what Israel was unable to do. Jesus is thus true Israel, and all who are found in him are heirs according to the promises God made to Abraham. Moreover, Jesus is revealed as the antitype of the Hebrew prophets through his preaching of repentance, his ministry of healing, his concern for the poor and the social outcasts, and his death near Jerusalem (see Luke 13:33). Though like the prophets in these ways, Jesus is demonstrated to be greater than all the previous prophets in the manner of his miraculous ministry, his claims to be God, and his vindication of those claims in his resurrection.[23]

This, of course, is not to confuse the biblical principle of typology with an allegorical method of biblical interpretation that ignores or rejects the historical nature of the Old Testament narratives. On the contrary, typology is firmly rooted in historical fact and always involves historical correspondence. As Stephen Sizer, author of *Christian Zionism: Road-map to Armageddon*, explains, "The difference between these two methods of interpretation is significant since the former [typology] places particular emphasis on the historical context of passages as well as upon the way Scripture interprets Scripture, whereas an allegorical approach finds eternal truths without reference to any historical setting." As Sizer further explains, "A typological approach also highlights the way New Testament writers see Jesus Christ to be the fulfillment of most Old Testament images and types."[24] Oxford Fellow K. J. Woollcombe has aptly pointed out, "Typological exegesis is the search for linkages between events, persons or things *within the historical framework of revelation*, whereas allegorism is the search for a secondary and hidden meaning underlying the primary and obvious meaning of a narrative."[25] Or, as Dr. Leonhard Goppelt puts it, "The historicity of what is reported and the literal meaning of the text are of no consequence for allegorical interpretation, but for typology they are foundational."[26] A type must therefore be a historical person, event, or institution that prefigures another reality in redemptive history, which is yet future. The typological approach to biblical interpretation is firmly committed to the theological truth that God is sovereign over history. Says Goppelt, "New Testament typology is an expression of a nonmystical view of history and the world that is based in faith and hope on the appearing and coming of Christ and that neither glorifies nor destroys history."[27]

Furthermore, biblical typology, as evidenced in the writings of the New Testament, always involves a heightening of the type in the antitype. It is not simply that Jesus replaces the temple as a new but otherwise equal substitute. No, Jesus is far greater than the temple! It is not as though Jesus is simply another in the line of prophets with Moses, Elijah, Isaiah, and Jeremiah. No, Jesus is much greater than the prophets! Contrary to popularists such as LaHaye, the new covenant is not a mere "plan B" that God instituted as a parenthesis between two phases of his redemptive work with Israel. The new covenant is far greater than the old covenant—"a better covenant" (Hebrews 7:22)—rendering the old "obsolete" (Hebrews 8:13)! "The type is not essentially a miniature version of the antitype, but is a prefiguration in a different stage of redemptive history that indicates the outline or essential features . . . of the future reality and that loses its own significance when that reality appears."[28]

Finally, it is important to point out that antitypes themselves may also function as types of future realities. Communion, for example, is the antitype of the Passover meal. Each year the Jews celebrated Passover in remembrance of God's sparing the firstborn sons in the homes of the Israelite families that were marked by the blood of the Passover lamb (see Luke 22; cf. Exodus 11–12). Jesus's celebration of the Passover meal with his disciples on the night of his arrest symbolically points to the fact that he is the ultimate Passover Lamb "who takes away the sin of the world" (John 1:29). Though the Last Supper and the corresponding sacrament of communion serve as the antitype of the Passover meal, they also point forward to their ultimate fulfillment in "the wedding supper of the Lamb" (Revelation 19:9; cf. Luke 22:15–18). On that glorious day the purified bride—true Israel—will be united with her Bridegroom in the new heaven and the new earth (see Revelation 21:1–2). Thus the fulfillment of the promise is itself a guarantee of the final consummation of the kingdom of God. Says Goppelt, this already-but-not-yet typological fulfillment is indicative of "an eschatological tension in NT typology. Salvation has come in Christ; therefore, the church possesses what the fathers longed for. This salvation is hidden with Christ and is coming; therefore, the church, together with the fathers, waits for the perfect antitypes to be revealed."[29]

It is not too much to say that the biblical principle of typology is anathema for Christian Zionists such as Tim LaHaye. In his view, to depart from a strictly literal interpretation leads the student of the Bible "to all forms of confusion and sometimes heresy." The reality is that the debate does not revolve around whether one reads the Bible literally or metaphorically but whether old covenant shadows find their final consummation in the person and work of Jesus Christ.

A classic case in point involves the words of Jesus, "Destroy this temple, and I will raise it again in three days" (John 2:19). The Jews believed Jesus to be speaking of Herod's temple. Thus, with sarcasm dripping from their voices, they respond, "It has taken forty-six years to build this temple, and you are going to raise it in three days?" (v. 20). However, says John, the temple Jesus had spoken of *was his body*" (v. 21). After Jesus had been "raised from the dead, his disciples recalled what he had said." "Then," says John, *"they believed the Scripture and the words that Jesus had spoken"* (v. 22).

Sizer astutely sums up the problem by saying that the essence of the matter is not whether one interprets the Bible literally or spiritually, but whether one understands the Bible in terms of old covenant types (shadows) or new covenant realities. "The failure to recognize this principle is the basic hermeneutical error which Christian Zionists make and from which flow the other distinctive doctrines that characterize the movement."[30] Nowhere is this more clearly seen than in Zionist misinterpretations regarding the promise God made to Abraham with respect to the land: "To your descendants I give this land, from the river of Egypt to the great river, the Euphrates—the land of the Kenites, Kenizzites, Kadmonites, Hittites, Perizzites, Rephaites, Amorites, Canaanites, Girgashites and Jebusites" (Genesis 15:18–21).

THE HOLY LAND

Two thousand years before Jesus was born in Bethlehem, God told Abram to leave his ancestral home in Basra (southern Iraq) and to "go to the land I will show you." God promised Abram:

> "I will make you into a great nation
>   and I will bless you;
> I will make your name great,
>   and you will be a blessing.
> I will bless those who bless you,
>   and whoever curses you I will curse;
>   and all peoples on earth
> will be blessed through you."
>
> (GENESIS 12:1–3)

When Abram was ninety-nine years old, God reiterated his promise:

"No longer will you be called *Abram*; your name will be *Abraham*, for I have made you a father of many nations. I will make you very fruitful; I will make nations of you, and kings will come from you. I will establish my covenant as an everlasting covenant between me and you and your descendants after you for the generations to come, to be your God and the God of your descendants after you. The whole land of Canaan, where you are now an alien, I will give as an everlasting possession to you and your descendants after you; and I will be their God." (Genesis 17:5–8)

Ironically, the only portion of the Promised Land Abraham ever took possession of was a cave in Hebron where he buried his wife Sarah. And even then he did not assume it by virtue of the promise but through payment of the value. When Ephraim the Hittite offered the land to Abraham as a gift, he responded, "Listen to me, if you will. I will pay the price of the field. Accept it from me so I can bury my dead there" (Genesis 23:13). In the end, for the sum of four hundred shekels of silver, "the field and the cave in it were deeded to Abraham by the Hittites as a burial site" (v. 20).

The promise of God regarding the land was not relegated to Abraham. During a time of great famine, he reiterated the promise to Abraham's son Isaac.

"To you and your descendants I will give all these lands and will confirm the oath I swore to your father Abraham. I will make your descendants as numerous as the stars in the sky and will give them all these lands, and through your offspring all nations on earth will be blessed, because Abraham obeyed me and kept my requirements, my commands, my decrees and my laws." (Genesis 26:3–5)

In like fashion, God confirmed the promise to Jacob in a riveting dream at Bethel. Jacob, whose name God would change to Israel (Genesis 32:28; cf. 35:10), saw a stairway that extended from earth to heaven and heard the voice of God saying:

> "I am the LORD, the God of your father Abraham and the God of Isaac. I will give you and your descendants the land on which you are lying. Your descendants will be like the dust of the earth, and you will spread out to the west and to the east, and to the north and to the south. All peoples on earth will be blessed through you and through your offspring." (Genesis 28:13–14)

Christian Zionists are convinced that these promises God made to Abraham, Isaac, and Jacob with respect to the land are unconditional and yet unfulfilled. Says LaHaye, "We believe that God must fulfill to Israel as a national entity those promises made through *unconditional* covenants like the Abrahamic, Davidic, and Land of Israel. If this is true, then they must be fulfilled literally, and that means many aspects are yet future."[31] Leading Christian Zionist Arnold Fruchtenbaum agrees. Israel must own all of the land from the river of Egypt in the north to the river Euphrates in the South. "Since God cannot lie, these things must yet come to pass."[32]

These Zionists are convinced that Israel will soon control not only the West Bank, Gaza, and Golan, but Iraq, Jordan, and Lebanon. Says John Hagee, "The Royal Land Grant that God, the original owner, gave to Abraham, Isaac, and Jacob and their seed forever, includes the following territory which is presently occupied by Israel, the West Bank, all of Lebanon, one half of Syria, two-thirds of Jordan, all of Iraq, and the northern portion of Saudi Arabia."[33] Even cream-of-the-crop dispensationalist scholars contend that the Bible presupposes Israel must yet control an area of land roughly thirty times its present size.[34]

This, however, is far from true. As we will see, Abraham was not merely promised a country thirty times its present size. He was promised the cosmos! As Paul, apostle to the Gentiles, underscores, "Abraham and his offspring received the promise that he would be *heir of the world*" (Romans 4:13). Thus, while Christian Zionists hyperventilate over tiny areas of land such as the Golan or Gaza, God promises them the globe. In the fore future, God fulfilled his promise when the children of Israel entered the Promised Land. In the far future God fulfilled his promise to true Israel through Christ, who forever sits on the throne of David. And, in the final future, the promises of God will reach their zenith as Paradise lost gives way to Paradise restored.

First, the land promises were fulfilled in the fore future when Joshua led the physical descendants of Abraham into Palestine. As the book of Joshua records, "The LORD gave Israel all the land he had sworn to give their forefathers, and they took possession of it and settled there." Indeed says Joshua, "Not *one* of all the LORD's good promises to the house of Israel failed; every one was fulfilled" (Joshua 21:43, 45). Even as the life ebbed from his body, Joshua reminded the children of Israel that the Lord had been faithful to his promises. "You know with all your heart and soul that *not one* of all the good promises the LORD your God gave you has failed. Every promise has been fulfilled; *not one has failed*" (Joshua 23:14).

Solomon, during whose reign the glorious temple was

constructed, was equally unambiguous. "Not one word has failed of all the good promises [the LORD] gave through his servant Moses" (1 Kings 8:56). In fact, at the height of the Solomonic kingdom, "the people of Judah and Israel were *as numerous as the sand on the seashore*; they ate, they drank and they were happy. And Solomon ruled over all the kingdoms from the River [Euphrates] to the land of the Philistines, as far as the border of Egypt" (4:20–21).

Even in the aftermath of Israel's exile into Babylon, Nehemiah extolled the faithfulness of God in fulfilling the land promises he had made to the patriarchs. As the temple was being rebuilt, Nehemiah entreated the Almighty to bless Judah and return it to its former glory. If there was ever a time to adjure God to fulfill an as yet unfulfilled promise, this was it! Yet far from appealing to the Abrahamic covenant as a reason for God to restore Judah to the land, Nehemiah humbly acknowledged that the loss of the land was due to the sin of the people of Israel, not to faltering faithfulness or delayed distribution on the part of God. In his impassioned prayer, Nehemiah praised the Lord for faithfulness to the Abrahamic covenant:

> "You found [Abraham's] heart faithful to you, and you made a covenant with him to give to his descendants the land of the Canaanites, Hittites, Amorites, Perizzites, Jebusites and Girgashites. You have kept your promise because you are righteous. . . . You gave them kingdoms and nations, allotting to them *even the remotest frontiers*. . . . *You made their sons as numerous as the stars in the sky, and you brought them into the land that you told their fathers to enter and possess.*" (Nehemiah 9:8, 22–24)[35]

Furthermore, the land promises are fulfilled in the far future through Jesus who provides true Israel with permanent rest from their wanderings in sin. In the irony of the ages, Christian Zionists view a Jewish return to the land as more significant than a Jewish return to the Lord. Dr. John Gerstner highlighted the irony, when with tongue firmly planted in cheek, he opined, "This certainly does make it hard on the Jews! When they might have had a glorious piece of real estate on the Mediterranean, all they end up with under this interpretation is Christ."[36]

It is truly tragic that Zionist leaders such as John Hagee place far more emphasis on returning Jewish pilgrims to the land than in turning Jewish people to the Lord. Says Hagee, "Let us put an end to this Christian chatter that 'all the Jews are lost' and can't be in the will of God until they convert to Christianity!"[37] Incredibly, Hagee takes the onus off of the Jewish community and places it squarely on the Jewish Christ: "If Jesus refused by his words or actions to claim to be the Messiah to the Jews," asks Hagee, "then *HOW CAN THE JEWS BE BLAMED FOR REJECTING WHAT WAS NEVER OFFERED?*"[38] Indeed, according to Hagee, "the [Jewish] people wanted him [Jesus] to be their Messiah, but he absolutely refused. . . . The Jews were not rejecting Jesus as Messiah, it was Jesus who was refusing to be the Messiah to the Jews!"[39]

Anyone who has read through the Gospels even once knows full well that Jesus emphatically contradicted such sentiments. Who can forget the emotionally charged words as he was walking away from the temple: "O Jerusalem, Jerusalem, you who kill the prophets and stone those sent to you, how often I have *longed to gather your children* together, as a hen gathers her chicks under her wings, but *you* were not willing" (Matthew 23:37). Or as John explains: "He came to that which was his own, but his own did not receive him" (John 1:11). It was the Jews who rejected Jesus, not the other way round (Mark 12:1–12).

To suggest, as Hagee does, that Jews are somehow entitled to building settlements in Gaza and yet excluded from the blessed salvation of the gospel might well be regarded as the height of anti-Semitism. Worse still is the Zionist preoccupation with herding Jews into the land, since in their view two-thirds of the Jewish population in Palestine—some say the world—will soon die in unbelief in a horrific Holy Land holocaust.[40] As previously demonstrated, both the idea that Jews in the twenty-first century will endure a holocaust for the first-century sins of their fathers and the ideology that Jews have a divine right to the land based on race are decidedly unbiblical.

As with the Levitical law, the promises concerning the land find ultimate fulfillment in the Lord. There is no biblical precedent for supposing that God favors Jews over Palestinians or vice versa. At the end of the day, our heavenly Father is not pro-Jew—he is pro-justice; he is not pro-Palestinian, he is pro-peace. In fact, the priceless material with which our feet are fitted for readiness in battle "against the rulers, against the authorities, against the powers of this dark world, and against the spiritual forces of evil in the heavenly realms" (Ephesians 6:12) is nothing less than a gospel of peace that works inexorably toward justice and equity. Only a gospel of peace and justice through faith in Jesus Christ is potent enough to break the stranglehold of anti-Semitism and racism fueled in part by bad theology.

This is made explicit through a vision of unclean food that Peter experienced in Joppa. Only after he encountered the gentile centurion Cornelius did Peter fully comprehend the import of the vision. "I now realize how true it is" said Peter, "that God does not show *favoritism* but accepts men from every nation who fear him and do what is right. You know the message God sent to the people of Israel, telling the good news of peace through Jesus Christ, who is Lord of *all*" (Acts 10:34–35).

Just as race is of no consequence in Christ, so too real estate should not be a primary consideration. When the disciples asked, "Lord, are you at this time going to restore the kingdom to Israel?" (Acts 1:6). Jesus reoriented their thinking from a restored Jewish state to a kingdom that knows no borders or boundaries. "My kingdom," he reiterated before Pilate, "is not of this world" (John 18:36). As our Lord typologically fulfilled and thus heightened the reality of the law, so too he fulfilled and thus heightened the reality of the land. The writer of Hebrews makes clear that the rest the descendants of Abraham experienced when they entered the land is but a type of the rest we experience when we enter an eternal relationship with the Lord. The land provided temporal rest for the *physical* descendants of Abraham, but the Lord provides eternal rest for the *spiritual* descendants of Abraham (see Hebrews 3 and 4). The land was never the focus of our Lord; instead, our Lord is forever the locus of the land.

Finally, the land promises are fully and finally fulfilled in the final future through Jesus who leads the spiritual descendants of Abraham into Paradise restored. In the fore future, the land promises were fulfilled when the children of Israel entered the Promised Land. In the far future, the promise is typologically fulfilled in the Lord who is the locus of the land. In the final future, the promise of the land will be fully and finally consummated when Paradise lost is reconstituted as Paradise restored. Canaan is thus typological of a renewed cosmos. Accordingly, Abraham was anything but a Zionist. Like Isaac and Jacob, he viewed living in the Promised Land in the same way that a stranger would view living in a foreign country. Why? Because as the writer of Hebrews makes plain, "He was looking forward to a city with foundations, whose architect and builder is God" (Hebrews 11:9–10). Abraham looked beyond binding borders and boundaries to a day in which the meek would "inherit the earth" (Matthew 5:5; cf. Psalm 37:11, 22).

THE HOLY CITY

Midnight, May 14, 1948, was a watershed moment for Zionist aspirations. What Theodor Herzl (1860–1904), the person most responsible for galvanizing Zionism into a cohesive cultural movement, and John Nelson Darby, the priest most responsible for growing Zionism into a cohesive Christian movement, had dreamed of was finally a tangible reality. As World War I drew to a close, British statesman Arthur James Balfour wrote a letter to British Baron Lord Rothschild, effectively committing Britain to a Jewish homeland in Palestine. If the Balfour Declaration (1917) was the golden key that unlocked the doors of Palestine,[41] the Abrahamic covenant was the stuff out of which the key was fashioned. Balfour, who was raised on a steady diet of dispensationalism, believed that the formation of a Jewish homeland, which happened to coincide with the best interests of British foreign policy, would be the key that unlocked the door of the biblical framework of prophecy.[42]

Not everyone was similarly convinced. As the door to premillennial prophecy swung open in 1948, dispensational publications such as the *Weekly Evangel* emphatically denounced cultural Zionism: "The Zionists will never get the Promised Land by their own political scheming and their own armed might. They will get it when they welcome Jesus of Nazareth back to earth as their Messiah."[43] The Old Testament prophets had proclaimed that entry to the land was contingent upon faith and obedience, just as exile from the land was rooted in unfaithfulness and disobedience.[44] In the words of dispensational heavyweight Stanley Ellisen, professor of biblical literature at Western Seminary: "Judged on biblical grounds, the nation [of Israel] today does not pass divine muster as a nation living in covenant obedience to God. The promise to possess the land is directly tied to the nation's response to Messiah. Though its international right to the land can be well defended, Israel's divine right by covenant to possess it today has only sentiment in its favor."[45]

Prophecy pundits, however, were quick to spin the Scriptures in the direction of political realities on the ground. Demonstrating remarkable revisionistic resolve, LaHaye reasoned that God had removed Israel from the land due to debauchery and defiance but would regather them from the nations in their disobedience and disbelief.[46] Hagee went so far as to suggest that prior to the establishment of the secular state of Israel, skeptics had reason to doubt the veracity of Scripture:

If Israel as a nation had not been reborn, if the Jews had not returned to the land, if the cities of Israel had not been rebuilt, if Judea and Samaria (the West Bank) had not been occupied, if the trees the Turks cut down had not been replanted, if the agricultural accomplishments of Israel had not been miraculous, there would be a valid reason to doubt that the Word of God is true.

However, in light of the above-mentioned miracles, none can doubt the absolute accuracy of the prophetic Scriptures concerning the rebirth and restoration of the Jewish state.[47]

In the dispensational mind-set, the return of the Jews to the land in defiance and disbelief not only vindicated Scripture but provided a basis for determining the exact timing of a two-phased return of Christ. As Lindsey says in *The Late Great Planet Earth*, "When the Jewish people, after nearly 2,000 years of exile, under relentless persecution, became a nation again on 14 May 1948 the 'fig tree' put forth its leaves. Jesus said that this would indicate that He was 'at the door,' ready to return. Then He said, 'Truly I say to you, *this generation* will not pass away until all these things take place.'" Lindsey goes on to conclude that "this generation" refers "obviously" to "the generation that would see the signs—chief among them the rebirth of Israel. A generation in the Bible is something like forty years. If this is a correct deduction, then within forty years or so of 1948, all these things could take place. Many scholars who have studied Bible prophecy all their lives believe that this is so."[48]

The founder of the Calvary Chapel movement, Chuck Smith, agreed. In a booklet titled *End Times*, Smith predicted the precise timing of the rapture and the second coming of Christ:

If I understand Scripture correctly, Jesus taught us that the generation which sees the "budding of the fig tree," the birth of the nation Israel, will be the generation that sees the Lord's return. I believe that the generation of 1948 is the last generation. Since a generation of judgment is forty years and the Tribulation

185

period lasts seven years, I believe the Lord could come back for his church any time before the Tribulation starts, which would mean any time before 1981 (1948 + 40 – 7 = 1981).[49]

As the time for the rapture and return of Christ came and went, the red-letter day in 1948 in which the secular state of Israel had been founded began to lose its luster. As historian Timothy Weber observes, dispensationalists were thrilled that the Jews were back in the land but perplexed with respect to its borders: "The new nation that had been declared in May 1948 looked nothing like the maps of ancient Israel found in the back of their Bibles or hanging on the walls of their Sunday school rooms."[50] Even more perplexing was the fact that Jews did not control the Holy City and had not been able to reinstitute the types and shadows of Old Testament sacrifice in a rebuilt temple on the site where the Muslim Dome of the Rock yet stood.

All of that changed, however, when June 10, 1967, replaced May 14, 1948, as the quintessential day in end-time speculation scenarios. The state of Israel launched preemptive attacks on Egypt, Syria, Iraq, and Jordan, and within six days occupied the Golan Heights, Gaza, the Sinai, the West Bank, and most important—Jerusalem. Weber documents the capture of Jerusalem as the ultimate accomplishment of the Six-Day War:

On Wednesday morning, June 7, the third day of the war, the IDF [Israeli Defense Force] surrounded the Old City of Jerusalem, then entered it from the northeast through St. Stephen's (or Lion's) Gate. It was a short distance from there to the Temple Mount. Jordanian troops put up a fight, but the IDF overwhelmed them quickly.

Soon hundreds of Israeli soldiers were swarming over the sacred site. A few of them raised an Israeli flag on the Dome of the Rock, but their real objective was the Western Wall. . . . The IDF's chief rabbi, Brigadier Shlomo Goren, arrived with a Torah scroll in one hand and a shofar in the other. . . .

According to Major General Uzi Narkiss, who had led the attack on the Old City, the initial reaction of Rabbi Goren was less than charitable. After stepping off what he believed were the outlines of the second temple, the rabbi urged General Narkiss to blow up the Dome of the Rock and clear the site once and for all, but the general refused. In fact, the Israelis moved quickly to assure Muslims that their holy places would be safe in an Israeli-controlled Jerusalem. Moshe Dayan, the Israeli defense minister, went to the Temple Mount the afternoon of its capture and ordered the lowering of the Israeli flag from the dome. He then conferred with Muslim leaders. Dayan promised that while officially the Temple Mount would remain in Israeli hands, Muslims would retain full control of their holy places there. Dayan insisted that the ban against Jews visiting the mount must be lifted, though he agreed that Jews would not be allowed to set up a place of worship there. Their holy site would be the Western Wall, over which Muslims would no longer have any control. . . .

While Muslims were relieved to retain control over the Dome of the Rock and the Al-Aqsa Mosque, they were outraged by what Israelis did to the area in front of the Western Wall. The war ended on Saturday, June 10. At midnight, dozens of bulldozers entered the Old

City and went to work on the Arab Mughrabi neigh-
borhood, which fronted the wall. By morning all the
homes were gone, and hundreds of Arab people were
homeless. The destruction was necessary, according to
Israeli officials, to accommodate all the Israelis who
wanted access to their most sacred space.[51]

The year 1967 not only reinvigorated the faith of
Christian Zionists, it renewed their fascination with timing
the two-pronged return of Christ. This time the math was
downright magical. Add forty to 1967, then subtract seven,
and 2000 emerges as the new date of destiny. Chuck Smith
saw this as more than accidental. "I think it is more than coin-
cidental that it was just about six thousand years ago that
Adam and Eve disobeyed God and sold the world into slavery.
According to biblical chronology, it was roughly 4000 BC
when Adam first ate of the forbidden fruit. That means the
world is coming very close to entering the 'seventh year' of its
captivity."[52] Smith subsequently recalibrated the date to not
later than 2014—this, said Smith, is "the maximum."[53]

While dispensationalists have come up with a variety of for-
mulas to explain away the fact that Christ has not yet returned,
1967, the year "the Jews took Jerusalem," has retained its significance. Jack Van Impe, for one, recalculated a generation to be
50 years—51.4 to be exact. "Add 51.4 to 1967 when the Jews
took Jerusalem and you come out to 2018," says Van Impe.
"Add the extra six months because it happened in June of 67 and
the 4/10ths and you come out to 2019 years and take away the
seven from that and you come out to 2012. Could it be that on
Christmas Day Jesus Christ would come at that moment?"[54]

As dates come and go, one thing remains unchanged. For

Christian Zionists, 1967 is a definitive date of destiny. As L. Nelson Bell put it a generation ago, "That for the first time in more than 2000 years Jerusalem is now completely in the hands of the Jews gives a student of the Bible a thrill and a renewed faith in the accuracy and validity of the Bible."[55] Or as John Hagee put it in our generation, "Jerusalem was reunited under Jewish leadership for the first time in two thousand years with Israel's victory in the Six-Day War of 1967. . . . If you listen closely, you can hear the footsteps of Messiah walking toward Israel."[56]

Hagee goes on to assert,

> The golden thread running through that blood-soaked historical tapestry is the unshakable association of the Jewish people with the sacred city. Jerusalem is sacred to Christians, Muslims, and Jews, but God has given Jerusalem *only to the Jews.* . . . Jerusalem is the city where God's presence dwells on the earth. I have traveled around the world several times and have visited the celebrated cities of the earth, but I have found that in Jerusalem there is a very special and powerful presence. It is the literal presence of the living God of Abraham, Isaac and Jacob.[57]

Such rhetoric raises a host of timely questions. Has God indeed given Jerusalem exclusively to the Jews? Is ethnic cleansing of Palestinians from Jerusalem a biblical axiom and a two-state solution a blasphemous abomination? Does the presence of God reside in Jerusalem in a special and powerful way? More to the point, is Jerusalem still to be regarded as the Holy City? If so, why do both Old and New Testaments label Jerusalem the harlot city? And what of the heavenly city Jerusalem? Why does the apostle Paul say, "the Jerusalem that is above is free, and she is our mother"? (Galatians 4:26).

To begin with, Jerusalem is regarded in the Judeo-Christian tradition as the Holy City because it was the place where God's glorious presence dwelt among the people. The city of Jerusalem is a type that pointed forward to the coming of Jesus, who dwelt among us in human flesh. It wasn't until David captured the city from the Jebusites a thousand years before Christ, however, that Jerusalem began to play a significant role in the history of the children of Israel (2 Samuel 5). David renamed Jerusalem the City of David, relocated the ark of the covenant to Jerusalem, and used Jerusalem to promote unity between the northern and southern tribes of Israel.

Following David's conquest of the city, "he became more and more powerful, because the LORD God Almighty was with him" (2 Samuel 5:10). Despite egregious sins, David stood in Hebrew history as the quintessential righteous king of Israel— a type of Christ, the "Son of David" (cf. Matthew 1:1; 12:23; 21:15; Luke 1:32). Thus, as the seat of David's throne and the eventual location of the temple built by David's son Solomon, Jerusalem symbolized all that Israel was to be. The city and its temple were holy and set apart from the pagan nations that surrounded Israel's borders. Set high as it was in the hill country, Jerusalem served as an apt reminder that the children of Israel were to be a light to the nations—a holy "city on a hill" that cannot be hidden (Matthew 5:14). Jerusalem is typological of the greater purposes of God to grant "rest to his people" and to dwell among them "forever" (1 Chronicles 23:25).

It is with these characteristics in mind that the Hebrew Psalms laud Jerusalem as "the hill of the LORD . . . his holy place" and "the city of the LORD Almighty" (Psalms 24:3; 48:8). Says the psalmist, "The LORD has chosen Zion, he has desired it for his dwelling: 'This is my resting place for ever and ever'" (132:13–14).[58] As God had covenanted with Abraham to bring his descendants into the Promised Land, so God covenanted with David to establish his throne in that land forever: "When your days are over and you go to be with your fathers, I will raise up your offspring to succeed you, one of your own sons, and I will establish his kingdom. He is the one who will build a house for me, and I will establish his throne for-ever" (1 Chronicles 17:11–12).

Furthermore, as Jerusalem was celebrated by the psalmists as the Holy City, so it would be condemned by the prophets as the harlot city. Like the Abrahamic covenant before it, the Davidic covenant was conditional.

> The LORD swore an oath to David,
>   a sure oath that he will not revoke:
> "One of your own descendants
>   I will place on your throne—
> *if* your sons keep my covenant
>   and the statutes I teach them,
> *then* their sons will sit
>   on your throne for ever and ever."
>
> (PSALM 132:11–12;
> CF. 2 CHRONICLES 6:16)

God reiterated the conditional nature of his covenants with Israel through the prophet Jeremiah, warning, "If you do not listen to me and follow my law, which I have set before you, and if you do not listen to the words of my servants and prophets, whom I have sent to you again and again (though you have not listened), then I will make . . . this city an object of cursing among all the nations of the earth" (Jeremiah 26:4–6).

Regrettably, David's descendants, beginning with his own son Solomon, rebelled against God and led Israel into idolatry. Intended to be a city on a hill—a light to the nations—Jerusalem became a mere microcosm of the surrounding pagan cultures. Though for a brief time it stood as a sacred place, Jerusalem became a symbol of spiritual prostitution—the harlot against whom the prophets pronounced great woes. The kings of Israel made unholy alliances with the rulers of pagan nations from Egypt to Babylon and, in the time of Christ, imperial Rome. They adopted the religions of foreign lands and built altars and shrines to pagan gods. Thus, far from serving as the holy resting place of God's presence among his people, Jerusalem became a bed of wickedness.

"You have lived as a prostitute with many lovers—
would you now return to me?"
declares the LORD.
"Look up to the barren heights and see.
Is there any place where you have not been ravished?
By the roadside you sat waiting for lovers,
sat like a nomad in the desert.
You defiled the land
with your prostitution and wickedness.
Therefore the showers have been withheld,
and no spring rains have fallen.
Yet you have the brazen look of a prostitute;
you refuse to blush with shame."

(JEREMIAH 3:1–3)

As demonstrated with the historical principle of Exegetical Eschatology, the apostle John goes so far as to refer to Jerusalem as "MYSTERY BABYLON THE GREAT THE MOTHER OF PROSTITUTES AND OF THE ABOMINATIONS OF THE EARTH" (Revelation 17:5). The harlotry of Jerusalem resulted in civil war, division of the kingdom, and ultimately the Assyrian exile of the northern kingdom of Israel in 722 BC, as well as the Babylonian exile of the southern kingdom of Judah in 597 BC. In the midst of the sixth-century BC Babylonian captivity, God revealed through Daniel his present and eternal purposes for Israel and the world. Daniel accurately predicted the progression of kingdoms from Babylon through the Median and Persian empires to the further persecution and suffering of the Jews under Antiochus IV Epiphanes, including his desecration of the Jerusalem temple and his untimely death, to freedom for the Jews under Judas Maccabeus in 165 BC.

Of significance is Daniel's vision of the seventy sevens, which symbolically refer to the lengthy period of extended exile beginning with the decree of King Cyrus of Persia (cf. Isaiah 44:28; Daniel 9:25). As prophesied by Jeremiah, Jerusalem would experience a partial restoration after seventy years of exile (Jeremiah 29:10; cf. Daniel 9:2); however, as revealed through the angel Gabriel, the return from exile was merely a type of the antitypical freedom that would be experienced through Judas Maccabeus, which itself was typological of the ultimate restoration through Jesus the Messiah. Cyrus's decree allowed for the return of the Jews to Jerusalem and the rebuilding of the temple (see Ezra 1:1); nevertheless, the people of Judah continued to be dominated by foreign powers. The symbolism of seventy sevens, a number repeated by Jesus in regard to the number of times we are to forgive others (Matthew 18:21–22; cf. Genesis 4:24), is grounded in the Hebrew redemptive year of Jubilee, in which all debts were canceled at the end of every forty-nine years (or seven periods of seven years; see Leviticus 25:8–17). Thus, the seventy sevens of Daniel encompass ten Jubilee eras and represent the extended exile of the Jews that would end in the fullness of time—the quintessential Jubilee—when the people of God would experience ultimate redemption and restoration, not in the harlot city, but in the holy Christ.

Christ echoed the judgments of the Hebrew prophets when he too identified Jerusalem as an unholy city. His unrequited love was profoundly expressed in the lament, "O Jerusalem, Jerusalem, you who kill the prophets and stone those sent to you, how often I have longed to gather your children together, as a hen gathers her chicks under her wings, but you were not willing. Look, your house is left to you desolate" (Matthew 23:37–38). Using the apocalyptic imagery of the Old Testament prophets, Jesus went on to predict Jerusalem's utter devastation within a generation. Colin Chapman, in *Whose Holy City?* comments:

> The fall of Jerusalem is to be an act of divine judgment, compared in a shocking way to the judgment on Babylon described by Isaiah. What seems to be most significant, therefore, is that whereas the Old Testament prophets predicted judgment, exile *and* a return to the land, Jesus predicts destruction and exile, *but says nothing about a return to the land.* Instead of predicting the restoration of Israel, he speaks about the coming of the kingdom of God through the coming of the Son of Man.[59]

Like his Master, the apostle John reflected a radical shift in thinking with respect to Jerusalem. In the book of Revelation, he goes so far as to liken Jerusalem to Sodom, Egypt, and Babylon (Revelation 11:8; 17:5). Indeed, by the end of the apostolic era, the focus of outreach and evangelism had shifted from Jerusalem to such faraway places as Rome.[60] Stephen Sizer explains:

> There is, therefore, no evidence that the apostles believed that the Jewish people still had a divine right to the land, or that the Jewish possession of the land would be important, let alone that Jerusalem would remain a central aspect of God's purposes for the world. On the contrary, in the christological logic of Paul, Jerusalem, as much as the land, has now been superseded. They have been made irrelevant in God's redemptive purposes.[61]

From the time of Jerusalem's destruction in AD 70 to the time that Constantine made Christianity the official religion of the Roman Empire, Jerusalem was a mere "byword among the nations." Jerusalem did not play a significant role in world history again until the fourth century when Constantine's mother, Queen Helena, refocused the attention of the Roman world on Jerusalem as the "holy" site of Jesus's crucifixion, burial, and resurrection.

In the seventh century, Jerusalem was captured by Caliph Omar Ibn al-Khatab and became a major focus of the Islamic world. Muslim control of Jerusalem continued on into the twentieth century interrupted only for relatively brief periods of time during the Crusades. "When the Crusaders captured

Jerusalem on 15 July 1099" says Chapman, "they slaughtered almost everyone in sight—Muslims, Jews and even Christians."[62] In light of the Crusades, "it is hardly surprising that the involvement of Britain and other Western powers in the Middle East in the twentieth and twenty-first centuries and their major role in creating the Middle East as it is today are seen by most Arabs and most Muslims as a continuation of the Crusades, in which the Christian West sought to defeat and control the Muslim and Arab East."[63]

Muslim rule of Jerusalem ended in 1917 when the Ottoman Turks were defeated by the British. Britain in turn relinquished control of Jerusalem in 1947 when the UN issued a partition plan for the establishment of distinct Jewish and Palestinian states with Jerusalem as an international city. Palestinian rejection of the UN partition plan resulted in the military siege of Jerusalem by Jordanian, Egyptian, and British forces. Having been divided between Jewish and Jordanian control for nineteen years, Jerusalem was fully captured by Israeli military in 1967 as a result of the Six-Day War. And so, after three hundred years of post-Constantinian Christian rule, thirteen centuries of Muslim control, and thirty years of British domination, Jerusalem is again under the control of a secular Jewish state.

While Christian Zionists see the fact that Jerusalem is now completely in the hands of the Jews as validation for the Bible, nothing could be further from the truth. Even if one ignores the typological fulfillment of Jerusalem in Jesus, the old covenant promise of return to the land is inviolately conditioned upon belief and faithfulness. Modern Israel fails to meet the biblical requirement for return to the land. As Moses unambiguously warned the children of Israel, disobedience against the Lord would result in dispersion (Deuteronomy 28:58–64; 29:23–28), while return to the land requires repentance: "*When* you and your children return to the LORD your God and obey him with all your heart . . . *then* the LORD your God will restore your fortunes and have compassion on you and gather you again from the nations where he scattered you" (Deuteronomy 30:2–3).

There is therefore no warrant for the Christian Zionists' claims that the recapturing of Jerusalem by modern Israel signifies the preliminary fulfillment of God's promises to Abraham.[64] While one might well defend the right of the secular state of Israel to exist, the contention that the modern state of Israel is a fulfillment of biblical prophecy is indefensible. In truth, since coming under the exclusive control of modern Israel, Jerusalem has demonstrated a far greater resemblance to the harlot city spoken of by the prophets than to the holy city spoken of by the psalmists.[65]

Thus, far from culminating in a supposed fulfillment of God's promise to Abraham, the unholy history of the once holy city bears out the reality of Jesus's words to the Samaritan woman: "A time is coming when you will worship the Father neither on this mountain *nor in Jerusalem*. . . . A time is coming and has now come when the true worshipers will worship the Father in spirit and truth" (John 4:22–23). History, like the New Testament, reveals that the Holy City—turned harlot city—is superseded by the holy Christ. Jesus is the antitype who fulfills all of the typology vested in Jerusalem. Thus, while Jerusalem remains an important historical site as the typological City of David and the "holy" birthplace of Christianity, there is neither biblical nor historical warrant for treating it as the object of our eschatological hope. Actually, it is in Jesus, not Jerusalem, that we come face-to-face with the glory and presence of the living God.

Finally, the New Testament reveals that the Holy City turned harlot city is a type that points forward to the heavenly city, "the new Jerusalem coming down out of heaven from God, prepared as a bride beautifully dressed for her husband" (Revelation 21:2). Biblical Christianity is not fixated on an earthly Jerusalem but on a heavenly "city with foundations, whose architect and builder is God" (Hebrews 11:10). The apostle John got a glimpse of this antitypical holy city when the Spirit showed him, "the Holy City, Jerusalem, coming down out of heaven from God. It shone with the glory of God, and its brilliance was like that of a very precious jewel, like a jasper, clear as crystal" (Revelation 21:10–11). As John gazed upon the splendor of this heavenly Jerusalem, his mind must surely have flashed back to the words of King Jesus as he stood before Pilate. "My kingdom" Jesus had said, "is not of this world. If it were, my servants would fight to prevent my arrest by the Jews. But now my kingdom is from another place" (John 18:36).

The quintessential point of understanding for John as well as for the rest of the disciples began to dawn at the time of Christ's postresurrection appearances. Previously they had been under the same misconceptions as modern-day Christian Zionists. They had expected Jesus to establish Jerusalem as the capital of a sovereign Jewish empire. The notion was so ingrained in their psyches that even as Jesus was about to ascend into heaven, they asked, "Lord are you at this time going to restore the kingdom to Israel?" (Acts 1:6).

Jesus not only corrects their erroneous thinking, but expands their horizons from a tiny strip of land on the east coast of the Mediterranean to the farthest reaches of the earth. "You will receive power when the Holy Spirit comes on you," said Jesus, as he was about to be taken up into heaven; "and you will be my witnesses in Jerusalem, and in all Judea and Samaria, *and to the ends of the earth*" (Acts 1:8). In effect, Jesus left his disciples with instructions to exit Jerusalem, embrace the earth, and never again entertain the thought of establishing an earthly Jerusalem.

The disciples are no longer permitted to view Israel in exclusivistic parochial categories; their sights instead must be elevated to an inclusive Israel. As Paul put it in the book of Romans, "Not all who are descended from Israel are Israel. Nor because they are his descendants are they all Abraham's children" (Romans 9:6–7). True Israel consists of people from "every tribe and language and people and nation" (Revelation 5:9).

At the Jerusalem council, James identifies this new covenant reality as the antitypical fulfillment of the well-known prophecy that God would "restore David's fallen tent" (Amos 9:11). Though Amos's prophecy was fulfilled in the fore future when a remnant of Israel was restored to the land, James interprets this fulfillment as a type that finds its ultimate resolution not in a future restoration of national Israel to the land, but in the inclusion of both Jews and Gentiles in the church. As James explains,

"Simon has described to us how God at first showed his concern by taking from the Gentiles a people for himself. The words of the prophets are in agreement with this, as it is written:

" 'After this I will return
    and rebuild David's fallen tent.
Its ruins I will rebuild,
    and I will restore it,
that the remnant of men may seek the Lord,
    and all the Gentiles who bear my name.' . . .

"It is my judgment, therefore, that we should not make it difficult for the Gentiles who are turning to God." (Acts 15:14–19)

James underscores the reality that Abraham was not to be the father of *a* nation but the father of *many* nations through whom all the world would be blessed (cf. Genesis 17:5). When God promises Abraham, "I will bless those who bless you, and whoever curses you I will curse; and all the peoples on earth will be blessed through you" (Genesis 12:3), such blessings and cursings pertain not simply to the faithful remnant of ethnic Israel, but to true Israel, which consists of every person who through faith has been adopted into the family of God.

Just as God's promise to Abraham was fulfilled when the gospel went out from Jerusalem to all the earth, so God's promise to David that his descendants would sit on the throne forever (see 2 Samuel 7:11–16; cf. Isaiah 9:7) was fulfilled when Christ, the "Son of David" (cf. Matthew 1:1; 12:23; 21:15; Luke 1:32), ascended to the throne of the heavenly Jerusalem and established his rule and reign over all the earth. The apostle Peter drove this point home on the day of Pentecost when he proclaimed to fellow Jews:

"[David] was a prophet and knew that God had promised him on oath that he would place one of his descendants on his throne. Seeing what was ahead, he spoke of the resurrection of the Christ, that he was not abandoned to the grave, nor did his body see decay. God has raised this Jesus to life, and we are all witnesses of the fact. Exalted to the right hand of God, he has received from the Father the promised Holy Spirit and has poured out what you now see and hear. For David did not ascend to heaven, and yet he said,

> "'The Lord said to my Lord:
> "Sit at my right hand
> until I make your enemies
> a footstool for your feet.'" [66]

"Therefore let all Israel be assured of this: God has made this Jesus, whom you crucified, both Lord and Christ" (Acts 2:30–36).

Just as Joshua is a type of Jesus who leads the true children of Israel into the eternal land of promise, so King David is a type of the "King of Kings and Lord of Lords" who forever rules and reigns from the New Jerusalem in faithfulness and in truth (Revelation 19:16; cf. 19:11). In each case, the lesser is fulfilled and rendered obsolete by the greater.

Moreover, as Peter makes clear, Jesus's reign has already been inaugurated in his resurrection and ascension to the throne of God. The apostle Paul affirmed the same message to his fellow Jews:

> "We tell you the good news: What God promised our fathers he has fulfilled for us, their children, by raising up Jesus. As it is written in the second Psalm:
>
> " 'You are my Son;
>   today I have become your Father.'

The fact that God raised him from the dead, never to decay, is stated in these words:

" 'I will give you the holy and sure blessings promised to David.'"

(ACTS 13:32–34)

Rather than focusing on an exclusively Jewish Jerusalem, Paul rejoices that Christ's reign extends to faithful Gentiles throughout the earth who, on account of Christ, "are no longer foreigners and aliens, but fellow citizens with God's people and members of God's household" (Ephesians 2:19).

In light of this christological reality, to now require that God must provide a literal throne in Jerusalem upon which Jesus will physically sit to rule over national Israel in a millennial semi-golden age is more than an anticlimactic step backward; it is an insult to the glory and grandeur of God's throne. What is greater, ruling the entire heavens and earth from God's very throne, or ruling over national Israel on David's throne? The answer should be obvious. As Peter Walker has well said, as a result of the Incarnation, "Jesus, not Jerusalem, would now become the central 'place' within God's purposes, the place around which God's true people would be gathered."[67] The earthly Jerusalem is thus a type that has been heightened by the greater reality of the heavenly city where Christ sits on the throne. It is toward the antitypical heavenly Jerusalem with Jesus on its throne that we are to direct our eschatological gaze.

Paul illustrates this typologically heightened fulfillment when he figuratively contrasts Sarah with Hagar. Says Paul, "These things may be taken figuratively, for the women represent two covenants. One covenant is from Mount Sinai and bears children who are to be slaves: This is Hagar. Now Hagar stands for Mount Sinai in Arabia and corresponds to the present city of Jerusalem, because she is in slavery with her children. *But the Jerusalem that is above is free, and she is our mother"* (Galatians 4:24–26). In saying this, Paul emphasizes that all who fixate on an earthly Jerusalem with a rebuilt temple and reinstituted temple sacrifices are in slavery to types and shadows. Conversely, all who recognize that the shadow of Jerusalem has found fulfillment in the substance of Christ are set free to inherit the earth (cf. Psalm 37:11; Matthew 5:5; Romans 4:13).

THE HOLY TEMPLE

One of the most riveting stories in the whole of Scripture involves construction of the traveling tabernacle. Shortly after liberation from bondage in Egypt, the Almighty instructed Moses to build a tabernacle of surpassing brilliance and beauty. And with the command came sovereign empowerment:

> "I have chosen Bezalel son of Uri, the son of Hur, of the tribe of Judah, and I have filled him with the Spirit of God, with skill, ability and knowledge in all kinds of crafts—to make artistic designs for work in gold, silver and bronze, to cut and set stones, to work in wood, and to engage in all kinds of craftsmanship. Moreover, I have appointed Oholiab son of Ahisamach, of the tribe of Dan, to help him. Also I have given skill to all the craftsmen to make everything I have commanded you." (Exodus 31:2–6)

After the divinely empowered craftsmen had completed their architectural artistry and Moses had consecrated the tabernacle and its furnishings, the shekinah glory of the Lord descended upon the tabernacle in a cloud. From that day onward, the children of Israel did not continue their travels until the presence of God as manifested in the cloud moved with them. "So the cloud of the LORD was over the tabernacle by day, and fire was in the cloud by night, in the sight of all the house of Israel during all their travels" (Exodus 40:38).

Throughout the Bible we can find passages that hark back to the wilderness tabernacle as the very place of God's presence on the earth. The apostle John actually used a verbal representation of the term *tabernacle* when he wrote: "The Word became flesh and made his dwelling [tabernacled] among us" (John 1:14). Similarly, Stephen, in his speech to the Sanhedrin, accused the Jews of turning the tabernacle into an object of idolatry by failing to recognize it as a type pointing forward to "the Righteous One" who had come to tabernacle among them (Acts 7:38–53). Revelation, likewise, refers back to furnishings of the wilderness tabernacle—golden lampstands (1:12), incense (5:8), altar (6:9), ark of the covenant (11:19), among other examples—as types pointing forward to the time that God would forever tabernacle among his people in Paradise restored.

The tabernacle, however, was but a temporary type of God's dwelling on the earth. During the golden age of Solomon, it gave way to a temple of surpassing splendor. Like the tabernacle before it, the temple would symbolize the dwelling of God among the people. In fact, after the ark of the covenant containing the Ten Commandments had been placed in the holy of holies "the glory of the LORD filled his temple" (1 Kings 8:11) as it had previously filled the tabernacle. Despite its grandeur, however, the temple paled in comparison to the effulgence of God's greatness and glory. As Solomon acknowledged in his dedicatory prayer, "The heavens, even the highest heaven, cannot contain you. How much less this temple I have built!" (1 Kings 8:27).

After the completion of the temple, the Lord appeared to Solomon a second time. On the first occasion he had granted Solomon "a wise and discerning heart" (1 Kings 3:12). On this occasion he gave Solomon a warning of disaster ahead. "If you or your sons turn away from me and do not observe the commands and decrees I have given you and go off to serve other gods and worship them, then I will cut off Israel from the land I have given them and will reject this temple I have consecrated for my Name. Israel will become a byword and an object of ridicule among all peoples" (1 Kings 9:6–7).

Despite world-class wisdom, Solomon failed to heed the warning. As a consequence, his peaceful and prosperous rule ended in idolatrous scandal and civil strife. "As Solomon grew old, his wives turned his heart after other gods. . . . He followed Ashtoreth the goddess of the Sidonians, and Molech the detestable god of the Ammonites. So Solomon did evil in the eyes of the LORD; he did not follow the LORD completely, as David his father had done" (1 Kings 11:4–6).

And so God appeared to Solomon one more time—this time in judgment. Solomon had played fast and loose with the covenants and decrees of the Almighty. Therefore, the Lord said to Solomon. "Since this is your attitude and you have not kept my covenant and my decrees, which I commanded you, I will most certainly tear the kingdom away from you and give it to one of your subordinates" (1 Kings 11:11). The words took on foreboding reality when Ahijah, the prophet of Shiloh, "took hold of the new cloak he was wearing and tore it into twelve pieces. Then he said to Jeroboam, 'Take ten pieces for yourself, for this is what the LORD, the God of Israel says: "See, I am going to tear the kingdom out of Solomon's hand and give you ten tribes. But for the sake of my servant David and the city of Jerusalem, which I have chosen out of all the tribes of Israel, he will have one tribe." '" (1 Kings 11:30–32).

Thus, after but a century (1031–931 BC) of relative peace and prosperity in Palestine, the united kingdom was torn in two. In accordance with the prophecy of Ahijah, a nation that had flourished under the rules of Saul, David, and Solomon became a divided kingdom—Israel (the ten tribes to the north) ruled by Solomon's subordinate Jeroboam, and Judah ruled by Solomon's son Rehoboam. In 722 BC Assyria conquered the northern kingdom of Israel and assimilated the ten tribes into Assyrian culture. Not long thereafter, Babylon enslaved the southern kingdom of Judah (beginning in 606 BC) and demolished Solomon's temple (586 BC).

It wasn't until 539 BC that Cyrus, king of Persia, conquered Babylon and decreed that the Jews be permitted to "go up to Jerusalem in Judah and build the temple of the LORD" (Ezra 1:3). Seventy years after its destruction, the temple was rebuilt under the leadership of Ezra and Nehemiah and later enlarged under the Roman Herod at the time of Christ. A mere ten years after the completion of its restoration, however, the second temple was utterly destroyed by Titus and the Roman army (AD 70). It was just as Jesus had prophesied: "I tell you the truth, not one stone here will be left on another; every one will be thrown down" (Matthew 24:2).

The destruction of the temple brought an end to the age of sacrifice for Jews. For Christians, however, the age of the temple—like the law and the land—had already come to an end with the sacrifice of Jesus.

Such a high priest meets our need—one who is holy, blameless, pure, set apart from sinners, exalted above the heavens. Unlike the other high priests, he does not need to offer sacrifices day after day, first for his own sins, and then for the sins of the people. He sacrificed for their sins once for all when he offered himself. For the law appoints as high priests men who are weak; but the oath, which came after the law, appointed the Son, who has been made perfect forever. (Hebrews 7:26–28)

As Hebrews goes on to explain, the tabernacle and the temple were but types. The priest offered sacrifices "at a sanctuary that is a *copy* and *shadow* of what is in heaven. This is why Moses was warned when he was about to build the tabernacle: 'See to it that you make everything according to the *pattern* shown you on the mountain.' But the ministry Jesus has received is as superior to theirs as the covenant of which he is mediator is superior to the old one, and it is founded on better promises" (8:5–6). Hebrews declares the utter futility of the sacrificial system in light of the Savior's sacrifice. "Day after day every priest stands and performs his religious duties; again and again he offers the same sacrifices, which can never take away sins" (10:11). Jesus, however, "offered for all time one sacrifice for sins" (v. 12). Jesus forever did away with the need for sacrifice, rendering the temple obsolete.

Despite the fact that Jesus forever dispensed with the need for temple, priest, and sacrifice two thousand years ago, Christian Zionists today are bent on stoking the embers of

Armageddon by scheming the construction of yet another temple—and that on the very spot where the Dome of the Rock now stands. As previously noted, LaHaye calls Mount Moriah, site of the ancient Jewish temple, "the most coveted ground in the world." In his words, "the deep significance of the 1967 Six-Day War is seen in the prospect that at long last Israel can rebuild its temple. This not just a national yearning—but a prophetic requirement of God's Word."[68]

LaHaye goes on to highlight the major obstacle: "The Muslims' multimillion-dollar Dome of the Rock is located on the spot where the temple should be."[69] He makes light of fellow dispensationalists who suggest that the Jewish temple could coexist with the Muslim mosque. "Some have tried to suggest that perhaps this location is not the only place in Jerusalem the temple could be built, and thus the Muslim mosque and the Jewish temple could coexist. No careful Bible student would accept that reasoning. . . . There is no substitute on the face of the earth for that spot."[70] Says LaHaye, "there is no other single factor so likely to unite the Arabs in starting a holy war as the destruction of the Dome of the Rock."[71]

Destruction of the Muslim mosque fits well in LaHaye's end-time scenario. As the story goes, a third temple will be built where the Dome of the Rock now stands. The Antichrist will desecrate the temple by standing in the holy of holies and declaring himself God (2 Thessalonians 2:3–4), thus becoming "the abomination that causes desolation" (Mathew 24:15). Jewish resistance in turn will lead to the greatest holocaust in Jewish history. Removing the mosque and rebuilding the temple, however, are only a piece of the puzzle. Temple furnishings, sacred garments, and tools suitable for slaughtering multiplied millions of animals must be fashioned in accord with Levitical law. In addition to all this, a new order of Levitical priests must be established and educated. Above all, before even the first stone of the temple is set in place, it is crucial to purify both the masons and the mount with the ashes of a red heifer.

Thus far the ashes of the red heifer have been a bitter pill for Christian Zionists to swallow. Thomas Ice, executive director of LaHaye's Pre-Trib Research Center, explained the twofold dilemma. "First, there are no red heifer ashes available today, and second, only a person who is ceremonially pure can conduct this ceremony, and no such person exists."[72] Before the fuse of Armageddon can be ignited, an unblemished heifer (dubbed by columnist David Landau of the Israeli newspaper *Ha'aretz*, "a four-legged bomb"[73]) and an unblemished human must be found or fashioned. The significance of this virgin heifer has been wryly compared to virgins in heaven. "You don't have to believe that a rust-colored calf could bring about the end of the world— or that 72 black-eyed virgins await the pious Islamic suicide bomber in paradise"—says Rod Dreher, "but there are many people who do, and are prepared to act on that belief."[74]

Among those prepared to act on the belief that a "rust-colored calf" must be produced in Palestine before a third temple can be rebuilt is Clyde Lott, "a Pentecostal cattleman from Canton Mississippi." As reported by historian Timothy Weber, Lott traveled to Jerusalem in 1990 to meet with Rabbis Chaim Richman and Yisreal Ariel. Although the Pentecostal rancher and Jewish rabbis seemed unlikely bed-fellows, they were locked at the hip in the objective of creating a heifer that met the Levitical requirements outlined in Numbers 19:2. "The original plan was to transport two hundred pregnant cows to Israel via ocean liners at two thousand dollars per head. By using the methods of genetic science, they were confident that the new herd would eventually produce the perfect red heifer."[75]

After founding the nonprofit organization Canaan Land Restoration of Israel, Inc., Lott began raising funds from fellow Christians to finance the red heifer project. A falling out over finances, however, along with discovery by Rabbi Richman that Lott intended to communicate Christian convictions in the course of creating the rust-colored calf, short-circuited the project. Lott, however, was not alone in attempts to produce the perfect heifer. Gershon Salomon of The Temple Faithful organization joined another cattleman in seeking to produce a red heifer. In doing so, he discovered the difficulties inherent in creating and caring for the cow were even more daunting than previously imagined. "A Red Heifer needs to be raised and handled in a very special way like a holy thing which is completely dedicated to G-d. It has to be raised in a very special, clean stall and to be fed with special food, and even to be spoiled. She cannot be raised with other calves and especially not with males."[76]

In the end, rabbis outran ranchers in the race for the red heifer. In 1996 "an all-red-heifer was born to a black and white Holstein that had been impregnated with semen from Switzerland"[77] at the Orthodox Kfar Hasidim agricultural center near Haifa. Declaration by rabbis that the cow was kosher set off a media frenzy. In addition to the press, preachers and prophecy pundits descended on the Kfar Hasidim en masse. Jack Van Impe, for one, noted that since Scripture requires that the heifer, nicknamed Melody, be sacrificed at age three, the ashes might well "be used for Temple purification ceremonies as early as 2000."[78] Unfortunately, cuphoric delight turned to utter dismay when Melody's eyebrows turned black and she sprouted white hairs on her tail and udder. In 2002 another red heifer was declared kosher only to be disqualified later. And so the search for the perfect red heifer continues.

Producing a ceremonially clean cow is one thing, producing a ceremonially clean child who can grow up to perform the purification process is quite another. Thomas Ice, however, notes a possible solution:

> What has been rumored is that special Israeli houses have been built on double arches to raise the dwelling off the ground so it does not come into contact with the land of Israel. This is because the land itself is defiled, and contact would cause the inhabitants raised in the house to also incur ritual impurity. It is claimed that children born to priestly families are being kept there in a state of quarantine and trained to perform the ceremony of purification.[79]

What is particularly troublesome is that everything mentioned thus far—from sacred garments to temple furnishings and from ceremonially clean children to correctly colored cows—is but a necessary evil to the necessary end of constructing a third temple that the Antichrist will desecrate sometime between the first and second phases of the second coming of Christ. Equally troubling is the fact that the entire rebuilt temple scenario, like a house of cards, rests on little more than inference. Such inference arises from the faulty assumption that Jesus, in the space of several sentences within the Olivet Discourse, predicts not simply the destruction of the second temple, but the desecration of a third temple as well. Indeed, according to the *Tim LaHaye Prophecy Study Bible*, Jesus predicts the destruction of the second temple in Matthew 24:2 and then without warning begins describing a twenty-first-century tribulation in which a third temple is desecrated. LaHaye, in concert with fellow Christian Zionists, and in conflict with his own commitment to strict literalism, invents and subsequently inserts a gap of two thousand years between Matthew 24:2 and Matthew 24:4.[80]

Likewise, LaHaye infers a third temple in the apostle Paul's warning to the Thessalonians that "the day of the Lord" will not come until "the man of lawlessness is revealed, the man doomed to destruction. He will oppose and will exalt himself over everything that is called God or is worshiped, so that he sets himself up in God's temple, proclaiming himself to be God" (2 Thessalonians 2:3–4). In projecting Paul's warning onto the landscape of the twenty-first century, LaHaye overlooks Paul's obvious allusion to Caesar Caligula. As N. T. Wright explains, "The Roman emperor Gaius Caligula, convinced of his own divinity, and angry with the Jews over various matters, ordered a huge statue of himself to be placed in the Temple in Jerusalem. Massive Jewish protests at all levels, and the anxious advice of his officers on the spot, failed to dissuade him from this provocative project. Only Gaius's sudden murder in January of AD 41 prevented a major disaster."

Wright goes on to explain that the events of the late AD 60s provided the near-future fulfillment of Paul's prophecy:

> It looks as though Paul, aware of what had nearly happened, envisaged that sooner or later some other megalomaniac would have the same idea. He speaks of a "man of lawlessness," who elevates himself to a position of divinity, exactly as the Roman emperors were beginning to do. Paul saw this danger on the horizon, and knew

212

that such idolatry would conflict disastrously with the true God and his Temple in Jerusalem. Had Paul lived until AD 70 he would have recognized the initial fulfillment of his words in this passage. Evil must reach its height, and then meet sudden doom. The Roman empire itself would go through unimaginable convulsions: the death of four emperors in quick succession during 68 and 69, followed by the destruction of the Jerusalem Temple, would certainly qualify, in Old Testament terms, for the title "the day of the Lord."[81]

As LaHaye misinterprets the words of Jesus and Paul, so too he misunderstands John's words in Revelation 11: "I was given a reed like a measuring rod and was told, 'Go and measure the temple of God and the altar, and count the worshipers there. But exclude the outer court; do not measure it, because it has been given to the Gentiles. They will trample on the holy city for 42 months'" (vv. 1–2). Again LaHaye misses the obvious. Writing prior to the destruction of Jerusalem, the only temple that John would have had in mind is the one he had known all his life—the one yet standing in Jerusalem that would soon be trampled on by the Gentiles!

Not only is the notion of a third temple an inference imposed on the Scriptures, but the New Testament warns that to revert back to the types and shadows of the old covenant is sheer apostasy (see Galatians 3–5; Hebrews 5:11–6:12; 10; 12:14–29).[82] In place of sacrificing holy cows, we are called to celebrate Holy Communion in remembrance of the sacrifice of the holy Christ. Scripture forbids Christians to partake in or encourage the building of a third temple, which would occasion the trampling of the holy Son of God underfoot by counting the blood of the covenant a common thing through the offering of unholy animal sacrifices (cf. Hebrews 10:29).

Despite the clear prohibition of Scripture, LaHaye not only teaches that the Muslim mosque will be replaced by a third temple during the Tribulation, but holds that during the Millennium, the Messiah will preside over animal sacrifices in still another temple. Most troubling of all is the fact that LaHaye's misguided literalism forces him to conclude that these temple sacrifices are not merely memorials but are absolutely necessary for the atonement of sins, such as ceremonial uncleanness.[83]

The Bible speaks of four Temples in Jerusalem. The first two, Solomon's and Herod's, have already been built and destroyed. The final two, the Tribulation Temple and the Millennial Temple, have yet to be built and are described in great detail in biblical prophecy. In the eternal state there will be no Temple because the new heavens and new earth are not polluted with sin, and God, who is holy, will be able to dwell openly with man.[84]

LaHaye quotes Jerry Hullinger to underscore the point: "Because of God's promise to dwell on earth during the millennium (as stated in the New Covenant), it is necessary that He protect his presence through sacrifice. . . . During the eternal state all inhabitants of the New Jerusalem will be glorified and will therefore not be a source of contagious impurities to defile the holiness of Yahweh."[85]

The writer of Hebrews explicitly counters all such contentions by saying that in Christ the old covenant order, including temple sacrifices, are "obsolete" and would "soon disappear"

(Hebrews 8:13). The logic is simple—if temple sacrifices in the Millennium are efficacious for ceremonial uncleanness, Christ's atonement on the cross was not sufficient to pay for all sin for all time. LaHaye's teaching that the temple must be rebuilt and that temple sacrifices must be reinstituted thus stands in direct opposition to the teaching of Hebrews and undermines the central hope of the Christian faith—the atoning sacrifice of Christ for all sins past, present, and future (cf. Hebrews 7:26–27; 9:12, 26, 28; 10:10–14).[86]

In light of the Zionist zeal for rebuilding the temple where the Dome of the Rock now stands, thus inflaming religious passions, threatening to ignite the fuse of Armageddon, and treating as an unholy thing the precious blood of Jesus Christ, we would do well to conclude this chapter by taking a closer look at what Scripture really teaches with respect to Solomon's temple, the second temple, and the spiritual temple in which the first and second temples find their fulfillment.

First, it is crucial to recognize in the context of ancient Israel that Solomon's temple stood as the glorious symbol of God's immanent presence on the earth. Appropriately, Solomon's temple is described in Scripture as a monument of unsurpassed magnificence: "Solomon covered the inside of the temple with pure gold, and he extended gold chains across the front of the inner sanctuary, which was overlaid with gold. So he overlaid the whole interior with gold. He also overlaid with gold the altar that belonged to the inner sanctuary" (1 Kings 6:21–22). It was in this magnificent structure in the heart of Jerusalem, made of the most precious metals and woods, that the holy and transcendent God of the universe condescended to dwell among the people of Israel (cf. 1 Kings 6:11–13). In fact, the temple actually represented the uniting of heaven and earth.

The psalmist expressed this reality by using parallelism to compare God's holy temple with God's heavenly throne: "The
LORD is in his holy temple; the LORD is on his heavenly
throne" (Psalm 11:4). As N. T. Wright explains, "The symbolism of the Temple was designed to express the belief that it
formed the centre not only of the physical world but also of the
entire cosmos, so that, in being YHWH's dwelling-place, it was
the spot where heaven and earth met."[87] Just as the shekinah
glory of God had traveled with the wandering Israelites in the
hallowed tabernacle, so it now rested among the Israelites in
the holy temple, set as it was in the religious and political heart
of the land of rest God had given his people.

As the place of God's holy presence, Solomon's temple func-
tioned as the primary location of communication between God
and his people. During the Israelites' wilderness wanderings,
God commanded Moses to appoint Aaron and his sons, from
the tribe of Levi, to serve as high priests who would mediate
such communication (see Exodus 28:1). In contrast with a synagogue or a modern Christian church, the tabernacle, and
subsequently the temple, was not a public place of worship.
The Israelites were restricted except on special occasions from
entering the inner sanctuary of the temple, and all were
expressly forbidden from entering the holy of holies except for
one day a year on which the high priest alone, after much ceremonial cleansing, would enter to atone for himself and the
people (cf. Hebrews 9:6–7) Thus, when Solomon built the
temple, it was the Aaronic priests who were to offer sacrifices on
the altar in atonement for the sins of the people, to offer prayers
on behalf of the people, and to watch over God's word and
guard his covenant (cf. Deuteronomy 33:8–9). The Aaronic
high priests, along with the rest of the Levitical priesthood, not

only mediated the communication of the Israelites with God, but also mediated God's communication with the people by teaching and guarding the law (i.e., the Torah).

Given their central role in the worship of Israel, every aspect of the priestly office, down to the color of the yarn used to fashion the garments of the high priest, was specially designed by God to instill reverence for his holiness in the hearts and minds of the Israelites. By living in a manner that was above reproach, the high priests were to remain holy examples of moral purity. Indeed, "for high priests and Levites alike, holiness (setting apart) was the chief distinguishing characteristic."[88] As God commanded, "They must be holy to their God and must not profane the name of their God. Because they present the offerings made to the LORD by fire, the food of their God, they are to be holy" (Leviticus 21:6).

One of the primary functions of the priests was to prepare and offer sacrifices on behalf of the people. God gave the Israelites the sacrificial system as a way of bridging the great chasm that separates the holy God from sinful humanity. To instill in the Israelites an awareness of the severity of sin, it was appropriate that God require the substitution of one life for the atonement of another: "For the life of a creature is in the blood, and I have given it to you to make atonement for yourselves on the altar; it is the blood that makes atonement for one's life" (Leviticus 17:11). As Hebrews explains, "the law requires that nearly everything be cleansed with blood, and without the shedding of blood there is no forgiveness" (9:22).

Just as God placed strict requirements on the moral and physical purity of the priests, so he placed strict requirements on the purity of the animals the priests were to accept as sacrifices. Foreseeing that the Israelites would be tempted to approach the sacrificial system without due reverence, God forbade them from offering as a sacrifice any animal that had a defect or blemish: "If any of you—either an Israelite or an alien living in Israel—presents a gift for a burnt offering to the LORD, either to fulfill a vow or as a freewill offering. . . . Do not bring anything with defect, because it will not be accepted on your behalf" (Leviticus 22:18–20). God concluded his warning by admonishing the priests to reject all such unworthy sacrifices: "Do not profane my holy name. I must be acknowledged as holy by the Israelites. I am the LORD, who makes you holy and who brought you out of Egypt to be your God. I am the LORD" (v. 32). Even the king was not exempt from these requirements. Thus, it was with great care and reverence that after Solomon had knelt before the altar of the Lord and dedicated the temple, "the king and all Israel with him offered sacrifices before the LORD" (1 Kings 8:62).

As exemplified by Solomon, the temple was not merely connected with the office of the priest; it was also integral to the office of the king. In the political economy of ancient Israel, the temple was as much a political symbol as it was a religious one. The temple and the ark of the covenant it housed symbolized the manifest presence of God among his chosen people, a presence that meant peaceful existence and victory in battle for the people if they remained faithful to God. It was not without political significance, therefore, when David relocated the ark of the covenant to Jerusalem and Solomon constructed the temple in the same city as his palace (see 2 Samuel 6–7; 1 Chronicles 21–22; 28–29). The temple was "a potent symbol of God's victory over his enemies."[89] As even the enemies of Israel were forced to acknowledge, God, not the king, was the ultimate ruler of Israel and the only one powerful enough to bring peace to the land. In fact, it was because the temple was to signify peace for the Israelites that David, a warrior, was not selected by God as its builder (cf. 1 Chronicles 28:3). Because of the connection between the king's political leadership of the people and God's ultimate sovereignty over the whole earth, the temple, even more than the palace, became the primary symbol of royalty. Wright points out that "when Solomon built the Temple, he established the pattern that would remain true for all subsequent generations up to and including the first century: the Temple-builder was the true king, and vice versa."[90]

Solomon's temple was thus the dwelling place of God's shekinah glory and the symbol for the Israelites of all the political and spiritual benefits it would bring. It was therefore a devastating blow to the spiritual and social identity of Israel when the Babylonians destroyed the temple in 586 BC. Says Wright: "The destruction of the Temple by the Babylonians was a catastrophe at every level, theological as well as political. It could only be explained in terms of YHWH having abandoned the Temple to its fate. The glory, the Shekinah, had departed; the Davidic monarchy had been cast aside; heaven and earth had been pulled apart, so that worship became impossible."[91]

Furthermore, as the shekinah glory departed Solomon's temple, severing the connectedness of heaven and earth, so the shekinah glory would depart the second temple. The temple that was rebuilt under the leadership of Ezra and Nehemiah had rapidly devolved from a divinely designated type to a degenerated den of tradition. In fact, as Jesus overturned the tables of the money changers and the benches of those selling doves, he cried out, "It is written, 'My house will be called a house of prayer,' but you are making it a 'den of robbers'" (Matthew 21:12–13). Just as robbers run to their dens to elude capture, so the unrepentant were running to the temple expecting that the sacrifice of a dove would protect them from their enemies and exempt them from the judgment of God. The words of Jesus echoed the sentiments voiced by Jeremiah prior to the time that Solomon's temple was destroyed. "Will you steal and murder, commit adultery and perjury, burn incense to Baal and follow other gods you have not known, and then come and stand before me in this house, which bears my Name, and say, 'We are safe'—safe to do all these detestable things? Has this house, which bears my Name, become a den of robbers to you? But I have been watching! declares the LORD" (Jeremiah 7:9–11).

As Jeremiah had prophetically pointed to the destruction of the first temple, so Jesus prophesied the destruction of the second temple. Just as in the days of Jeremiah, the Jews had prostituted the temple. Like their forefathers, they had failed to heed God's warning, "Reform your ways and your actions, and I will let you live in this place. Do not trust in deceptive words and say, 'This is the temple of the LORD, the temple of the LORD, the temple of the Lord!'" (Jeremiah 7:3–4). They had failed to recognize that temple, priest, and sacrifice were but types that pointed to something—no, someone—far greater, someone even now standing in their midst. Incredibly, "when the chief priests and the teachers of the law saw the wonderful things he did and the children shouting in the temple area, 'Hosanna to the Son of David,' *they were indignant*" (Matthew 21:15).

Thus, while Jesus never uttered a single word regarding a third temple, he emphatically pronounced the ruin of the second. After pronouncing seven woes upon the teachers of the law and the Pharisees, calling them "hypocrites," "blind guides," "whitewashed tombs," "snakes," and "a brood of vipers" he departed the temple saying, "O Jerusalem, Jerusalem, you who kill the prophets and stone those sent to you, how often I have longed to gather your children together, as a hen gathers her chicks under her wings, but you were not willing. *Look, your house is left to you desolate*" (Matthew 23:37–38).

Finally, the shekinah glory of God that departed the second temple, thus leaving it desolate, forever dwells within the spiritual temple. The shekinah glory of God will never again descend upon a temple constructed of lifeless stones, for it forever dwells within "the living Stone—rejected by men but chosen by God" (1 Peter 2:4). As the apostle Peter goes on to explain, "You, also, like living stones, are being built into a *spiritual house* to be a holy priesthood, offering *spiritual sacrifices* acceptable to God through Jesus Christ" (v. 5).

Incredibly, Peter uses the very language once reserved for national Israel and applies it to spiritual Israel. "But *you*" says Peter, "are a chosen people, a royal priesthood, a holy nation, a people belonging to God, that you may declare the praises of him who called you out of darkness into his wonderful light. Once you were not a people, but now you are *the* people of God" (1 Peter 2:9–10). The type and shadow of the first-century temples find their substance not in a Tribulation temple followed by a millennial temple, but in church built out of living stones comprised of Jews and Gentiles with Jesus Christ himself as the capstone.

For in Scripture it says:

> "See, I lay a stone in Zion,
>   a chosen and precious cornerstone,
> and the one who trusts in him
>   will never be put to shame."

Now to you who believe, this stone is precious. But to those who do not believe,

> "The stone the builders rejected
> has become the capstone."
>
> (vv. 6–7)

Says Sizer, "The New Testament portrays the temple as a temporary edifice, a shadow and type anticipating the day when God will dwell with people of all nations because of the atoning work of the true temple, Jesus Christ. The purpose of the temple, therefore, finds its ultimate significance and fulfillment not in another man-made sanctuary but in Jesus Christ and his church."[92]

Jesus made his typological relationship to the earthly sanctuary explicit when he pronounced, "One greater than the temple is here" (Matthew 12:6). This reality is aptly underscored in a conversation between our Lord and a woman at Jacob's well in Samaria. "Our fathers," said the Samaritan woman, "worshiped on this mountain, but you Jews claim that the place where we must worship is in Jerusalem." Jesus corrected her faulty presuppositions with a liberating truth: "Believe me, woman," he said, "a time is coming when you will worship the Father neither on this mountain nor in Jerusalem. . . . Yet a time is coming and has now come when the true worshipers will worship the Father in spirit and truth" (John 4:20–21, 23). Put another way, the time for temple worship had come to an end. As Goppelt explains, the teaching of Jesus and the apostles is that "in his own person Christ takes the place of temple and sacrifice and every other OT means of salvation. He is not simply the mediator of God's New

Covenant; he is the incarnation of it. His place in typology becomes clear only when we realize there is no typology that by-passes Christ; he is the antitype of the entire OT."[93]

Nowhere is the typological fulfillment of the temple and the rest of the old covenant more directly and dramatically underscored than in the book of Hebrews. "When Christ came as high priest of the good things that are already here, he went through the greater and more perfect tabernacle that is not man-made, that is to say, not a part of this creation. He did not enter by means of the blood of goats and calves; but he entered the Most Holy Place once for all by his own blood, having obtained eternal redemption" (9:11–12).

Hebrews highlights that Jesus is the antitype not only of the temple and the high priest, but he is the antitypical sacrifice as well: "The blood of goats and bulls and the ashes of a heifer sprinkled on those who are ceremonially unclean sanctify them so that they are outwardly clean. How much more, then, will the blood of Christ, who through the eternal Spirit offered himself unblemished to God, cleanse our consciences from acts that lead to death, so that we may serve the living God!" (9:13–14). Indeed, even the sacred ashes of the red heifer, like the blood of bulls and goats, find their ultimate antitypical fulfillment in the blood of Jesus Christ. It is for this reason that the writer of Hebrews explains in no uncertain terms that to revert to a sacrificial system is to trample the Son of God under foot, to treat as an unholy thing the blood of the covenant and to insult the Spirit of grace (Hebrews 10:29; cf. Galatians 3–5; Hebrews 5:11–6:12).

The New Testament's typological interpretation of the Old Testament thus stands as the ultimate corrective to Zionist zeal. Sizer has well said:

The movement in the progressive revelation of Scripture is always from the lesser to the greater. It is never reversed. The New Testament repeatedly sees such Old Testament concepts as the temple, high priest and sacrifice as "types" pointing to and fulfilled in Jesus Christ. Typology in Scripture never typifies itself, nor is it ever greater than that which it typifies. It is therefore argued that Christians who advocate the rebuilding of the temple are regressing to a pre-Christian sacrificial system, superseded and annulled by the finished work of Jesus Christ.[94]

The coming of Christ has forever rendered the notion of an earthly temple obsolete. It is the Savior and the saved who form the sanctuary in which the Spirit of the living God now dwells. Says Sizer:

To suggest, therefore, that the *Shekinah* is to return to a single local shrine in Jerusalem to which Jews and Christians must come to worship is to regress from the reality to the shadow, to re-erect the dividing curtain of the temple and to commit apostasy, since it impugns the finished work of Christ. The preoccupation, therefore, among Christian Zionists with locating the site of the temple, with training temple priests, with breeding red heifers and raising funds for the temple treasury is at best a distraction, and at worst a heresy.[95]

The conclusion of the matter is this: All of the types and shadows of the old covenant, including the holy land of Israel, the holy city Jerusalem, and the holy temple of God, have been fulfilled in the Holy Christ. It is Paradise—a new heaven and a new earth—not Palestine for which our hearts yearn. It is "the Holy City, the new Jerusalem, coming down out of heaven from God, prepared as a bride beautifully dressed for her husband" (Revelation 21:2) upon which we fix our gaze. And it is the Master Teacher, not a majestic temple, that forever satisfies our deepest longings. While John saw the New Jerusalem coming down out of heaven from God, he

> did not see a temple in the city, because the Lord God Almighty and the Lamb are its temple. The city does not need the sun or the moon to shine on it, for the glory of God gives it light, and the Lamb is its lamp. The nations will walk by its light, and the kings of the earth will bring their splendor into it. On no day will its gates ever be shut, for there will be no night there. The glory and honor of the nations will be brought into it. Nothing impure will ever enter it, nor will anyone who does what is shameful or deceitful, but only those whose names are written in the Lamb's book of life." (Revelation 21:22–27)

Truly, it is the risen Christ, at once the capstone of the spiritual temple and its heavenly architect, who ever sits upon the throne of David as King of Kings and Lord of Lords (cf. Acts 2:30; Revelation 19:16). In light of the Incarnation, the Zionist suggestion that the modern land of Palestine, along with its capital Jerusalem, is to be reserved exclusively for a single ethnicity, or that the temple must be rebuilt and its sacrificial system reinstituted, borders on blasphemy. Moreover, while the modern state of Israel has a definitive right to exist, to suggest that native Palestinians—many of whom are our sisters and brothers in Christ—must be forcibly removed from the land is not only unbiblical but unethical. By standing on the steps of the Capitol and protesting a two-state solution in the Middle East, Christian Zionists are creating a roadblock on the pathway to peace.

Just as it is a grievous sin to turn a blind eye to the evil of anti-Semitism, so it is a grievous sin to turn a blind eye to a theology that divides people on the basis of race rather than uniting them on the basis of righteousness, justice, and equity. Those who presumptuously appeal to the words of Moses—"I will bless those who bless you, and whoever curses you I will curse" (Genesis 12:3)—as a pretext for unconditionally supporting a secular state that prohibits the advance of the gospel while simultaneously disregarding the plight of the Palestinians should, according to their own hermeneutical standard, heed the words of the prophet Jeremiah:

"This is what the LORD Almighty, the God of Israel, says: Reform your ways and your actions, and I will let you live in this place. Do not trust in deceptive words and say, 'This is the temple of the LORD, the temple of the LORD, the temple of the Lord!' If you really change your ways and your actions and deal with each other justly, *if you do not oppress the alien*, the fatherless or the widow and do not shed innocent blood in this place, and if you do not follow other gods to your own harm, then I will let you live in this place, in the land I gave your forefathers for ever and ever. But look, you are trusting in deceptive words that are worthless." (Jeremiah 7:3–8)

7

——❧❧❧——

SCRIPTURAL SYNERGY:
The Code Breaker

*I don't know what science fiction he is reading; we believe
the Rapture is going to come, not [Hank Hanegraaff's] nonsense that Christ came back in AD 68*

—TIM LAHAYE[1]

*"I don't know about you, but the more I think about the new
heaven and new earth, the more excited I get! It is incredible to think that one day soon we will not only experience the
resurrection of our carcasses, but the renewal of the cosmos
and the return of the Creator. We will literally have heaven
on earth. Eden lost will become Eden restored and a whole
lot more! Not only will we experience God's fellowship as
Adam did, but we will see our Savior face to face. God
incarnate will live in our midst. And we will never come to
the end of exploring the infinite, inexhaustible I AM or the
grandeur and glory of his incomparable creation.*

—HANK HANEGRAAFF, *RESURRECTION*

IN NOVEMBER 2004 AN ARTICLE APPEARED IN THE
Dallas Morning News titled "Last Disciple vs. Left Behind:
New Take on Rapture Puts Authors in Apocalyptic Feud." In

227

the article, Tim LaHaye supposed that I subscribe to the "nonsense that Christ came back in AD 68."[2] As the charge was circulated via newspapers and the Internet, I was summarily branded a "preterist."[3] Worse still, LaHaye's contention raised the specter of self-contradiction. *The Last Disciple* allegedly forwarded the notion that "Christ came back in AD 68," while my book *Resurrection* communicates that Christ's second coming is as yet future.[4]

R. C. Sproul has said, "The simple canons of common decency should protect any author from unwarranted charges of self-contradiction. If I have the option of interpreting a person's comments one of two ways, one rendering them consistent and the other contradictory, it seems that the person should get the benefit of the doubt."[5] This rule is particularly pertinent to Scripture. In fact, it may rightly be deemed the principal imperative in the art and science of biblical interpretation. Says Sproul, "This means, quite simply, that no part of Scripture can be interpreted in such a way as to render it in conflict with what is clearly taught elsewhere in Scripture. For example, if a given verse is capable of two renditions or variant interpretations and one of those interpretations goes against the rest of Scripture while the other is in harmony with it, then the latter interpretation must be used."[6]

This in a nutshell is what the principle of scriptural synergy is all about. It means that the whole of Scripture is greater than the sum of its individual parts. We cannot comprehend the Bible as a whole without comprehending individual passages, and we cannot comprehend individual passages apart from comprehending the Bible as a whole. Individual passages of Scripture are synergistic rather than deflective with respect to the whole of Scripture. Indeed, scriptural synergy demands that individual Bible passages may never be interpreted in such a way as to conflict with the whole of Scripture. Nor may we assign arbitrary meanings to words or phrases that have their referent in biblical history. The biblical interpreter must keep in mind that all Scripture, though communicated through various human instruments, has one single Author. And that Author does not contradict himself nor does he confuse his servants.

Proper application of the biblical principle of scriptural synergy might well have deterred Bart Ehrman's evolution from fundamentalist Christian to fundamentalist atheist. When Ehrman read that Jesus told Caiaphas and the court that condemned him to death, "In the future you will see the Son of Man sitting at the right hand of the Mighty One and coming on the clouds of heaven" (Matthew 26:64), he should not for a moment have supposed that Jesus was predicting that his generation would experience the end of the world. Even the most basic comparison of Scripture with Scripture reveals that clouds are a common Old Testament symbol that pointed to God as the sovereign Judge of the nations. In the words of Isaiah, "See, the LORD rides on a swift *cloud* and is *coming* to Egypt. The idols of Egypt tremble before him, and the hearts of the Egyptians melt within them" (Isaiah 19:1). Jesus, like the Old Testament prophets, wielded the symbolism of "clouds" to warn his hearers that as judgment fell on Egypt, so too it would soon befall Jerusalem and its temple. In the destruction of Jerusalem the court that condemned Jesus to death would comprehend that Christ was Judge over earth and sky.

As the principle of scriptural synergy should have prevented Ehrman from disparaging Jesus as a false prophet, so too it should have prohibited LaHaye from supposing that Christ's "coming on clouds" metaphor was directed toward a twenty-first-century audience. Said Jesus, "I say to all of *you*: In the future *you* will *see* the Son of Man sitting at the right hand of the Mighty One and coming on the clouds of heaven" (Matthew 26:64). The generation that crucified Christ would *see* the day that he was exalted and enthroned at "the right hand of the Mighty One." John makes this point explicit in Revelation 1:7: "Look, he is *coming with the clouds*, and *every eye will see him, even those who pierced him*; and all the peoples of the earth will mourn because of him. So shall it be! Amen." "The crucifiers would see Him coming in judgment—that is, they would *experience* and *understand* that His Coming would mean wrath on the Land.... In the destruction of their city, their civilization, their Temple, their entire world-order, they would understand that Christ had ascended to His Throne as Lord of heaven and earth."[7]

SUPREME RULE

In thinking back through the letters of the LIGHTS acronym, it becomes readily apparent that scriptural synergy is crucial to reading the Scriptures for all they are worth. Indeed, scriptural synergy, or what the Reformers referred to as the "analogy of faith," may rightly be referred to as "the primary rule of hermeneutics."[8] The code breaker for apocalyptic passages does not reside in subjective flights of fancy but in examining Scripture in light of Scripture. Indeed, if there is a code in the apocalyptic passages of the New Testament, more often than not the code breaker is found in their Old Testament referents.

As discussed in chapter 2, the literal principle of Exegetical Eschatology demands that we interpret the Bible as literature. Simply put, this means that we are to interpret Scripture just as we interpret other forms of communication—in its most obvious and natural sense. Thus, when a biblical writer uses a symbol or an allegory, we do violence to his intentions if we interpret what is symbolic in a strictly literal manner. For example, when the apostle John describes Satan as a "dragon" and an "ancient serpent," we would be seriously mistaken to suppose that he intends to communicate that Satan is literally a smoke-spouting snake. Indeed, the symbolism of a dragon or a snake is not designed to tell us what Satan *looks* like but to teach us what Satan *is* like.

Conversely, it would be peculiarly prejudicial to pontificate that Dr. Luke is intending to pen a parable when he begins his gospel narrative with these words: "Many have undertaken to *draw up an account* of the things that have been fulfilled among us, just as they were handed down to us by those who from the first were *eyewitnesses* and servants of the word. Therefore, since I myself have *carefully investigated everything from the beginning*, it seemed good also to me *to write an orderly account* for you, most excellent Theophilus" (Luke 1:1–4).

The consequences of reading the Bible literalistically rather than synergistically are disastrous. When Jesus said, "Destroy this temple, and I will raise it again in three days" (John 2:19), the Jews interpreted his words in a woodenly literal fashion. They understood the plain or commonsense meaning of Jesus's words to refer directly and specifically to the destruction of their temple, which had "taken forty-six years to build" (John 2:20). Jesus, however, spiritualized his prophecy. As the apostle John explains, "The temple he had spoken of was his body" (v. 21)

Chapter 3—Illumination Principle of e^2 contains an equally graphic example of what occurs when the principle of scriptural synergy is neglected in the course of biblical interpretation. For example, when Jesus in his Olivet Discourse prophesied a tribulation "unequaled from the beginning of the world until now—and never to be equaled again" (Matthew 24:21), he was clearly using prophetic hyperbole. If this literary reality is not comprehended, Scripture devolves into hopeless contradiction.

Daniel said, "Under the whole heaven nothing has ever been done like what has been done to Jerusalem" (Daniel 9:12). Likewise, God the Father said, "I will do to you what I have *never* done before and will *never* do again" (Ezekiel 5:9). If Israel faced its greatest tribulation during the Babylonian exile, Christ would be gravely mistaken to predict a greater tribulation in the future. Moreover, one can scarcely imagine a greater tribulation in the future than the tribulation of the Flood in the past. Pressing the words of Jesus into a wooden, literal labyrinth inevitably leads to self-contradiction.

Failure to properly apply the principle of scriptural synergy in the same discourse causes dispensationalists to miss the fact that Christ uses the words sun, moon, and stars in precisely the same way as did the Old Testament prophets. As documented under the grammatical principle in chapter 4, when Jesus declared "the sun will be darkened, and the moon will not give its light; the stars will fall from the sky, and the heavenly bodies will be shaken" (Matthew 24:29; cf. Mark 13:24–25; Luke 21:25), he was quoting the prophet Isaiah.

> See, the day of the LORD is coming
>   —a cruel day, with wrath and fierce anger—
> to make the land desolate
>   and destroy the sinners within it.
> *The stars* of heaven and their constellations
>   will not show their light.

The rising *sun will be darkened*
and the moon will not give its light.

(ISAIAH 13:9–10)

Surely no one supposes that the stars went into supernova when Isaiah pronounced judgment on Babylon in 539 BC. Instead, as Isaiah used the sun, moon, and stars as judgment metaphors against Babylon, our Lord used them as judgment images against Jerusalem. Indeed, only when we interpret Scripture in light of Scripture rather than Scripture in light of the daily newspaper do we perceive its perspicuous meaning.

If the significance of scriptural synergy is heightened anywhere, it is in the book of Revelation. In chapter 5 on the historical principle of $\boxed{e^2}$, I emphasize that Revelation contains symbols deeply rooted in Old Testament history. We mistake their meanings when we fail to hear the background music of the Old Testament.[9] The *tree of life* referred to in Jesus's letter to the church in Ephesus first appears in Genesis; the *ten days of testing* in Smyrna find their referent in Daniel; the heavenly *manna* promised to the church of Pergamum first fell from heaven in Exodus; the *Jezebel* who promoted sexual immorality in Thyatira is the mirror image of the idolatrous Jezebel in Kings; the *seven spirits* of the letter to the church in Sardis hark back to the Spirit as described by Zechariah; the *key of David* referenced in the letter to Philadelphia echoes the words of Isaiah; and Christ's rebuke to the church in Laodicea alludes to the words of Proverbs, "My son, do not despise the LORD's discipline and do not resent his rebuke" (3:11).

As the letters of Christ to his *persecuted bride* utilize images deeply embedded in language of the Bible, so the judgment of Christ against a *prostituted bride*—written on a seven-sealed

233

scroll, announced with seven trumpets, and depicted by seven plagues—finds its referent in the history of the Old Testament Scriptures. The pattern of sevenfold judgment against unfaithfulness on the part of Israel is spelled out in dreadful detail in Leviticus. Four times God tells his covenant people, "I will punish you for your sins seven times over."[10] In like fashion, the imagery of sevenfold judgment against apostate Israel is unveiled on four occasions in Revelation. The pronouncement of judgment for unfaithfulness in the seven churches is followed by the judgments of the seven seals, seven trumpets, and seven bowls.

On the heels of the judgment of the seven bowls is the judgment of the *prostituted bride*. She is said to be "the great prostitute, who sits on many waters. With her the kings of the earth committed adultery" (Revelation 17:1–2). John continues his description in verses 3–5:

> I saw a woman sitting on a scarlet beast that was covered with blasphemous names and had seven heads and ten horns. The woman was dressed in purple and scarlet, and was glittering with gold, precious stones and pearls. She held a golden cup in her hand, filled with abominable things and the filth of her adulteries. This title was written on her forehead:
>
> MYSTERY
> BABYLON THE GREAT
> THE MOTHER OF PROSTITUTES
> AND OF THE ABOMINATIONS OF THE EARTH.

Neglect of the principle of scriptural synergy inevitably leads to a case of mistaken identity. LaHaye, for one, is absolutely certain that the mother of prostitutes and the abominations of the earth covered with blasphemous names is none other than the Roman Catholic Church. Not even Dan Brown's *The Da Vinci Code* approaches the invective launched by LaHaye against this already vulnerable target. In biblical history, however, only one nation is inextricably linked to the moniker "harlot."[11] *And that nation is ancient Israel!*

Anyone who has read the Bible even once must surely have flashbacks to the graphic images of apostate Israel when they first encounter the great prostitute of Revelation. From the Pentateuch to the Prophets, the image is repeated endlessly. The biblical link between Ezekiel 16 and Revelation 17 in itself is enough to preclude misidentification. Had LaHaye interpreted Scripture in light of Scripture, the Roman Catholic Church would not have suffered yet another gratuitous broadside.

SUBSTANCE OR SHADOW

Perhaps the most egregious error dispensationalists commit by failing to appropriately consider the import of scriptural synergy is to revert to Old Testament types that have been gloriously fulfilled in Jesus Christ. Despite the clear prohibition of Scripture, LaHaye not only teaches that the Muslim Dome of the Rock will be replaced by a third temple, but holds that during the Millennium the Messiah will preside over animal sacrifices in yet another temple. Most troubling of all is the fact that LaHaye's misguided literalism forces him to conclude that these temple sacrifices are not merely memorial but are absolutely necessary for the atonement of sins, such as ceremonial uncleanness.

The writer of Hebrews explicitly counters all such contentions by writing that in Christ, the old covenant order, including temple sacrifices, are "obsolete" and would "soon disappear" (Hebrews 8:13). The type and shadow of the first and second temples do not find their substance in a Tribulation temple followed by a millennial temple, but in a church built out of living stones comprised of Jew and Gentile with Jesus Christ himself the capstone. Jesus made his typological relationship to the temple explicit when he pronounced, "One greater than the temple is here" (Matthew 12:6). All old covenant types and shadows including the Holy Land, the Holy City, and the holy temple have been fulfilled in the holy Christ. There is no need or room for a rebuilt temple with reinstituted temple sacrifices.

Failure to interpret Scripture in light of Scripture creates a genuine conundrum for Christian Zionists. If temple sacrifices in the Millennium are efficacious for ceremonial uncleanness, Christ's atonement on the cross was insufficient to pay for all sin for all time. The teaching that the temple must be rebuilt and that temple sacrifices must be reinstituted not only stands in direct opposition to the book of Hebrews but undermines the central hope of the Christian faith—the atoning sacrifice of Christ for all sins past, present, and future (cf. Hebrews 7:26–27; 9:12, 26, 28; 10:10–14).

SACRIFICING TRADITIONS

If the evangelical death march toward the endgame of Armageddon is subverted, it will be because believers recommit themselves to *faithful exegesis*—to mining what the Spirit has breathed into the Scriptures as opposed to superimposing our models onto the Scriptures. We must fervently pray that the Holy Spirit gives us clear minds and open hearts as we plug into the power of scriptural synergy daily by interpreting

Scripture in light of Scripture. The question we must ask is this: are we willing to sacrifice our treasured traditions on the altar of biblical fidelity, or has tradition become our god?

I began *The Apocalypse Code* by underscoring the truth that the entire Bible is eschatological. From Genesis to Revelation, it is the chronicling of God's redemptive plan for a fallen humanity. Eschatology is the thread that runs through the tapestry of the entire text of Scripture. When eschatological models are imposed on the text, the tapestry is undone and the loose ends dangle ignominiously. When scriptural synergy takes precedence, the majesty of Scripture culminates in "the new Jerusalem, coming down out of heaven from God, prepared as a bride beautifully dressed for her husband." And "a loud voice from the throne saying, 'Now the dwelling of God is with men, and he will live with them. They will be his people, and God himself will be with them and be their God'" (Revelation 21:2–3).

Notes

Introduction

1. The book of Revelation derives its name from the Greek *apokalupsis* (ἀποκάλυψις), which translated is "revelation" (see Revelation 1:1).
2. Hal Lindsey, *Apocalypse Code* (Palos Verdes, CA: Western Front, 1997), back cover.
3. Ibid., 37 (emphasis added).
4. Ibid., 33.
5. Ibid., 36.
6. Ibid., 41 (emphasis added).
7. The emphasis is Lindsey's in his quotation of Revelation 9:7–10 (NIV) (ibid.). Lindsey explains that these qualifying terms ("looked like," "resembled," and so on) indicate that John "was aware of describing vehicles and phenomena far beyond his first-century comprehension" (41–42).
8. Ibid., 42.
9. Ibid., 43–44.
10. Ibid., back cover.
11. Hal Lindsey with C. C. Carlson, *The Late Great Planet Earth* (Grand Rapids: Zondervan, 1970).
12. See Bruce M. Metzger, *Breaking the Code: Understanding the Book of Revelation* (Nashville: Abingdon, 1993), 13.
13. Lindsey, *Apocalypse Code*, 32.
14. Tim LaHaye, "Introduction," in Mark Hitchcock and Thomas Ice, *The Truth Behind Left Behind: A Biblical View of the End Times* (Sisters, OR: Multnomah, 2004), 7.
15. The Left Behind series, co-authored by the theologian-novelist team of Tim LaHaye and Jerry B. Jenkins, is a fiction series set in the near future that depicts an invisible rapture of Christians from the earth followed by a seven-year period of tribulation led by the Antichrist, as well as other prophetic events entailed by the currently popular end-times theology of premillennial dispensationalism, which originated with John Nelson Darby.
16. See Tim LaHaye and Jerry B. Jenkins, *The Indwelling: The Beast Takes Possession* (Wheaton: Tyndale, 2000), 363–68. Lest this aberrant view be rationalized as literary license in fiction, LaHaye defends his view that "Antichrist will die and be resurrected" in his commentary on Revelation, *Revelation Unveiled*, dubbed on its back cover as "the biblical foundation for the best-selling Left Behind series." Commenting on Revelation 17:11, LaHaye writes, "He [the Antichrist] will die in the middle of the Tribulation period, duplicate the resurrection of Jesus Christ by coming back to life, but at the end of the Tribulation will be destroyed (19:20)" (Tim LaHaye, *Revelation Unveiled* [Grand Rapids: Zondervan, 1999], 262; see also 211–12). Thomas Ice defends LaHaye's view in "The Death and Resurrection of the Beast," http://www.pre-trib.org/article-view.php?id=239 (accessed December 26, 2006).
17. Paragraph adapted from Hank Hanegraaff and Sigmund Brouwer, *The Last Disciple* (Wheaton: Tyndale, 2004), 394.

239

18. LaHaye would no doubt deny that he holds to a dualistic worldview in which Satan is God's equal. He might say God is sovereignly allowing Satan this one-time miracle of miracles. Such a concession nonetheless undermines his profession of monotheism.

19. Tim LaHaye and Thomas Ice, *Charting the End Times* (Eugene, OR: Harvest House, 2001), 46, emphasis added. LaHaye believes there are essentially three classes, namely, Israel and the church, with the church subdivided into true believers and "Christendom." In his words, "Scripture speaks of three classes of people throughout prophecy and history. We find all three in 1 Corinthians 10:32." The second class is composed of "two aspects of the church—true believers and Christendom." From LaHaye's perspective, true believers are "the body of Christ, which began on the Day of Pentecost and will go to heaven in the Rapture." "Christendom, by contrast, will be left behind to enter into the Tribulation period and is being prepared to serve as Satan's harlot" (LaHaye and Ice, *Charting the End Times,* 46–50).

20. Tim LaHaye, *The Beginning of the End* (Wheaton: Tyndale, 1972), 45.

21 Arnold G. Fruchtenbaum, "The Little Apocalypse of Zechariah," in Tim LaHaye and Thomas Ice, eds., *The End Times Controversy* (Eugene, OR: Harvest House, 2003), 262. It should be noted that Fruchtenbaum here points out that it may well be that the judgment of God against two-thirds of the Jews involves the slaughter of not only those in the land of Israel but two-thirds of all Jews worldwide.

22. LaHaye, *Beginning of the End,* 38–39, emphasis in original. LaHaye argued that World War I uniquely fulfilled the prophecy of Matthew 24:7, which in his mind was the sign to indicate "the beginning of the end."

23. See, e.g., ibid., chapter 3, "The First Sign of the End," and chapter 15, "Is This the Last Generation?"

24. Ibid., 165.

25. Ibid., 164.

26. See, e.g., Tim LaHaye and Jerry B. Jenkins, *Are We Living in the End Times?* (Wheaton: Tyndale, 1999). LaHaye explains his two main objectives for writing this book: "1. To provide a basic companion outline of the end-time events and scriptural verification of the personages fictionalized in the Left Behind series; 2. To show that we have more reason than any generation before us to believe Christ may return in our generation" (xi). Moreover, as of 1999, LaHaye had not ruled out the possibility that the generation that saw World War I is the prophesied generation that would not pass away until the Lord returns, saying that scenario "should not be ruled out completely for another five years or so" (59).

27. See, e.g., LaHaye and Ice, *Charting the End Times,* 84–87; see also chap. 6, n. 43, below.

28. Gary Burge writes, "According to U.N. records in June 1999, about 3.6 million Palestinian refugees are the victims of Israel's nationhood" (Gary M. Burge, *Whose Land? Whose Promise? What Christians Are Not Being Told about Israel and the Palestinians* [Cleveland: Pilgrim, 2003], x). Human Rights Watch says, "Palestinians are the world's oldest and largest refugee population, and make up more than one-fourth of all refugees" (http://hrw.org/doc/?t=refugees&document [accessed December 26, 2006]). Cf. Jimmy Carter, *Palestine Peace not Apartheid* (New York: Simon & Schuster, 2006).

29. Burge, *Whose Land?* 109.

30 Ibid., 141.

31. Ibid.

32. Quoted in ibid., 39.

33. Quoted in ibid.

34. Brother Andrew and Al Janssen, *Light Force: A Stirring Account of the Church Caught in the Middle East Crossfire* (Grand Rapids: Revell, 2004), 110. Andrew and Janssen report the number of Palestinians killed at Deir Yassin as 250, citing Benny Morris, *The Birth of the Palestinian Refugee Problem, 1947-1949* (Cambridge: Cambridge University Press, 1987), 113-115. Morris has revised this figure to 100–110 (Ari Shavit, "Survival of the Fittest? An Interview with Benny Morris" *Haaretz*, January 9, 2004, http://www.haaretz.com/hasen/pages/ShArt.jhtml?itemNo=380986&contrassID=2 [accessed Dec. 2, 2006]; also available in PDF online at http://www.logosjournal.com/morris.pdf [accessed November 29, 2006]); but see chap. 6, n. 3, below.

35. Burge, *Whose Land?* 81.

36. Ibid., 92.

37. "Address by Prime Minister Benjamin Netanyahu," The Feast of Tabernacles Conference, October 5, 1998, National Christian Leadership Conference for Israel Web site, http://www.nclci.org/NETANYAHU-Tabernacles.htm (accessed December 26, 2006); also quoted in Timothy P. Weber, *On the Road to Armageddon: How Evangelicals Became Israel's Best Friend* (Grand Rapids: Baker, 2004), 217.

38. LaHaye, *Beginning of the End*, 50.

39. Ibid., 51.

40. Ibid., 58.

41. Ibid., 55–56.

42. LaHaye and Ice, *Charting the End Times*, 95 (emphasis in original).

Chapter 1: Exegetical Eschatology [e²]

1. Moreover, Louis Berkhof writes, "It is not sufficient that we understand the meaning of the secondary authors (Moses, Isaiah, Paul, John, etc.); we must learn to know the mind of the Spirit" (Louis Berkhof, *Principles of Biblical Interpretation* [Grand Rapids: Baker, 1950], 11–12). Thus, vital to the task of interpreting the Bible is the recognition that it is divinely inspired.

2. To study Scripture is to study eschatology, for all of God's work in redemption—past, present, and future—moves toward eternal redemption. So, to study eschatology is to study the past, present, and future (i.e., the whole of Scripture).

3. The basic principles that compose the method I call Exegetical Eschatology and that are codified by the acronym LIGHTS are not new. Rather, they have been the staple of the historic Christian church's hermeneutical diet from the time of the apostles.

4. See Tim LaHaye, ed., *Tim LaHaye Prophecy Study Bible* (Chattanooga: AMG Publishers, 2000), 1389.

5. Such is the logical extension of LaHaye's view (see chapter 4, "Grammatical Principle," pp. 70–94).

6. See Revelation 1:1, 3; 2:16; 3:11; 11:14; 22:6, 7, 10, 12, 20.

7. Tim LaHaye and Thomas Ice, *Charting the End Times* (Eugene, OR: Harvest House, 2001), 35.

8. Tim LaHaye and Jerry B. Jenkins, *Are We Living in the End Times?* (Wheaton: Tyndale, 1999), 95-96.

9. In the original Greek, the second person and vocative (signifying address) are used throughout Matthew 23:13–39.

10. Carson continues, "Even if 'generation' by itself can have a slightly larger semantic range, to make '*this* generation' refer to all believers in every age, or the generation of believers alive when eschatological events start to happen, is highly artificial" (D. A. Carson, "Matthew," in Frank E. Gaebelein, ed., *The Expositor's Bible Commentary*,

vol. 8 [Grand Rapids: Zondervan, 1984], 507, emphasis in original; and in Gary DeMar, "Letting the Bible Speak for Itself—The Literal Meaning of 'This Generation': A Response to Ed Hindson's 'The New Last Days Scoffers,'" pt. 6, American Vision Web site, http://www.americanvision.org/articlearchive/06-17-05.asp# [accessed January 2, 2007]).

11. LaHaye, ed., *Tim LaHaye Prophecy Study Bible*, 1040, emphasis added.

12. Tim LaHaye, "Introduction: Has Jesus Already Come?" in Tim LaHaye and Thomas Ice, eds., *The End Times Controversy* (Eugene, OR.: Harvest House, 2003), 13.

13. LaHaye's derisive remarks are not only leveled at the notion that Revelation was written prior to AD 70, but they directly attack the assertion that Nero is the Antichrist (see LaHaye, "Introduction," in Mark Hitchcock and Thomas Ice, *The Truth Behind Left Behind: A Biblical View of the End Times* (Sisters, OR: Multnomah, 2004), 13.

14. See chapter 6, "Typological Principle."

15. LaHaye presents such a version of the mark of the Beast in the Left Behind series. See Tim LaHaye and Jerry B. Jenkins, *The Mark: The Beast Rules the World* (Wheaton: Tyndale, 2000), 85.

Chapter 2: Literal Principle

1. Quoted in Cathleen Falsani, "The God Factor," *Chicago Sun-Times*, October 24, 2004, News 16.

2. Tim LaHaye, "Introduction," in Mark Hitchcock and Thomas Ice, *The Truth Behind Left Behind: A Biblical View of the End Times* (Sisters, OR: Multnomah, 2004), 7.

3. R. C Sproul, *Knowing Scripture* (Downers Grove, IL: InterVarsity Press, 1977), 48. Sproul continues, "That is, the natural meaning of a passage is to be interpreted according to the normal rules of grammar, speech, syntax and context. . . . and above all we must be carefully involved in what is called 'genre analysis.'" I discuss genre, or form, below, pages 20–23.

4. Sometimes, however, the most natural sense to a first-century Jewish believer is not obvious to a 21ˢᵗ century believer in the West. Hence the need for taking into account not only genre but the gamut of hermeneutical principles codified in LIGHTS.

5. Tim LaHaye, *No Fear of the Storm* (Sisters, OR: Multnomah, 1992), 240.

6. Ibid.

7. Tim LaHaye, ed., *Tim LaHaye Prophecy Study Bible* (Chattanooga: AMG Publishers, 2000), 1151.

8. LaHaye, "Introduction," 8, emphasis added.

9. See Timothy P. Weber, *On the Road to Armageddon: How Evangelicals Became Israel's Best Friend* (Grand Rapids: Baker, 2004), 24.

10. Ibid., 25.

11. Emphasis added. See further discussion below, chapter 4, "Grammatical Principle," pp. 70–94.

12. LaHaye, "Introduction," 7.

13. Ibid., emphasis added.

14. While Jesus is purposely ambiguous with the word "temple," he does not allow the word to be a mere abstraction or void of objective meaning. Rather, as a wise teacher, he offers the truly spiritual meaning of the word "temple," namely, that the earthly temple in Jerusalem was merely a type of the true temple that is Christ's body and, in fact, himself. See chapter 6, "Typology Principle."

15. G. B. Caird, *The Language and Imagery of the Bible* (Grand Rapids: Eerdmans, 1980, 1997 ed.), 157.

16. LaHaye and Ice, *Charting the End Times*, 94–95.
17. See further discussion on this point in The Holy Temple section of Chapter 6: Typology Principle (pp. 203–26).
18. LaHaye, ed., *Tim LaHaye Prophecy Study Bible*, 1389.
19. See Revelation 17:9–10 and 1:20, respectively.
20. David Chilton, *The Days of Vengeance: An Exposition of the Book of Revelation* (Tyler, TX: Dominion, 1987), 376.
21. Dennis E. Johnson, *Triumph of the Lamb: A Commentary on Revelation* (Phillipsburg, NJ: P & R, 2001), 11.
22. Ibid., 12. For further discussion on genre analysis, see Grant R. Osborne, *The Hermeneutical Spiral: A Comprehensive Introduction to Biblical Interpretation* (Downers Grove, IL: InterVarsity, 1991), 149ff.
23. Gene Edward Veith Jr., *Reading Between the Lines: A Christian Guide to Literature* (Wheaton: Crossway, 1990), 84.
24. N. T. Wright, *Jesus and the Victory of God*, vol. 2, *Christian Origins and the Question of God* (Minneapolis: Fortress, 1996), 321.
25. Discussion adapted in part from Hank Hanegraaff, *The Bible Answer Book* (Nashville: Nelson, 2004), 186–87.
26. Gary DeMar, *Last Days Madness: Obsession of the Modern Church* (Atlanta: American Vision, 1994), 159, emphasis added; cf. the fourth revised edition published in 1999, page 165.
27. Chilton, *Days of Vengeance*, 66, emphasis in original.
28. Sproul, *Knowing Scripture*, 55.
29. Caird, *Language and Imagery of the Bible*, 165.
30. Ibid, emphasis added.
31. Ibid, emphasis added.
32. See Genesis 6–9; cf. Matthew 24:38–39; 1 Peter 3:20; 2 Peter 2:5.
33. Cf. Norman L. Geisler, *Systematic Theology*, vol. 4, "Church, Last Things" (Minneapolis: Bethany House, 2005), 639. Geisler suggests that Jesus is prophesying here that actual stars will fall from the sky.
34. George B. Caird, *Jesus and the Jewish Nation* (London: Athlone, 1965), 22, quoted in Wright, *Jesus and the Victory of God*, 341.
35. Revelation 12:3.
36. Revelation 9:7.
37. Revelation 13:2.
38. Gene Edward Veith Jr., "Good Fantasy and Bad Fantasy," *Christian Research Journal* 23, no. 1:16, available online at www.equip.org.
39. Gordon D. Fee and Douglas Stuart, *How to Read the Bible for All Its Worth: A Guide to Understanding the Bible*, 2nd ed. (Grand Rapids: Zondervan, 1993), 233.
40. William Gurnall, *The Christian in Complete Armour*, vol. 2, rev. and abridged Ruthanne Garlock, Kay King, Karen Sloan, and Candy Coan (Edinburgh: Banner of Truth Trust, 1988 [originally published in 1658]), 150, emphasis added.
41. Johnson, *Triumph of the Lamb*, 181.
42. Ibid., 190.

Chapter 3: Illumination Principle

1. Charles Darwin, *The Descent of Man*, chap. 6, "On the Affinities and Genealogy of Man," in Robert Maynard Hutchins, ed., *Great Books of the Western World*, vol. 49, *Darwin* (Chicago: Encyclopedia Britannica, 1952), 336.

2. Arthur Keith, *Evolution and Ethics* (New York: Putnam, 1947), 230, http://reactor-core.org/evolution-and-ethics.html (accessed January 25, 2007).

3. Daniel Goleman, "Lost Paper Shows Freud's Effort to Link Analysis and Evolution," *New York Times*, February 10, 1987, C1. Goleman explains further, "The evolutionary idea that Freud relied on most heavily in the manuscript is the maxim that 'ontogeny recapitulates phylogeny,' that is, that the development of the individual repeats the evolution of the entire species." Cf. Henry M. Morris, *The Long War Against God: The History and Impact of the Creation/Evolution Conflict* (Grand Rapids: Baker, 1989), 33.

4. Henry M. Morris and Gary E. Parker, *What Is Creation Science?* rev. ed. (El Cajon, CA: Master Books, 1987), 67; see also Stephen Jay Gould, "Dr. Down's Syndrome," *Natural History* (April 1980): 142–48.

5. Marvin L. Lubenow, *Bones of Contention: A Creationist Assessment of Human Fossils*, rev. ed. (Grand Rapids: Baker, 2004), 62.

6. A concise overview on the history of eugenics is Michael Crichton's "Why Politicized Science is Dangerous," appendix 1 in his novel *State of Fear* (New York: HarperCollins, 2004), 575–80.

7. Ibid., 576.

8. See Jeremiah 30:7; Matthew 24:21.

9. Timothy P. Weber, *On the Road to Armageddon: How Evangelicals Became Israel's Best Friend* (Grand Rapids: Baker, 2004), 136, 146; see 129ff.

10. Arno Clemens Gaebelein, *The Conflict of the Ages: The Mystery of Lawlessness, Its Origin, Historic Development, and Coming Defeat* (Vienna, VA: The Exhorters, n.d., uncensored reprint ed.), 147.

11. Weber, *On the Road to Armageddon*, 135–36.

12. See ibid., 130ff.

13. James M. Gray, "The Jewish Protocols," *Moody Bible Institute Monthly* 22 (October 1921): 598, quoted in Weber, *On the Road to Armageddon*, 132.

14. Gaebelein, *Conflict of the Ages*, 99; see also discussion in Weber, *On the Road to Armageddon*, 134.

15. Weber, *On the Road to Armageddon*, 142.

16. Charles C. Cook, "The International Jew," *King's Business* 12 (November 1921): 1087, quoted in Weber, *On the Road to Armageddon*, 132.

17. Harry A. Ironside, "Are the Jews as a People Responsible for the So-Called Protocols of the Elders of Zion?" *Chosen People* 39 (March 1934): 5–7, quoted in Weber, *On the Road to Armageddon*, 138.

18. John Walvoord, *Israel in Prophecy* (Grand Rapids: Zondervan, 1968), 107, 113–14, quoted in Weber, *On the Road to Armageddon*, 149, emphasis added.

19. Hal Lindsey with C. C. Carlson, *The Late Great Planet Earth* (Grand Rapids: Zondervan, 1970 [40th printing May 1974]), 110; and in Weber, *On the Road to Armageddon*, 151.

20. Tim LaHaye and Thomas Ice, *Charting the End Times* (Eugene, OR: Harvest House, 2001), 63.

21. Tim LaHaye and Jerry B. Jenkins, *Are We Living in the End Times?* (Wheaton: Tyndale, 1999), 146.

22. LaHaye and Ice, *Charting the End Times*, 58.

23. Referring to his state of mind upon leaving England aboard the HMS *Beagle*, Darwin wrote, "I did not then in the least doubt the strict and literal truth of every word in the Bible" (F. Darwin, ed., *The Life and Letters of Charles Darwin*, vol. 1 [London: John Murray, 1888], 45, quoted in Michael Denton, *Evolution: A Theory in*

NOTES

Crisis [Bethesda, MD: Adler & Adler, 1986], 25). The notion that Darwin was ever a Bible-believing creationist is widely disputed. In fact, his grandfather Erasmus—the real inventor of the theory of evolution—was an eighteenth-century rationalist.

24. Timothy P. Weber, *Living in the Shadow of the Second Coming: American Premillennialism, 1875–1982* (Chicago: University of Chicago Press, 1983 ed.), 6. Weber cites Winthrop S. Hudson, Martin E. Marty, William Warren Sweet, and Sydney Ahlstrom.

25. My principal sources for the following discussion are Weber, *Living in the Shadow of the Second Coming*; Weber, *On the Road to Armageddon*; Ernest R. Sandeen, *The Roots of Fundamentalism: British and American Millenarianism 1800–1930* (Chicago: University of Chicago Press, 1970); and George Eldon Ladd, *The Blessed Hope* (Grand Rapids: Eerdmans, 1956).

26. Sandeen, *Roots of Fundamentalism*, 42, 47–48.

27. See Tim LaHaye, *The Beginning of the End* (Wheaton: Tyndale, 1972), 38–39; also see the whole of chapter 3, "The First Sign of the End," and chapter 15, "Is This the Last Generation?" LaHaye argued that World War I uniquely fulfilled the prophecy of Matthew 24:7, which in his mind was the sign to indicate "the beginning of the end." In 1999 LaHaye coauthored with Jerry B. Jenkins *Are We Living in the End Times?* (Wheaton: Tyndale, 1999), in which he had not yet ruled out the possibility that the generation that saw World War I would not pass away until the Lord returns, saying that scenario "should not be ruled out for another five years or so" (59).

28. Ladd, *The Blessed Hope*, 41.

29. S. P. Tregelles, *The Hope of Christ's Second Coming: How Is It Taught in Scripture? and Why?* (Chelmsford, Eng.: The Sovereign Grace Advent Testimony, 6th ed., n.d. [1st ed. 1864]), 35; and in Ladd, *Blessed Hope*, 41.

30. According to historian Timothy Weber, Darby himself explained that "the doctrine of the pretribulational rapture virtually jumped out of the pages of the Bible once he understood and consistently maintained the absolute distinction between Israel and the church in the prophetic plans of God" (*On the Road to Armageddon*, 25).

31. Ladd, *Blessed Hope*, 130.

32. Ibid., 41.

33. Weber, *On the Road to Armageddon*, 39.

34. LaHaye and Ice, *Charting the End Times*, 81.

35. Weber, *On the Road to Armageddon*, 15.

36. Ironically, Christian Zionist John Hagee contends that the biblical allusion to stars and dust is proof that God has two distinct people—one heavenly (stars) and the other earthly (dust). Says Hagee, "God mentions two separate and distinct elements: stars of the heaven and sand of the seashore. . . . Stars are heavenly, not earthly. They represent the church, spiritual Israel. The 'sand on the seashore,' on the other hand, is earthly and represents an earthly kingdom with a literal Jerusalem as the capital city. Both stars and sand exist at the same time, and neither ever replaces the other. Just so, the nation of Israel and spiritual Israel, the church, exist at the same time and do not replace each other" (John Hagee, *Final Dawn over Jerusalem* [Nashville: Nelson, 1998], 108–9). Interpreting Scripture in light of Scripture, however, utterly undermines Hagee's contention. The prophet Nehemiah, for example, extolled the trustworthiness of God in fulfilling his promises by making Abraham's descendants as numerous as the stars in the sky (Nehemiah 9:23; cf. Genesis 15:5; 22:17).

37. LaHaye and Ice, *Charting the End Times*, 48.

38. Keith A. Mathison, *Dispensationalism: Rightly Dividing the People of God?* (Phillipsburg, NJ: P & R, 1995), 29, emphasis in original.

39. See Revelation 5:9; 7:9.

40. LaHaye and Ice, *Charting the End Times*, 87.

41. Ibid., 90.

42. Ibid., 48, emphasis added.

43. Ibid., 27.

44. Ibid., 46.

45. Weber, *On the Road to Armageddon*, 24, first emphasis only is added.

46. H. A. Ironside, *The Mysteries of God* (New York: Loizeaux, 1946), 50–51, quoted in Gary DeMar, *End Times Fiction: A Biblical Consideration of the Left Behind Theology* (Nashville: Nelson, 2001), 20.

47. As in Tim LaHaye, "Introduction: Has Jesus Already Come?" in Tim LaHaye and Thomas Ice, eds., *The End Times Controversy* (Eugene, OR: Harvest House, 2003), 11, emphasis added.

48. Tim LaHaye and Jerry B. Jenkins, *Are We Living in the End Times?* (Wheaton: Tyndale, 1999), 114.

49. Grant R. Jeffrey, "A Pretrib Rapture Statement in the Early Medieval Church," in Thomas Ice and Timothy Demy, gen. eds., *When the Trumpet Sounds* (Eugene, OR: Harvest House, 1995), 108, 109.

50. Norman L. Geisler, "A Friendly Response to Hank Hanegraaff's Book, *The Last Disciple*," http://www.ses.edu/NormGeisler/lastdisciple.htm (accessed January 25, 2007).

51. Norman L. Geisler, *Systematic Theology*, vol. 4, *Church, Last Things* (Minneapolis: Bethany House, 2005), 658.

52. Geisler, "Friendly Response."

53. LaHaye and Jenkins, *Are We Living in the End Times?* 114, emphasis added.

54. For a thorough discussion, see "Postscript: Pseudo-Ephraem on Pretrib Preparation for a Posttrib Meeting with the Lord," in Robert Gundry, *First the Antichrist* (Grand Rapids: Baker, 1997), 161–88.

55. LaHaye and Jenkins, *Are We Living in the End Times?* 95–96, emphasis added.

56. See 1 Corinthians 15:51–52; 1 Thessalonians 4:14–17.

56. N. T. Wright, "Farewell to the Rapture," *Bible Review*, August 2001, http://www.ntwrightpage.com/Wright_BR_Farewell_Rapture.pdf (accessed January 26, 2007).

58. The *Tim LaHaye Prophecy Study Bible* is explicit in saying that Jesus in John 14:1–3 does not have his second coming in mind but his secret coming in mind. See Tim LaHaye, ed., *Tim LaHaye Prophecy Study Bible*, 1151.

59. LaHaye, *No Fear of the Storm* (Sisters, OR: Multnomah, 1992), 188.

60. Thomas D. Ice, "The Origin of the Pretrib Rapture: Part II," *Biblical Perspectives*, March–April 1989, 5, quoted in Gary DeMar, *End Times Fiction: A Biblical Consideration of the Left Behind Theology* (Nashville: Nelson, 2001), 20. Elsewhere Thomas Ice writes, "No single Bible verse says precisely when the Rapture will take place in relation to the Tribulation or the Second Coming in a way that would settle the issue to everyone's satisfaction." Ice goes on to argue that the teaching in Scripture on the pretribulational rapture is like that of the Incarnation or the Trinity, which are "the product of harmonizing the many passages that relate to these matters." While he thinks the Scriptures teach "a clear position" on the pretribulation rapture, he acknowledges that this doctrine depends on "four affirmations," none of which is uncontroversial. Says Ice, "Four affirmations provide a biblical framework for the Pretribulational Rapture: They are (1)

consistent literal interpretation, (2) Premillennialism, (3) futurism, and (4) a distinction between Israel and the church. These are not mere suppositions, but rather are important biblical doctrines upon which the doctrine of the Rapture is built" (Thomas Ice, "Why I Believe the Bible Teaches Rapture Before Tribulation," http://www.pre-trib.org/pdf/Ice-WhyIBelieveTheBibleTe.pdf [accessed December 30, 2006], emphasis in original). Moreover, Gary DeMar elegantly refutes likening the pretrib rapture to the doctrines of the Incarnation and Trinity: "The incarnate nature of Christ can be proved by citing just two verses: 'In the beginning was the Word, and the Word was with God, and *the Word was God*. . . . And *the Word became flesh*, and dwelt among us, and we beheld his glory, glory as of the only begotten from the Father, full of grace and truth' (John 1:1, 14). The Trinity is equally easy to prove: the Father is God (1 Cor. 8:6); Jesus is God (John 1:1); the Holy Spirit is God (Acts 5:3–4); and there is only one God (1 Tim. 2:5). Unlike the pretrib Rapture, these two doctrines have been part of church history for centuries" (DeMar, *End Times Fiction*, 219n4).

61. Our Lord's use of the Flood illustration makes it clear that the unrighteous are taken in judgment while the righteous are left behind. The force of this argument is such that even Tim LaHaye acknowledges that Luke 17:34–36 "is not a reference to the Rapture" and that the "taken" are unbelievers experiencing judgment not raptured saints (see LaHaye, ed., *Tim LaHaye Prophecy Study Bible*, 1113).

62. LaHaye, "The Tribulation," in LaHaye, ed., *Tim LaHaye Prophecy Study Bible*, 1374.

63. The single phrase that LaHaye pretends is Daniel 9:27—"He will confirm a covenant with many for one seven" (see Ibid.). *The Popular Encyclopedia of Bible Prophecy* maintains that "Daniel's prophecy of the 70 weeks (Hebrew, *shavuah*, 'sevens') in Daniel 9:24-27 provides the indispensable chronological key to Bible prophecy" (Randall Price and Thomas Ice, "Seventy Weeks of Daniel," in Tim LaHaye and Ed Hindson, gen. eds., *The Popular Encyclopedia of Bible Prophecy* [Eugene, Ore.: Harvest House, 2004], 356.). At best, the seventy weeks prophecy is very difficult to interpret—so difficult that no interpretation should be held with dogmatism. Furthermore, the dispensational interpretation is the least plausible of the several competing interpretations that Christ-honoring scholars have offered of this passage. Thus, this passage cannot serve as the firm foundation dispensationalism requires. To gain an appreciation for how difficult the seventy weeks prophecy is to interpret, especially in light of the Book of Daniel as a whole, compare and contrast the relevant expositions found in the following: Kim Riddlebarger, *A Case for Amillennialism: Understanding the End-Times* (Grand Rapids: Baker Books, 2003), 149-56; Edward J. Young, *The Prophecy of Daniel: A Commentary* (Eugene, Ore.: Wipf and Stock, 1998, originally published 1949); Milton S. Terry, *Biblical Hermeneutics: A Treatise on the Interpretation of the Old and New Testaments* (Grand Rapids: Zondervan, [n.d.] reprinted 1974); Milton S. Terry, *Biblical Apocalyptics: A Study of the Most Notable Revelations of God and of Christ in the Canonical Scriptures* (Eugene, Ore.: Wipf and Stock Publishers, 2001), 181-212, esp. 200-207; Gary DeMar, *Last Days Madness: Obsession of the Modern Church*, 4th edition (Atlanta: American Vision, 1999), 323-35; Richard L. Pratt, Jr., "Hyper-Preterism and Unfolding Biblical Eschatology," in Keith A. Mathison, ed., *When Shall These Things Be: A Reformed Response to Hyper-Preterism* (Phillipsburg, NJ: P & R, 2004), 121-54, esp. 144-46; J. Dwight Pentecost, *Things to Come: A Study in Biblical Eschatology* (Grand Rapids: Zondervan, 1958), 239-250.

64. LaHaye, "The Tribulation," in LaHaye, ed., *Tim LaHaye Prophecy Study Bible*, 1374.

65. It is widely agreed that seven symbolizes totality or completeness (see, e.g., Richard Bauckham, *The Climax of Prophecy: Studies on the Book of Revelation* [Edinburgh: T. & T. Clark, 1993], 30–31, 405; Dennis E. Johnson, *Triumph of the Lamb: A Commentary on Revelation* [Phillipsburg, NJ: P & R, 2001], 14).

66. See also discussion in chapter 2, "Literal Principle," pp. 30–32.

67. For an extensive list of titles, including "The Time of Jacob's Trouble," "The Great Tribulation," "The Day of Israel's Calamity," "The Day of Clouds," The Hour of Judgment," which LaHaye enjoins to this future seven-year tribulation, see LaHaye and Ice, *Charting the End Times*, 56.

68. Paul Benware, "The Marriage of the Lamb," in LaHaye, ed., *Tim LaHaye Prophecy Study Bible*, 1395.

69. Cf. Stephen Sizer, *Christian Zionism: Road-map to Armageddon?* (Leicester: Inter-Varsity, 2004), 138.

70. LaHaye and Jenkins, *Are We Living in the End Times?* 231.

71. Ibid.

72. Ibid., 231–32.

73. Ibid., 231.

74. This was the incredible scenario depicted in *Left Behind: The Movie* (Cloud Ten Pictures, 2000).

75. LaHaye and Jenkins, *Are We Living in the End Times?* 185–86. LaHaye and Jenkins are quoting Revelation 6:14 and interpreting it literally.

76. Ibid., 186.

77. Ibid., 187.

78. Ibid., emphasis added.

79. Ibid., 188.

80. Ibid., 189.

81. Ibid., 191, 192.

82. Ibid., 191.

83. Ibid., 192.

84. Ibid., 193, emphasis added.

85. Ibid., 195.

86. Ibid., 138–42.

87. Ibid., 198.

88. Ibid., 201.

89. See Ibid., 198–203.

90. Ibid., 206.

91. Ibid., 207.

92. Ibid., 208.

93. Ibid., 218.

94. Ibid., 219.

95. Ibid., 226–27.

96. Ibid., 229.

97. Ibid., 231.

98. Citing Isaiah 65:20, LaHaye and Jenkins write, "We believe this means that believers will live throughout the entire period but that the unregenerate will be given one hundred years to repent and accept Christ as their Lord; if they refuse to do so, they will die. This will result in an enormous population by the end of the Millennium, the vast majority of whom will be saved. In fact, we believe that because of the Millennium, there may be more people in heaven than in hell" (ibid., 240).

99. Ibid., 245.

100. John Hagee, *Should Christians Support Israel?* (San Antonio, TX: Dominion, 1987), 1, 73.

101. Ibid., 132, emphasis added.

Chapter 4: Grammatical Principle

1. "Videotaped Testimony of William Jefferson Clinton, President of the United States, Before the Grand Jury Empanelled for Independent Counsel Kenneth Starr," August 17, 1998, transcript by the Office of the Independent Counsel released September 21, 1998, online at JURIST: The Law Professors' Network, http://jurist.law.pitt.edu/transcr.htm (accessed December 31, 2006).

2. Report of the Independent Counsel to Congress, September 9, 1998, online at http://www.gooddocuments.com/icreport/jan171998.htm (accessed December 31, 2006).

3. Steven Pinker, *The Language Instinct: How the Mind Creates Language* (New York: HarperPerennial, 1994), 276, see 39–45, 262–76.

4. While the specific rules of English differ from those of the original languages in which the Bible was written, we are indebted to a host of skilled linguists whose painstaking efforts over hundreds of years have produced for us many outstandingly accurate English translations of the biblical texts. Though familiarity with the original languages is an invaluable skill for any interpreter of the Bible, the availability of such excellent English translations of the Bible, together with the accessibility of a variety of study aids, such as Bible dictionaries, concordances, and lexicons, have made it possible for the student of Scripture to plumb the depths of the meaning of biblical texts without a thoroughgoing knowledge of the original languages. Thus, the true meanings of the eschatological passages under consideration in this book are ascertainable through an application of the rules of English grammar to the texts of any reputable English translation of the Bible.

5. Matthew 24:6–34.

6. The entire corpus of LaHaye's eschatological writings implies this conclusion, but for a virtually explicit acknowledgment, see note 22 of this chapter; cf. also note 24 of this chapter.

7. See chapter 6, "Typology Principle," 161–226.

8. Bertrand Russell, in Paul Edwards, ed., *Why I Am Not a Christian: And Other Essays on Religion and Related Subjects* (New York: Simon & Schuster, 1957), 16. Russell also wrote that "there are a great many texts [in the Gospels] that prove" that Jesus believed he would return within the lifetime of his original hearers, but he cites only two: "I tell you the truth, you will not finish going through the cities of Israel before the Son of Man comes" (Matthew 10:23), and "I tell you the truth, some who are standing here will not taste death before they see the Son of Man coming in his kingdom" (Matthew 16:28; cf. Luke 9:27). Other texts Russell may have had in mind include: "And so upon you will come all the righteous blood that has been shed on earth, from the blood of righteous Abel to the blood of Zechariah son of Berekiah, whom you murdered between the temple and the altar. I tell you the truth, all this will come upon this generation" (Matthew 23:35–36); "I tell you the truth, this generation will certainly not pass away until all these things have happened" (Matthew 24:34); and "But I say to all of you: In the future you will see the Son of Man sitting at the right hand of the Mighty One and coming on the clouds of heaven" (Matthew 26:64). There is no question that the Lord Jesus indicates in these passages that at least some of his disciples as well as enemies would remain alive until the prophesied events unfolded. What Russell missed through his negligent dismissal of Scripture was a correct understanding of what Jesus actually predicted would happen within the near future: not his bodily return to earth in the second coming, but his coronation as the true King by his death, resurrection, and ascension to the right hand of God, the manifestation of his kingdom through the power of the Holy Spirit, and climactically his vindication in the judgment on unbelieving Israel. Russell and others, such as C. S. Lewis, who have struggled with the implications of such passages of Scripture, are also cited in

Gary DeMar, *Last Days Madness: Obsession of the Modern Church* (Atlanta: American Vision, 1999, 4th rev. ed.), 46–49; and R. C. Sproul, *The Last Days According to Jesus: When Did Jesus Say He Would Return?* (Grand Rapids: Baker, 1998), 12–13.

9. Albert Schweitzer, *Out of My Life and Thought: An Autobiography* (New York: Henry Holt, 1933), 7. Former evangelical minister and atheist activist Dan Barker claims Christ is not reliable because "Jesus told his disciples that they would not die before his second coming: 'There be some standing here, which shall not taste of death, till they see the Son of man coming in his kingdom' (Matthew 16:28). 'Behold, I come quickly' (Revelation 3:11). It's been 2,000 years, and believers are still waiting for his 'quick' return" (Dan Barker, "Why Jesus?" Nontract #12, Freedom from Religion Foundation, Inc. http://ffrf.org/nontracts/jesus.php [accessed December 31, 2006]).

10. Gerald Sigal, "Question: What does 'this generation' mean in the verse, 'Truly I say to you this generation' will not pass away until all these things take place' (Matthew 24:32, Mark 13:30, Luke 21:32)?" Jews for Judaism Web site, http://www.jewsforjudaism.org/web/faq/faq114.html (accessed December 31, 2006), emphasis added.

11. Gerald Sigal, "Question: How does the passage of time effect [*sic*] the Christian claim of a 'second coming of Christ'?" Jews for Judaism Web site, http://www.jewsforjudaism.org/web/faq/faq116.html (accessed December 31, 2006), emphasis added.

12. A standard New Testament Greek lexicon defines the Greek word translated "this" in Matthew 24:34 as follows: "[*houtos, haute, touto*] demonstrative pronoun, used as adjective and substantive: *this*, referring to something comparatively near at hand, just as *ekeinos* ["that"] refers to something comparatively far away; cf. Luke 18:14; James 4:15; Mandate 3:5." W. Bauer, W. F. Arndt, and F. W. Gingrich, *A Greek-English Lexicon of the New Testament and Other Early Christian Literature* (Chicago: University of Chicago Press, 1957), 600 (abbreviations expanded).

13. Thomas Ice and Kenneth L. Gentry Jr., *The Great Tribulation: Past or Future? Two Evangelicals Debate the Question* (Grand Rapids: Kregel, 1999), 28.

14. C. I. Scofield, ed., *The Scofield Study Bible*, readers ed. (New York: Oxford University Press, 1996, originally published 1917), 1034, note on Matthew 24:34.

15. Scofield, ed., *The Scofield Study Bible*, 1034, note on Matthew 24:34.

16. DeMar, *Last Days Madness*, 186.

17. Ibid.

18. In the original Greek, the second person and vocative (signifying address) are used throughout Matthew 23:13–39.

19. George B. Caird, *Jesus and the Jewish Nation* (London: Athlone, 1965), 22, quoted in N. T. Wright, *Jesus and the Victory of God*, vol. 2, *Christian Origins and the Question of God* (Minneapolis: Fortress, 1996), 341.

20. See DeMar, *Last Days Madness*, 69–71.

21. Wright, *Jesus and the Victory of God*, 342, emphasis in original.

22. LaHaye writes concerning Revelation 1:1, "Further on in the verse we find that this is the revelation of Jesus Christ 'to show his servants what must soon take place.' Again we see that the emphasis of the book is on future events" (Tim LaHaye, *Revelation Unveiled* [Grand Rapids: Zondervan, 1999], 25).

23. Tim LaHaye and Jerry B. Jenkins, *Are We Living in the End Times?* (Wheaton: Tyndale, 1999), 59.

24. Concerning Revelation 22:7, "Behold, I am coming soon!" LaHaye writes, "Three times we find this expression in the last verses of this book. Some have been confused about the literal meaning of the expression because it was uttered almost two thousand years ago. It is more accurately translated, 'Behold, I come

suddenly.' This saying does not refer to an appointed time soon to come but means that His coming will take place suddenly and without warning." (LaHaye, *Revelation Unveiled*, 371. Cf. Tim LaHaye, ed., *Tim LaHaye Prophecy Study Bible* (Chattanooga: AMG Publishers, 2000), 1404, 1405, notes on Revelation 22:7 and 22:20.) The reality, however, is that the plain reading of such words as "near," "soon," "the time is at hand," as found in Revelation 1:1, 3; 2:16; 3:11; 11:14; 22:6, 7, 10, 12, 20, is that the events prophesied were to occur within John's near future. For further discussion, see DeMar, *Last Days Madness*, 379–95.

25. Tim LaHaye and Thomas Ice, *Charting the End Times* (Eugene, OR: Harvest House, 2001), 45.

26. LaHaye believes that each of the seven churches in Revelation 2–3 represents a particular period within church history. The Philadelphia age of church history is said to cover the period from about 1750 to the time of the rapture. It is the church of Philadelphia Jesus promised to deliver from the coming tribulation, which LaHaye interprets as a promise to rapture the universal church prior to the trial that will overtake the whole world. See LaHaye, *Revelation Unveiled*, 78–83; and LaHaye and Ice, *Charting the End Times*, 107.

27. For further discussion, see DeMar, *Last Days Madness*, 379–95.

28. Richard Bauckham, *The Climax of Prophecy: Studies on the Book of Revelation* (Edinburgh: T. & T. Clark, 1993), 263. It should be noted that Bauckham does not share my general view of Revelation.

Chapter 5: Historical Principle

1. See Dan Vergano and Cathy Lynn Grossman, "Long-Lost Gospel of Judas Recasts 'Traitor,'" *USA Today*, April 6, 2006, http://www.usatoday.com/news/religion/2006-04-06-judas_x.htm?rss (accessed July 7, 2006).

2. *The Gospel of Judas*, National Geographic Channel, aired April 16, 2006, see http://channel.nationalgeographic.com/channel/gospelofjudas/index.html (accessed July 7, 2006).

3. Vergano and Grossman, "Long-Lost Gospel of Judas."

4. Ibid.

5. See *Gospel of Judas*, National Geographic Channel.

6. See Bart Ehrman, *Misquoting Jesus: The Story Behind Who Changed the Bible and Why* (San Francisco: HarperSanFrancisco, 2005), 1–8.

7. See *Gospel of Judas*, National Geographic Channel.

8. See Dan Brown, *The Da Vinci Code* (New York: Doubleday, 2003), 231ff.

9. Michael Baigent, Richard Leigh, and Henry Lincoln, *Holy Blood, Holy Grail* (New York: Delacorte, 1982); Michael Baigent, *The Jesus Papers: Exposing the Greatest Cover-Up in History* (San Francisco: HarperSanFrancisco, 2006).

10. Quoted in Stacy Meichtry, "New Views of Judas Reflect New Views on Evil," Religion News Service, April 6, 2006, http://religionnews.com/ArticleofWeek040606.html (accessed December 18, 2006).

11. Funk was interviewed on *Peter Jennings Reporting, The Search for Jesus*, ABC, aired June 26, 2000.

12. Crossan was interviewed on *Peter Jennings Reporting, The Search for Jesus*, ABC, aired June 26, 2000.

13. Daniel B. Wallace, "The Gospel of John: Introduction, Argument, Outline," http://www.bible.org/page.asp?page_id=1328 (accessed July 7, 2006); see also John A. T. Robinson, *Redating the New Testament* (Eugene, OR: Wipf and Stock, 2000, originally published by SCM Press, 1976), 277–78.

14. The only existing manuscript of the Gospel of Judas is written in Coptic and is dated to c. AD 280. The circumstances surrounding its unveiling are suspicious, but it was probably discovered in Upper Egypt. See *Gospel of Judas*, National Geographic Channel.

15. To read the Gospel of Judas for yourself, go to http://www.earlychristianwritings.com/gospeljudas.html (accessed July 7, 2006).

16. For further discussion on genre analysis, see Grant R. Osborne, *The Hermeneutical Spiral: A Comprehensive Introduction to Biblical Interpretation* (Downers Grove, IL: InterVarsity, 1991), 149ff.

17. See *Gospel of Judas*, National Geographic Channel.

18. Bart Ehrman explains, "Perhaps the most common reason to forge writing in antiquity was to get a hearing for one's own views. . . . If you wrote in your own name (Mark Aristedes, or whatever), no one would be much intrigued or feel compelled to read what you had to say, but if you signed your treatise 'Plato,' then it might have a chance." (Bart D. Ehrman, *The New Testament: A Historical Introduction to the Early Christian Writings*, 3rd ed. [New York: Oxford University Press, 2004], 373).

19. For further discussion, see Craig Blomberg, "The Historical Reliability of the New Testament," in William Lane Craig, *Reasonable Faith: Christian Truth and Apologetics*, rev. ed. (Wheaton: Crossway, 1994), 193–231.

20. For further discussion on the Gnostic gospels, see Gregory A. Boyd, *Cynic Sage or Son of God?* (Wheaton, IL: BridgePoint, 1995).

21. Gospel of Thomas, 114, in Robert W. Funk, Roy W. Hoover, and the Jesus Seminar, *The Five Gospels* (New York: Macmillan, 1993), 532. For further discussion on the Gnostic gospels, see Douglas Groothuis, "Gnosticism and the Gnostic Jesus," *Christian Research Journal*, Fall 1990, http://www.equip.org/free/DG040-1.pdf; and Douglas Groothuis, "The Gnostic Gospels: Are They Authentic?" *Christian Research Journal*, Winter 1991, http://www.equip.org/free/DG040-2.htm; see also James Patrick Holding, "Mary Magdalene's Modern Makeover," *Christian Research Journal* 29, no. 2: 6–8.

22. See *Gospel of Judas*, National Geographic Channel.

23. If John had recorded his gospel after the destruction of Jerusalem and its centerpiece, the temple, he would not have failed to reference the most apocalyptic event in Jewish history. Such neglect would be tantamount to writing a history of New York City after September 11, 2001, and failing to mention the destruction of the World Trade Center. Not only so, but had John written his gospel after the destruction of the temple, he surely would have highlighted the fulfillment of his Master's most audacious prophecy, "I tell you the truth, not one stone here will be left on another; every one will be thrown down. . . . I tell you the truth, this generation will certainly not pass away until all these things have happened. Heaven and earth will pass away, but my words will never pass away" (Matthew 24:2; 34–35). Cf. Daniel B. Wallace, "The Gospel of John: Introduction, Argument, Outline," http://www.bible.org/page.asp?page_id=1328 (accessed July 7, 2006).

24. The early church fathers say Paul was martyred under Nero. Writing in the early fourth century, Eusebius cites Dionysius of Corinth (writing c. AD 170), Tertullian (writing c. AD 200), and Origen (writing c. AD 230–250). See Gary R. Habermas and Michael R. Licona, *The Case for the Resurrection of Jesus* (Grand Rapids: Kregel, 2004), 56–59, 224; cf. Ben Witherington, *The Paul Quest: The Renewed Search for the Jew of Tarsus* (Downers Grove, IL: InterVarsity, 1998), 324–27.

25. Acts ends with Paul under house arrest in Rome. With the emphasis Luke puts on Paul's ministry in Acts, it is inexplicable that he did not record Paul's execution under Nero if Acts was written after Paul's death.

26. See Craig Blomberg, *The Historical Reliability of the Gospels* (Downers Grove, IL: InterVarsity, 1987), 12–18. Journalist Lee Strobel interviews New Testament scholar Craig Blomberg, who presents this basic argument for the early dating of these New Testament books in Lee Strobel, *The Case for Christ: A Journalist's Personal Investigation of the Evidence for Jesus* (Grand Rapids: Zondervan, 1998), 32–34.

27. See Leon Morris, *The First Epistle of Paul to the Corinthians: An Introduction and Commentary* (Leicester: Inter-Varsity, 1985), 31; John A. T. Robinson, *Redating the New Testament* (Eugene, OR: Wipf and Stock, 2000, previously published by SCM Press, 1976), 54; Bart D. Ehrman, *The New Testament: A Historical Introduction to the Early Christian Writings*, 3rd ed. (New York: Oxford University Press, 2004), 288.

28. William Lane Craig, "Did Jesus Rise from the Dead?" in Michael J. Wilkins and J. P. Moreland, eds., *Jesus Under Fire: Modern Scholarship Reinvents the Historical Jesus* (Grand Rapids: Zondervan, 1995), 147, 153; William Lane Craig, *Reasonable Faith: Christian Truth and Apologetics* (Wheaton: Crossway, 1994), 273.

29. Gary R. Habermas, *The Historical Jesus: Ancient Evidence for the Life of Christ* (Joplin, Mo.: College Press, 1996), 154; cf. Craig L. Blomberg, "Where Do We Start Studying Jesus?" in Wilkins and Moreland, *Jesus Under Fire*, 42–43. As philosopher and New Testament historian Gary Habermas points out, evidences that lead scholars to such an unusual consensus are myriad. Paul employs technical Jewish terminology used to transmit oral tradition when he uses such words as *delivered* and *received*. Paul's use of the Aramaic word *Cephas* for Peter points to an extremely early Semitic source. (These details and much more are found in Habermas, *The Historical Jesus*, 152–57.) Additionally, Oxford scholar and philosopher Terry Miethe explains, "Most New Testament scholars point out that one of the ways we know [1 Corinthians 15:3–7] is a creedal statement is that it appears to have been in a more primitive Aramaic, and it's also in hymnic form. This means it was stylized Greek, non-Pauline words, and so on, which indicates that it predated Paul and was . . . universally acknowledged" (Gary R. Habermas and Antony G. N. Flew, *Did Jesus Rise from the Dead?* [San Francisco: Harper & Row, 1987], 86).

Not only so, but Peter, Paul, and the rest of the apostles claimed that Christ appeared to hundreds of people who were still alive and available for cross-examination. Paul received this creed from the believing community (1 Corinthians 15:3), perhaps from Peter and James in Jerusalem in AD 36 (see Galatians 1:18–19), if not sooner (see Habermas, *Historical Jesus*, 155; Craig, *Reasonable Faith*, 273). It would have been one thing to attribute these supernatural experiences to people who had already died. It was quite another to attribute them to multitudes who were still alive. As the famed New Testament scholar of Cambridge University C. H. Dodd points out, "There can hardly be any purpose in mentioning the fact that most of the five hundred are still alive, unless Paul is saying, in effect, 'The witnesses are there to be questioned.'" In sharp contrast to the Nag Hammadi Library of apocryphal Gnostic gospels like Judas, Philip, and Thomas, the canonical Gospels are free from legendary corruption and indubitably grounded in eyewitness testimony (see C. H. Dodd, "The Appearances of the Risen Christ: A Study in the Form Criticism of the Gospels," in *More New Testament Studies* [Manchester: University of Manchester, 1968], 128, quoted in William Lane Craig, *Reasonable Faith: Christian Truth and Apologetics* [Wheaton: Crossway, 1994], 282).

30. Craig writes, "The writings of Herodotus enable us to determine the rate at which legend accumulates, and the tests show that even two generations is too short a time span to allow legendary tendencies to wipe out the hard core of historical facts. Julius Müller challenged scholars of the mid-nineteenth century to show anywhere in history where within thirty years a great series of legends had accumulated around a historical individual and had become firmly fixed in general belief. Muller's challenge has never been met" (Craig, *Reasonable Faith*, 285; see

284–85). A fortiori, three to eight years is too little time for the possibility of legendary corruption.

31. Crossan was interviewed on *Peter Jennings Reporting, The Search for Jesus*, ABC, aired June 26, 2000.

32. Bart D. Ehrman, *Jesus: Apocalyptic Prophet of the New Millennium* (New York: Oxford University Press, 1999), 244, emphasis in original.

33. See pp. 83–84.

34. Ehrman, *Misquoting Jesus*, 9–10.

35. Bart D. Ehrman, *Jesus: Apocalyptic Prophet of the New Millennium* (New York: Oxford University Press, 1999), 130–31; and Bart D. Ehrman, *The New Testament: A Historical Introduction to the Early Christian Writings*, 3rd ed. (New York: Oxford University Press, 2004), 128–29.

36. The phrase "From now on the Son of Man will be seated at the right had of the power of God" alludes to the messianic Psalm 110:1, just as in the parallel passages, Matthew 26:64 and Mark 14:62. Ehrman does not realize, however, that his literalistic interpretation of the Jewish clouds metaphor is precisely the misinterpretation Luke was trying to steer his predominantly gentile audience away from by leaving out the metaphor. Luke could not expect his literal-minded gentile readers to know that "coming on clouds" *means* having the sovereign authority of Yahweh himself and has nothing to do with physically riding on a moving cloud. So, Luke simply omitted it, recognizing that its meaning is already captured in the readily understood allusion to Psalm 110:1.

37. Luke often translates Jewish allusions for the sake of his gentile audience. For another example, instead of the very Jewish, "When you see standing in the holy place 'the abomination that causes desolation,' spoken of through the prophet Daniel—let the reader understand—then let those who are in Judea flee to the mountains" (Matthew 24:15–16), Luke writes the gentile-friendly, "When you see Jerusalem being surrounded by armies, you will know that its desolation is near. Then let those who are in Judea flee to the mountains. . ." (Luke 21:20–21). New Testament historian N. T. Wright explains, "Luke (21.20) has cashed out the apocalyptic imagery in Matthew (24.15) and Mark (13.14) in terms of Jerusalem's being surrounded with armies. This for his gentile readers makes far more sense: faced with a cryptic allusion to Daniel, they would not be in a position to obey the command of Mark 13.14b, 'Let the reader understand.' Luke's reading of Mark is quite clear: all this language refers to the fall of Jerusalem, which is to be understood in terms of the scriptural background of the predicted destruction of Babylon" (N. T. Wright, *Jesus and the Victory of God* [Minneapolis: Fortress Press, 1996], 359).

38. See above, pp. 73–81.

39. Tim LaHaye, *Revelation Unveiled* (Grand Rapids: Zondervan, 1999), 25.

40. Tim LaHaye, "Introduction: Has Jesus Already Come?" in Tim LaHaye and Thomas Ice, eds., *The End Times Controversy* (Eugene, OR: Harvest House, 2003), 9, emphasis added.

41. Ibid., 13.

42. Ibid.

43. LaHaye, *Revelation Unveiled*, 27. LaHaye reasons that "Nero is a poor excuse for an Antichrist" and dismisses the early dating of Revelation, concluding that both are "historically ridiculous" notions (LaHaye, "Introduction," in LaHaye and Ice, *End Times Controversy*, 13.).

44. See Arnold G. Fruchtenbaum, "The Little Apocalypse of Zechariah," in LaHaye and Ice, eds., *The End Times Controversy* (Eugene, OR: Harvest House, 2003), 262. Cf. Tim LaHaye, ed., *Tim LaHaye Prophecy Study Bible* (Chattanooga: AMG Publishers, 2000), 991, note on Zechariah 13:7–9. Further, regarding Revelation 12,

LaHaye writes, "Chapter 12 introduces the fact that in the middle of the Tribulation period Israel will be confronted with the worst wave of anti-Semitism the world has ever seen. Yet 'God is faithful' as usual!" (LaHaye, *Revelation Unveiled*, 197).

45. According to the *Dictionary of Biblical Imagery*, "Of the numbers that carry symbolic meaning in biblical usage, seven is the most important. It is used to signify completeness or totality. Underlying all such use of the number seven lies the seven-day week, which, according to Genesis 1:1–2:3 and Exodus 20:11, belongs to the God-given structure of creation" (Leland Ryken, James C. Wilhot, Tremper Longman III, eds., *Dictionary of Biblical Imagery* [Downers Grove, IL: InterVarsity, 1998], 774). If so, and given the prominence seven plays in the book of Revelation, it is highly probable that the seven churches together represent the totality of the Christian church.

46. C. I. Scofield, ed., *The Scofield Study Bible*, readers ed. (New York: Oxford University Press, 1917, reissued 1996), 1331–32, note on Revelation 1:20, emphasis in original.

47. Ibid., 1332, note on Revelation 1:20.

48. The following details concerning the Caesars and emperor worship are found in David Chilton, *Days of Vengeance: An Exposition of the Book of Revelation* (Tyler, TX: Dominion, 1987), 6–10, 218; and Kenneth L. Gentry, *Before Jerusalem Fell: Dating the Book of Revelation* (Atlanta: American Vision, 1998), 261–84.

49. Julius Caesar was titled Jupiter Julius by the Roman Senate as a means of identifying him with none other than Jupiter, chief god of the Romans.

50. See John 18:28–19:16.

51. I allude to the hymn by Reginald Heber, "The Son of God Goes Forth to War."

52. See, e.g., Robert H. Mounce, *The Book of Revelation* (Grand Rapids: Eerdmans, 1977), 75; Dennis E. Johnson, *Triumph of the Lamb* (Phillipsburg, New Jersey: P & R, 2001), 56; John F. Walvoord, *The Revelation of Jesus Christ* (Chicago: Moody, 1966), 41.

53. The following details concerning Patmos are found in Gordon Franz, "The King and I: The Historical Setting of Revelation 1:9 and the Apostle John on Patmos," http://www.pre-trib.org/pdf/Franz-TheKingAnsITheHistor.pdf (accessed July 11, 2006).

54. In the *Tim LaHaye Prophecy Study Bible*, John C. Whitcomb writes, "The seventh and last of these kings 'is not yet come; and when he comes, he must continue for a short space' ([Revelation] 17:10). This will be the revived Roman Empire, the final phase of the great image of Daniel 2 (the ten toes) and the Beast in Daniel 7 (the ten horns and the eleventh 'little horn' who will arise 'among them' [7:8])" (p. 898). And Tim LaHaye and Thomas Ice write, "In the last days, there will be a world government led by ten kings or heads of regions (Daniel 2:40–43; 7:23–24)" (Tim LaHaye and Thomas Ice, *Charting the End Times* [Eugene, OR: Harvest House, 2001], 120).

55. Roman historians inevitably began their count with Julius—Father of his country. For example, Roman biographer, Gaius Suetonius Tranquillus, in his *Lives of the Twelve Caesars*, begins with Julius and records Nero as sixth in succession.

56. So Gentry, *Beast of Revelation*, 138–39.

57. LaHaye, "Introduction," in LaHaye and Ice, *End Times Controversy*, 13.

58. To better grasp the horror that was Caesar Nero, read the documentary novel by Paul L. Maier, *The Flames of Rome* (Grand Rapids: Kregel, 1981); and also the historical fiction series I coauthored with Sigmund Brouwer beginning with *The Last Disciple* (Wheaton: Tyndale, 2004), and *The Last Sacrifice* (Wheaton: Tyndale, 2005).

59. Tacitus, *The Annals*, 15:44. See the online translation by Alfred John Church and William Jackson Brodribb at http://classics.mit.edu/Tacitus/annals.11.xv.html (accessed July 11, 2006).

60. See Philostratus, *Life of Apollonius* 4:38, quoted in Gentry, *Beast of Revelation*, 53. Apollonius of Tyana was a first-century pagan writer. Gentry quotes or cites many other ancient writers who testify to Nero's "beastial nature," including Lactantius (AD 240–320), *On the Death of the Persecutors* 2:2; Sulpicious Severus (AD 360–420), *Sacred History* 2:28; and the Jewish *Sibylline Oracles* 5:343 (c. AD 80–130).

61. C. Suetonius Tranquillus, *The Lives of the Twelve Caesars: The Life of Nero*, 39 (Loeb Classical Library, 1914), http://penelope.uchicago.edu/Thayer/E/Roman/Texts/Suetonius/12Caesars/Nero*.html.

62. Regarding Revelation 3:10, the *Tim LaHaye Prophecy Study Bible* states, "This is the most specific guarantee from our Lord Himself that Christian believers will not go into that seven-year Tribulation period He is about to unveil (Rev. 6–18)" (LaHaye, ed., *Tim LaHaye Prophecy Study Bible*, 1370; cf. LaHaye, *Revelation Unveiled*, 81).

63. I first heard this metaphor from New Testament scholar N. T. Wright. If we are not conscious of the music of the Old Testament playing in the background as we play that of the New, we are in danger of producing only discordant noise and not harmonious music at all. "Let him who has ears to hear. . . ."

64. Leviticus 26:18, 21, 24, 28.

65. See LaHaye, *Revelation Unveiled*, 266–77, emphasis added.

66. J. Ramsey Michaels, *Revelation* (Downers Grove, IL: InterVarsity, 1997), 191–201, especially 200.

67. Richard Bauckham, *The Climax of Prophecy: Studies on the Book of Revelation* (Edinburgh: T. & T. Clark, 1993), 343.

68. Even the two exceptions once worshiped the one true God of Israel. Nineveh was transformed through the preaching of Jonah (Jonah 3) and Tyre assisted Solomon in the construction of the Jewish temple (1 Kings 5). Thus, their apostasy is associated with harlotry. See Chilton, *Days of Vengeance*, 424; cf. J. Massyngberde Ford, *Revelation* (Garden City, NY: Doubleday, 1975), 283–84.

69. Cf. Chilton, *Days of Vengeance*, 425–28.

70. For further study and refutation of the teachings of the Jehovah's Witnesses, see the many resources available on the Web site of the Christian Research Institute at www.equip.org. See also the relevant entries in my two books, *The Bible Answer Book* (Nashville: J. Countryman, 2004) and *The Bible Answer Book, Volume 2* (Nashville: J. Countryman, 2006).

71. See LaHaye, *Revelation Unveiled*, 148–50.

72. Of course, the most well known use of the symbolic number "thousand" in Scripture is found in John's encouraging promise to the persecuted first-century church that the saints who would be martyred for resisting the mark of the Beast would reign in glory with Christ for "a thousand years" (Revelation 20:1-7). Failing to read Revelation in its appropriate historical and literary context, many have misconstrued John's words in Revelation 20 as a literal prophetic chronology according to which Satan will literally be bound for one thousand years while the resurrected martyrs reign with Christ until the end of the "millennium" at which time the rest of the dead will be raised and Satan will be released to wage war against Christ and the resurrected saints. Rather than allowing one metaphorically rich passage in the apocalyptic letter of Revelation to override the rest of the clear passages in Scripture that teach a single, general resurrection of the dead (e.g., John 5.28-29, 1 Corinthians 15:51-52; 1 Thessalonians 4:14-17), we must be willing to interpret this markedly symbolic passage in light of the rest of Scripture. When we do so, it becomes clear that in keeping with the traditional use of "a thousand" as a numeric symbol of ultimate completion, John is simply here promising his readers that though God would allow the Beast to execute his reign

of terror for "ten days"—a relatively short time—God would vindicate the martyred believers by allowing them to reign with Christ for "a thousand years"— a comparatively limitless time. By suggesting that Satan would be bound during this period and that the rest of the dead would not be resurrected until after the thousand years had ended (vv. 2-3, 5, 7), John was simply using symbolic chronological bookends to highlight the qualitatively (as opposed to quantitatively) unique vindication that the martyrs of this great persecution will experience at the general resurrection of the dead. John's vision of the vindication of "the souls of those who had been beheaded because of their testimony for Jesus and because of the word of God" (20:4) is thus the climactic answer to the prayer for vindication—"How long, Sovereign Lord, holy and true, until you judge the inhabitants of the earth and avenge our blood?"—that was called out in chapter six by "the souls of those who had been slain because of the word of God and the testimony they had maintained" (6:9-10).

73. G. K. Beale, *The Book of Revelation: A Commentary on the Greek Text*, New International Greek Testament Commentary (Grand Rapids: Eerdmans, 1999), 39.

74. LaHaye, *Revelation Unveiled*, 188.

75. Peter, like John, is writing prior to the destruction of Jerusalem. As such, the primary referent of the prophets' apocalyptic language is the great and terrible destruction of Jerusalem that Jesus had promised would happen before the generation of his contemporaries had passed away. However, as will be made clearer in the discussion of typology in chapter 6, the destruction of Jerusalem in AD 70 and the prophecies thereof serve as types that at once point forward to and guarantee a day of ultimate judgment when Christ will appear a second time to judge the living and the dead.

76. LaHaye, *Revelation Unveiled*, 147.

77. Beale, *Book of Revelation*, 34.

78. Ehrman, *New Testament*, 468.

79. Ibid., 469.

80. R. C. H. Lenski, *Commentary on the New Testament: The Interpretation of St. John's Revelation* (Peabody, MA: Hendrickson, 2001, originally published by Augsburg, 1943), 9.

81. Donald Guthrie, *New Testament Introduction* (Downers Grove, IL: InterVarsity, 1970), 936.

82. Papias writes, "If . . . any one who had attended on the elders came, I asked minutely after their sayings,—what Andrew or Peter said, or what was said by Philip, or by Thomas, or by James, or by John, or by Matthew, or by any other of the Lord's disciples: which things Aristion and the presbyter John, the disciples of the Lord, say. For I imagined that what was to be got from books was not so profitable to me as what came from the living and abiding voice" (fragment quoted in Eusebius, *Church History*, iii.39.4; see also the discussion in Guthrie, *New Testament Introduction*, 886–87).

83. William Hendriksen, *More Than Conquerors: An Interpretation of the Book of Revelation* (Grand Rapids: Baker Books, 1967, 1998), 12.

84. Guthrie, *New Testament Introduction*, 934–35.

85. Ibid., 940.

86. Chilton, *Days of Vengeance*, 2. Chilton maintains that the use of "numbers in a symbolic sense that transcends their literal significance" is "obvious in Revelation;" he then cites the following references in John's Gospel for comparison: John 2:6, 19-20; 5:2, 5; 6:7, 9, 13; 8:57; 13:38; 19:14, 23; 21:11, 14, 15-17. See also Austin Farrer, *The Revelation of St. John The Divine: A Commentary on the English Text* (London: Oxford University Press, 1964), 41ff.

87. Bauckham, *Climax of Prophecy*, ix.

88. Quoted in Guthrie, *New Testament Introduction*, 941n3.

89. James Moffatt, *The Revelation of St. John The Divine*, in W. Robertson Nicoll, ed., *The Expositor's Greek Testament* (reprint, Grand Rapids: Eerdmans, 1976), 337.

90. Ehrman, *Misquoting Jesus*, 39. Elsewhere Ehrman writes, "The book of Acts suggests that John, the son of Zebedee, was uneducated and unable to read and write (the literal meaning of the Greek phrase 'uneducated and ordinary'; Acts 4:13)" (*The New Testament*, 174).

91. Craig L. Blomberg, Review Entry # 0206, *Bart D. Ehrman. Misquoting Jesus: The Story Behind Who Changed the Bible and Why*, Richard S. Hess, ed., *Denver Journal: An Online Review of Current Biblical and Theological Studies*, vol. 9, 2006, http://www.denverseminary.edu/dj/articles2006/0200/0206 (accessed November 29, 2006).

92. Cf. 2 Timothy 2:15. If Paul admonished Timothy to study the Scriptures, a fortiori would the original apostles have devoted themselves to such study.

93. Suetonius, *Lives of the Twelve Caesars: The Life of Nero*, 39.

94. Bauckham, *Climax of Prophecy*, 386; Gentry, *Beast of Revelation*, 40. The full Greek for the cryptogram is Νεόψηφον· Νέρων ἰδίαν μδτέρα ἀπέκτεινε, which Richard Bauckham renders as "A new calculation: Nero killed his own mother." Bauckham comments, "The word νεόψηφον (not otherwise known) must invite the reader to discover that the numerical value of the name Nero (1005) is the same as that of 'killed his own mother.' Thus the popular rumour, following the death of Agrippina, that Nero had been responsible for her murder is confirmed by isopsephism" (Bauckham, *Climax of Prophecy*, 386). "Nero" in Greek (Νέρων) adds up to 1,005 = (N=50) + (έ=5) + (ρ=100) + (ω=800) + (ν=50). The reader can check the numerical value for the Greek phrase "murdered his own mother" (ἰδίαν μδτέρα ἀπέκτεινε) by the following chart of numerical values assigned to Greek and Hebrew letters used in ancient gematria:

α = 1 = א	ι = 10 = '	ρ = 100 = ק
β = 2 = ב	κ = 20 = כ	σ = 200 = ר
γ = 3 = ג	λ = 30 = ל	τ = 300 = ש
δ = 4 = ד	μ = 40 = מ	υ = 400 = ת
ε = 5 = ה	ν = 50 = ן or מ	φ = 500 = ךת
ς = 6 = ו	ξ = 60 = ס	χ = 600
ζ = 7 = ז	ο = 70 = ע	ψ = 700
η = 8 = ח	π = 80 = פ	ω = 800
θ = 9 = ט	ϙ = 90 = צ	

95. See Craig L. Blomberg, *Jesus and the Gospels* (Nashville: Broadman & Holman, 1997), 199.

96. Austin Farrer, *A Rebirth of Images: The Making of St. John's Apocalypse* (Westminster: Dacre Press, 1949), 259-60; and in Chilton, *Days of Vengeance*, 348-49.

97. F.W. Farrar, *The Early Days of Christianity* (New York: Cassell & Co., 1889), 470-71, emphasis in original; and in Chilton, *Days of Vengeance*, 348-49. Cf. Bauckham, *Climax of Prophecy*, 390ff.

98. For fuller discussion, see Gentry, *Beast of Revelation*, 37-47; or better yet, Kenneth L. Gentry Jr., *Before Jerusalem Fell: Dating the Book of Revelation* (Atlanta: American Vision, rev. ed., 1998), 193-212; see also Bauckham, *Climax of Prophecy*, 384-90.

99. See Paul L. Maier, *The Flames of Rome* (Grand Rapids: Kregel, 1981), 432-34. For ancient sources, see Tacitus, *Annals*, xv, 38ff.; Suetonius, *Lives of the Twelve Caesars: Nero*, 38; Dio Cassius, 62.16-18; Pliny, *Natural History*, 17.5; Seneca, *Octavia*, 831ff.

100. Tacitus, *Annals*, 15.44, trans. Alfred John Church and William Jackson Brodribb, eBooks@Adelaide, 2004, http://etext.library.adelaide.edu.au/t/tacitus/t1a/annals12.html (accessed December 1, 2006). See also, Suetonius, *Lives of the Twelve Caesars: Nero*, 16.

101. See Maier, *Flames of Rome*, esp. 317–31, 435–37.

102. Tacitus, *Annals*, 15.44.

103. LaHaye, "Introduction: Has Jesus Already Come?" in LaHaye and Ice, *End Times Controversy*, 13.

104. Maier, *Flames of Rome*, 433–34.

105. Tacitus, *Histories* 1:2–3, trans. Alfred John Church and William Jackson Brodribb, eBooks@Adelaide, 2004, http://etext.library.adelaide.edu.au/t/tacitus/t1h/hist1.html (accessed December 1, 2006).

106. Josephus, *Jewish War* 6, in Paul L. Maier, trans. and ed., *Josephus: The Essential Works* (Grand Rapids: Kregel, 1988), 371.

107. Ibid.

108. Ibid., 372.

109. Ibid., 376.

110. Josephus writes, "Now as soon as the army had no more people to slay or to plunder, because there remained none to be the objects of their fury, (for they would not have spared any, had there remained any other work to be done,) Caesar gave orders that they should now demolish the entire city and temple, but should leave as many of the towers standing as were of the greatest eminency; that is, Phasaelus, and Hippicus, and Mariamne; and so much of the wall as enclosed the city on the west side. This wall was spared, in order to afford a camp for such as were to lie in garrison, as were the towers also spared, in order to demonstrate to posterity what kind of city it was, and how well fortified, which the Roman valor had subdued; but for all the rest of the wall, it was so thoroughly laid even with the ground by those that dug it up to the foundation, that there was left nothing to make those that came thither believe it had ever been inhabited. This was the end which Jerusalem came to by the madness of those that were for innovations; a city otherwise of great magnificence, and of mighty fame among all mankind." Josephus, *War of the Jews* 7.1.1, trans. William Whiston, http://www.ccel.org/ccel/josephus/works/files/war-7.htm (accessed December 1, 2006).

111. LaHaye, "Introduction," 13.

112. LaHaye writes, "It is difficult to understand why anyone would question the AD 95 date for the writing of Revelation when it was so readily accepted by the early church. No other date was offered for almost four centuries, and even then it was not taken seriously. Irenaeus, a disciple of Polycarp (who was a disciple of the Apostle John) wrote *Against Heresies* around AD 180. He is accepted by all scholars as a reliable authority on the first 150 years of Christianity. He wrote that John received the book of Revelation on the Isle of Patmos 'toward the end of Domitian's reign.' And it is a known fact of history that Domitian was murdered in the year AD 96. . . . Irenaeus's statement was accepted as accurate by such early church fathers as Clement, Victorinus, Tertullian, Jerome, Eusebius, and others. The fact that he was only one generation removed from the Apostle John has traditionally carried great weight with historians. . . . For most students of Revelation, it is easier to accept the clear statement of highly regarded Irenaeus, supported by several of the other early church fathers that supported his view of the AD 95 date of the writing of the book, than the early date suggestion of those who lived eighteen hundred years removed from the events" (LaHaye, *Revelation Unveiled*, 28).

Elsewhere, LaHaye claims he is "better served by accepting the time-honored belief of the early church; that the apostle John did indeed write the book of Revelation in AD 95" (LaHaye, "Introduction," 16; cf. Mark Hitchcock, "The Stake in the Heart: The A.D. 95 Date of Revelation," in Tim LaHaye and Thomas Ice, eds., *The End Times Controversy* (Eugene, OR: Harvest House, 2003), 123–50).

The Achilles' heel of this view is that the alleged "time-honored belief of the early church" is itself dependent on Irenaeus's testimony. Irenaeus is "the fountain of tradition," as Gentry puts it. "Several scholars of note argue that the strong external witness to the late date of Revelation most likely may be traced back to Irenaeus' lone witness" (Gentry, *Before Jerusalem Fell*, 64, see 64–66; see also Gentry, *Beast of Revelation*, 203–4 and 220, in which Gentry presents a formidable list of contemporary scholars who either cite only Irenaeus or rely heavily on Irenaeus in assessing the historical evidence to infer a late date for Revelation).

Better that we take seriously the pre–AD 70 dating of Revelation advanced by scholars who have grappled with internal evidences from the book of Revelation itself. Gentry cites many dozens of scholars who advocate the early dating of Revelation, including F. F. Bruce, *New Testament History* (Garden City, NY: Doubleday, 1969), 411; John A. T. Robinson, *Redating the New Testament* (Philadelphia: Westminster, 1976); Philip Schaff, *History of the Christian Church*, 3rd ed., vol. 1: *Apostolic Christianity* (Grand Rapids: Eerdmans, [1910] 1950), 834; Milton S. Terry, *Biblical Hermeneutics* (Grand Rapids: Zondervan, [n.d.] reprinted 1974), 467; Brooke Foss Westcott, *The Gospel According to St. John* (Grand Rapids: Eerdmans, [1882] 1954); and R. C. Sproul, *The Last Days According to Jesus: When Did Jesus Say He Would Return?* (Grand Rapids: Baker, 1998), 140–49; see Gentry, *Before Jerusalem Fell*, 29–38.

113. The sentence in question is found in Irenaeus, *Against Heresies*, 5.30.3. For a helpful discussion, see Gentry, *Beast of Revelation*, 204–9; and, for an in-depth discussion, Gentry, *Before Jerusalem Fell*, 45–67.

114. See Irenaeus, *Against Heresies*, 2.22.5. See Gentry's discussion in *Beast of Revelation*, 208–9.

115. LaHaye's derisive remarks are not only leveled at the notion that Revelation was written prior to AD 70 but directly attack the assertion that Nero is the Antichrist (see LaHaye, "Introduction," 13).

116. These are not instances of the informal logical fallacy known as the argument from silence. Rather, the unacknowledged event in each case is so significant as to warrant the expectation of its being mentioned. Thus, these are instances of a cogent argument from significant silence.

117. Paul L. Maier, trans. and ed., *Josephus: The Essential Works* (Grand Rapids: Kregel, 1988), 371.

118. Norman L. Geisler and Frank Turek, *I Don't Have Enough Faith to Be an Atheist* (Wheaton: Crossway, 2004), 237–38, italics in original.

119. Ibid., 238, 425n.20.

120. Milton S. Terry, *Biblical Hermeneutics: A Treatise on the Interpretation of the Old and New Testaments* (reprint, Grand Rapids: Zondervan, 1985), 495–96.

Chapter 6: Typology Principle

1. Dietrich Bonhoeffer, *The Cost of Discipleship* (New York: Simon & Schuster, 1995 ed.; first published in German in 1937), 25.

2. Ibid., 89.

3. Benny Morris, *The Birth of the Palestinian Refugee Problem, 1947–1949* (Cambridge: Cambridge University Press, 1987). After further documents were released by the Israeli government, Morris revised his estimate of those who were murdered at Deir Yassin to 100–110. In a revealing, provocative interview, Morris was asked, "How many acts of Israeli massacre were perpetrated in 1948?" He responded:

"Twenty-four. In some cases four or five people were executed, in others the numbers were 70, 80, 100. . . . The worst cases were Saliha (70–80 killed), Deir Yassin (100–110), Lod (250), Dawayima (hundreds) and perhaps Abu Shusha (70). There is no unequivocal proof of a large-scale massacre at Tantura, but war crimes were perpetrated there. At Jaffa there was a massacre about which nothing had been known until now. The same at Arab al Muwassi, in the north. About half the acts of massacre were part of Operation Hiram [in the north, in October 1948]: at Safsaf, Saliha, Jish, Eilaboun, Arab, al Muwasi, Deir al Asad, Majdal Krum, Sasa. In Operation Hiram there was an unusually high concentration of executions of people against a wall or next to a well in an orderly fashion. That can't be chance. It's a pattern. Apparently, various officers who took part in the operation understood that the expulsion order they received permitted them to do these deeds in order to encourage the population to take to the roads. The fact is that no one was punished for these acts of murder. Ben-Gurion silenced the matter. He covered up for the officers who did the massacres" (Ari Shavit, "Survival of the Fittest? An Interview with Benny Morris," *Haaretz*, January 9, 2004, http://www.haaretz.com/hasen/pages/ShArt.jhtml?itemNo=380986&contrassID=2 [accessed Dec. 2, 2006]; also available in PDF at http://www.logosjournal.com/morris.pdf [accessed November 29, 2006]).

4. Shavit, "Survival of the Fittest?"

5. Brother Andrew and Al Janssen, *Light Force: A Stirring Account of the Church Caught in the Middle East Crossfire* (Grand Rapids: Revell, 2004), 140–41.

6. Ibid., 142–43.

7. Ibid., 141, 143.

8. Gary Burge writes, "According to U.N. records in June 1999, about 3.6 million Palestinian refugees are the victims of Israel's nationhood" (Gary M. Burge, *Whose Land? Whose Promise? What Christians Are Not Being Told about Israel and the Palestinians* (Cleveland: Pilgrim Press, 2003), x). Human Rights Watch says, "Palestinians are the world's oldest and largest refugee population, and make up more than one fourth of all refugees" (http://hrw.org/doc/?t=refugees&document [accessed December 26, 2006]).

9. The following details and descriptions of Nora Kort's account are found in Burge, *Whose Land? Whose Promise?* 208-10.

10. Burge, *Whose Land? Whose Promise?* 41.

11. Morris, *Birth of the Palestinian Refugee Problem*, 25.

12. Colin Chapman, *Whose Promised Land?* (Grand Rapids: Baker Books, 2002), 84.

13. John Nelson Darby, "The Hopes of the Church of God in Connection with the Destiny of the Jews and the Nations as Revealed in Prophecy," in William Kelly, ed., *The Collected Writings of J. N. Darby*, vol. 2, *Prophetic 1* (Kingston on Thames: Stow Hill Bible and Trust Depot, 1962), 380, quoted in Stephen Sizer, *Christian Zionism: Road-map to Armageddon?* (Leicester: Inter-Varsity, 2004), 162.

14. John Hagee, *Jerusalem Countdown: A Warning to the World* (Lake Mary, FL, Frontline, 2006), 47 (emphasis in the original).

15. CNN.com, "Robertson Suggests God Smote Sharon," January 6, 2006, http://www.cnn.com/2006/US/01/05/robertson.sharon (accessed December 4, 2006). While Robertson is resolutely opposed to a two-state solution in the Middle East, he did apologize to family members of Sharon for his insensitive remarks (see Julie Stahl, "Robertson Asks Forgiveness From Sharon's Family, Israel," CNSNews.com, January 12, 2006)..

16. CNN.com, "Robertson Suggests God Smote Sharon."

17. Michael D. Evans, *The American Prophecies: Ancient Scriptures Reveal Our Nation's Future* (New York: Warner Faith, 2004), 193.

18. "President Bush Discusses Iraq Policy at Whitehall Palace in London," The White House, Office of the Press Secretary, November 19, 2003, http://www.whitehouse.gov/news/releases/2003/11/20031119-1.html (accessed December 4, 2006).

19. See Evans, *American Prophecies*, 230ff.

20. Ibid., 27.

21. *John Hagee Today*, Trinity Broadcasting Network, September 26, 2006.

22. Twentieth-century German biblical scholar Leonhard Goppelt has noted in this regard, "For our understanding of the OT, typology provides a framework that is determined not only by the NT but also by the OT itself; one that unites the two Testaments with one another and that facilitates the understanding of each by pointing to the other" (Leonhard Goppelt, Donald H. Madvid, trans., *Typos: The Typological Interpretation of the Old Testament in the New* [Grand Rapids: Eerdmans, 1982], 237). And, as Earl Ellis explains, "The NT's understanding and exposition of the OT lies at the heart of its theology, and it is primarily expressed within the framework of a typological interpretation" (idem, foreword, xx).

23. The importance of understanding typology can hardly be overstated. This is especially true with respect to messianic prophecy. For example, the interconnection of typology and messianic prophecy is unmistakable in Isaiah's "virgin birth" prophecy. The prophecy in Isaiah 7—"The virgin will be with child and will give birth to a son, and will call him Immanuel"—was fulfilled in Isaiah 8. As Isaiah makes clear, this prophecy was fulfilled when Isaiah "went to the prophetess, and she conceived and gave birth to a son" named Maher-Shalal-Hash-Baz (v. 3). In context, Judah "was shaken" as two powerful kingdoms sought the nation's demise (see 7:1–2). God, however, promised that the birth of Maher-Shalal-Hash-Baz was a sign that Judah would be spared. In the words of Isaiah, "Before the boy knows enough to reject the wrong and choose the right, the land of the two kings you dread will be laid waste" (7:16; cf. 8:4).

Though Isaiah's wife, unlike Mary, was not a virgin when she gave birth, she nonetheless was the fore-future fulfillment of Isaiah's prophecy. "Virgin" (*almah*) was simply a term used to refer to the prophetess prior to her union with Isaiah, not to indicate that she would give birth to a child *as* a virgin. By way of analogy, it would have been true in 1999 to say that "the governor of Texas will one day lead this country," but this obviously does not mean that George W. Bush would lead the United States *as* the governor of Texas. Thus, while the Holy Spirit may have revealed to Isaiah that his prophecy pointed forward to Jesus (see John 12:41), it was not until after the miraculous virginal conception and birth of Jesus about seven hundred years later that it became entirely clear that the fore-future fulfillment of Isaiah's prophecy was a type, the antitype of which is Jesus the Messiah (Matthew 1:22–23). While Maher-Shalal-Hash-Baz signified temporal salvation for Judah, Jesus Christ—the literal "Immanuel" ("God with us")—embodied eternal salvation for true Israel.

Furthermore, Moses' prophecy that God would raise up a prophet like him from among the Israelites typologically points forward to *the* Prophet, Jesus Christ (Deuteronomy 18:15–19). Within the context of the Old Testament, however, the prophecy that God would raise up another prophet like Moses was fulfilled in the fore-future in Joshua who succeeded Moses and led the people into the Promised Land (see Deuteronomy 31). As foretold by Moses, God used Joshua as his mouthpiece to relay his commands to the Israelites (Deuteronomy 18:18; cf., e.g., Joshua 1). In fact, the Lord promised Joshua, "As I was with Moses, so I will be with you, I will never leave you nor forsake you" (Joshua 1:5), and the Israelite leaders appropriately expressed their allegiance to Joshua as the prophet "from among their own brothers" who would succeed Moses by saying, "Whatever you have commanded us we will do, and wherever you send us we will go. Just as we fully obeyed Moses, so we will obey you. Only may the LORD your God be with you as he was with Moses" (Joshua 1:16–17).

In addition to its near-future fulfillment in Joshua, this prophecy came to be understood as pointing forward to an eschatological prophet who would lead the people of God as a new Moses and a new Joshua. The Gospel of John reveals that this hope was alive and well in the first century (cf. John 1:21; 6:14; 7:40), and Stephen implicitly identifies Jesus as the ultimate fulfillment of this prophecy in his impassioned sermon for which he was martyred (Acts 7:37–38). In this way, both Moses's prophecy and its near-future fulfillment in Joshua serve as types of the great Prophet of God who not only spoke the words of God, but was himself the Word become flesh (John 1:14; cf. Hebrews 1:1–2).

Finally, the typological nature of messianic prophecies is evidenced in Psalm 22. This psalm of David is one of the most well-known prophecies of the suffering Messiah, but rarely is it observed that David was referring in this poetic song to his own historical circumstances. Fearing his own death and feeling abandoned by God to the evil men who sought his demise, David begins this psalm by exclaiming, "My God, my God, why have you forsaken me? Why are you so far from saving me, so far from the words of my groaning?" (v. 1). David proceeds with a poetic lament over his impending doom: "Dogs have surrounded me; a band of evil men has encircled me, they have pierced my hands and my feet. I can count all my bones; people stare and gloat over me. They divide my garments among them and cast lots for my clothing" (vv. 16–18). As a dramatic poem, we should not expect that every detail of this description was literally true of David, but rather that by making references to his enemies' casting of lots for his clothes, for example, David was poetically expressing his anxiety over what he in his desperation imagined as his undoing.

As recorded by Matthew, however, this particular detail of David's song actually was fulfilled literally in Jesus as he was being crucified (Matthew 27:35). That Jesus himself also understood David's psalm as fulfilled in his own crucifixion is evidenced by Jesus's dying words: "My God, my God, why have you forsaken me?" (Matthew 27:46). Thus, David's lament over his suffering serves as a divinely designed prefiguring of the suffering in righteousness of the crucified Lord. As David was able even in his desperation to praise God and trust in his faithfulness in the second half of the psalm, so all the more could Jesus who was raised from the dead and seated at the right hand of God affirm, "For he has not despised or disdained the suffering of the afflicted one; he has not hidden his face from him but has listened to his cry for help" (Psalm 22:24).

24. Sizer, *Christian Zionism*, 123.

25. K. J. Woollcombe, "The Biblical Origins and Patristic Development of Typology," in G. W. H. Lampe and K. J. Woollcombe, *Essays on Typology*, Studies in Biblical Theology (Naperville, IL: Allenson, 1957), 40, emphasis in original.

26. Goppelt, *Typos*, 18.

27. Ibid., 167.

28. Ibid., 177. Goppelt helpfully codifies these first two principles of typological interpretation in the following way: "Only historical facts—persons, actions, events, and institutions—are material for typological interpretation: words and narratives can be utilized only insofar as they deal with such matters. These things are to be interpreted typologically only if they are considered to be divinely ordained representations or types of future realities that will be even greater and more complete. If the antitype does not represent a heightening of the type, if it is merely a repetition of the type, then it can be called typology only in certain instances and in a limited way" (Goppelt, 17–18).

29. Ibid., 175.

30. Sizer, *Christian Zionism*, 135.

31. Tim LaHaye and Thomas Ice, *Charting the End Times* (Eugene, OR.: Harvest House, 2001), 78, emphasis added.

32. See Sizer, *Christian Zionism*, 162.

33. John Hagee, *Should Christians Support Israel?* (San Antonio, TX: Dominion, 1987), 99.

34. See Ronald B. Allen, "The Land of Israel," in H. Wayne House, ed., *Israel: The Land and the People: An Evangelical Affirmation of God's Promises* (Grand Rapids: Kregel, 1998), 24.

35. God's faithfulness in fulfilling the promises made to Abraham is also acknowledged in the New Testament when Paul recounts that "[God] overthrew seven nations in Canaan and gave their land to his people as their inheritance" (Acts 13:19; cf. 7:17, 45).

36. John H. Gerstner, *Wrongly Dividing the Word of Truth: A Critique of Dispensationalism* (Brentwood, TN: Wolgemuth & Hyatt, 1991), 44.

37. Hagee, *Should Christians Support Israel?* 125 (emphasis in original).

38. Ibid., 63.

39. Ibid., 67–68.

40. The amount of time and money that Christian Zionists have invested in relocating Jews to Israel is staggering. As noted by Timothy Weber, John Hagee, for example, claims to have spent $3.7 million to relocate over six thousand Jews (Timothy P. Weber, *On the Road to Armageddon: How Evangelicals Became Israel's Best Friend* [Grand Rapids: Baker, 2004], 227).

41. I paraphrase the oft-quoted line by Chaim Weizmann, a leader of the Zionist movement, who said before a Jewish audience a couple years after the Balfour Declaration was issued, that it is "the golden key which unlocks the doors of Palestine and gives you the possibility to put all your efforts into the country" (quoted in *Chaim Weizmann: Excerpts from His Historic Statements, Writings and Addresses* [New York: The Jewish Agency for Palestine, 1952], 302, quoted in Chapman, *Whose Promised Land?* 57).

42. See Weber, *On the Road to Armageddon*, 155–86, esp. 156–60, 166–71; and Sizer, *Christian Zionism*, 63–66. Sizer notes that Balfour was committed to the Zionist agenda without any intention of consulting with the indigenous Arab inhabitants of the land. In a letter to Lord Curzon, Balfour conceded, "The Four Great Powers are committed to Zionism. And Zionism, be it right or wrong, good or bad, is rooted in age-long traditions, in present needs, in future hopes of far profounder import than the desires or prejudices of the 700,000 Arabs who now inhabit that ancient land" (quoted in Sizer, *Christian Zionism*, 64–65). The fact that tens of thousands of the Palestinians were Christian was of little consequence to Balfour and the British.

43. Weber, *On the Road to Armageddon*, 169.

44. Recall that only two of the original generation (over the age of twenty) rescued out of Egypt by God through Moses were allowed to enter the Promised Land; because of unbelief, the others perished in the Sinai wilderness (Numbers 14:26–34). Also, dispensationalist scholar H. Wayne House writes, "The covenant of the land was an everlasting covenant, but any generation which refused to comply with the covenant code of Moses would be cast out of the land (Deut. 29:25)" (H. Wayne House, "The Church's Appropriation of Israel's Covenant Blessings," in H. Wayne House, ed., *Israel: The Land and the People: An Evangelical Affirmation of God's Promises* [Grand Rapids: Kregel, 1998], 81). Here are Moses's ominous words, to which House refers: "The whole land will be a burning waste of salt and sulfur—nothing planted, nothing sprouting, no vegetation growing on it. It will be like the destruction of Sodom and Gomorrah, Admah and Zeboiim, which the LORD overthrew in fierce anger. All the nations will ask: 'Why has the LORD done this to this land? Why this fierce, burning anger?' And the answer will be: 'It is because this people abandoned the covenant of

the LORD, the God of their fathers, the covenant he made with them when he brought them out of Egypt'" (Deuteronomy 29:23–25; cf. Leviticus 26:33; Deuteronomy 4:25–31; 28:64; Nehemiah 1:8).

Concerning the condition for returning to the land, Moses writes: "When all these blessings and curses I have set before you come upon you and you take them to heart wherever the LORD your God disperses you among the nations, and when you and your children return to the LORD your God and obey him with all your heart and with all your soul according to everything I command you today, then the LORD your God will restore your fortunes and have compassion on you and gather you again from all the nations where he scattered you. Even if you have been banished to the most distant land under the heavens, from there the LORD your God will gather you and bring you back. He will bring you to the land that belonged to your fathers, and you will take possession of it. He will make you more prosperous and numerous than your fathers" (Deuteronomy 30:1–5).

45. Stanley A. Ellisen, *Who Owns the Land? The Arab-Israeli Conflict*, rev. by Charles H. Dyer (Wheaton: Tyndale, 2003), 137. Ellisen's original wording has been slightly altered for clarity, not substance, in the revised edition. Here is the quote from the original edition: "Judged on biblical grounds, the nation [of Israel] today does not pass divine muster. The promise of the land is directly tied to the nation's response to Messiah. Though her international right to the land can be well defended, her divine right by covenant has only sentiment in its favor" (Stanley A. Ellisen, *The Arab-Israeli Conflict: Who Owns the Land?* [Portland, OR: Multnomah, 1991], 174, quoted in Ronald B. Allen, "The Land of Israel," in House, ed., *Israel: The Land and the People*, 26). Dispensationalist scholar Ronald Allen affirms Ellisen's assessment and also quotes approvingly Louis Goldberg along the same lines. Goldberg writes, "Some Israelis lay claim to the land now, but it will only be a reality when everyone in Israel undergoes the experience of having their heart of stone removed and a heart of flesh implanted in them (Ezek. 36:26)" (Louis Goldberg, "The Borders of the Land of Israel According to Ezekiel," *Mishkan* 26 [1997], http://www.caspari.com/mishkan/zips/mishkan26.pdf [accessed Dec. 11, 2006]). Allen comments, "Israel certainly has the right to exist as a nation. Israel has a right to remain in the land that became hers through the international actions of the United Nations following World War II. But a critical factor seems to be lacking for one to declare the present State of Israel to be the ultimate fulfillment of biblical prophecy for the return of the Jewish people to their ancient land—that factor is faith in the Savior of the Scriptures, the Lord Jesus, the Messiah. Nonetheless, neither may one minimize the significance of two facts that seem to be almost unbelievable: (1) the perseverance of the Jewish people through the centuries and (2) the formation of the Jewish State of Israel in the land long ago promised to them by God. Israel is a modern miracle. The very fact of the existence of the state is simply astonishing" (Allen, "Land of Israel," 26).

46. LaHaye and Ice acknowledge the biblical reasons for Israel's dispersion among the nations: "The threat of dispersion throughout the nations appears as early as the Mosaic Law (Leviticus 26:33; Deuteronomy 4:27; 28:64; 29:28). Nehemiah said, 'Remember the word which You commanded Your servant Moses, saying, "If you are unfaithful I will scatter you among the peoples"' (Nehemiah 1:8). Similar statements appear many times throughout the prophets." They go on to assert nonetheless that "In 1948 when the modern state of Israel was born, it not only became an important stage-setting development but began an actual fulfillment of specific Bible prophecies about an international regathering of the Jews in unbelief before the judgment of the Tribulation." In defense of this radical claim they cite the following passages: Ezekiel 20:33–38; 22:17–22; 36:22–24; 38–39; Isaiah 11:11–12; Zephaniah 1:14–18; 2:1–2. (Tim LaHaye and Thomas Ice, *Charting the End Times* [Eugene, OR: Harvest House, 2001], 84–85).

Hal Lindsey argues similarly: "Right here a careful distinction must be made between 'the physical restoration' to the land of Palestine as a nation, which clearly occurs shortly before the Messiah's coming, and the 'spiritual restoration' of all Jews who have believed in the Messiah just after His return to this earth. The 'physical restoration' is accomplished by unbelieving Jews through their human effort. As a matter of fact, the great catastrophic events which are to happen to this nation during 'the tribulation' are primarily designed to shock the people into believing in their true Messiah (Ezekiel 38; 39)" (Hal Lindsey with C. C. Carlson, *The Late Great Planet Earth* [Grand Rapids: Zondervan, 1970, 40th printing May 1974], 48.

LaHaye and Lindsey are fairly representative of Christian Zionist thinking in this area. Basically, the idea is to understand prophecies concerning the return from Babylonian captivity in the sixth century BC as finding their real fulfillment in modern Israel. Just as Ezra and Nehemiah describe distinct stages in the ancient return from exile, so we should not be surprised to see distinct stages in the modern return, even if a significant stage involves utter unbelief and disobedience. Colin Chapman soundly refutes this reasoning by comparing and contrasting the return from Babylon with the formation of modern Israel.

First, Chapman explains that the ancient Jewish exiles returned to their ancestral homes with the expectation of living with non-Israelites, "aliens," in their midst who would enjoy full rights of inheritance (Ezra 2:1; Ezekiel 47:21–23). Yet, he concludes, the process of forming and sustaining modern Israel has more closely resembled Joshua's conquest than the peaceful return from Babylon (see Isaiah 35:9–10). As such, the formation of modern Israel is not a recapitulation of the return from Babylon and thus is not the fulfillment of those prophecies.

Furthermore, the claim that unrepentant modern Israel fulfills prophecies of return from exile contradicts Moses's teaching in Deuteronomy. Chapman explains that Moses directly proclaimed that disobedience against the Lord results in dispersion (Deuteronomy 28:58–64; 29:23–28), and returning to the land requires repentance: "When you and your children return to the LORD your God and obey him with all your heart . . . *then* the LORD your God will restore your fortunes and have compassion on you and gather you again from the nations where he scattered you. Even if you have been banished to the most distant land under the heavens, from there the LORD your God will gather you and bring you back. He will bring you to the land that belonged to your fathers, and you will take possession of it. He will make you more prosperous and numerous than your fathers" (Deuteronomy 30:1–5).

Chapman then cites Daniel and Nehemiah as exemplars of genuine repentance who confess the sins of the people (e.g., Daniel 9:1–19; Nehemiah 1:4–11). "Thus," writes Chapman, "when God brings the remnant back to the Land, he does so in accordance with the conditions described in Deuteronomy. The people confess their sins corporately at a later stage after the return (e.g., Ezra 10:1–4; Neh 9:1–37). But before the return, a significant number of individuals have expressed repentance on behalf of the people."

To those who argue that Ezekiel 33–39 in particular justifies the teaching that repentance and belief will eventually follow the physical reoccupation of the land, Chapman seems to understand how those specific chapters can be read that way. "Something like this can perhaps be seen in Ezekiel," he says—but he quickly points out that cleansing and resettling coincide. As the Lord says, "On the day I cleanse you from all your sins, I will resettle your towns, and the ruins will be rebuilt" (Ezekiel 36:33). And, again, Deuteronomy's foundational condition for return is repentance.

Chapman concludes, "If the temple was destroyed in AD 70 and Jews exiled from the Land, as Jesus taught, as a judgment for their failure to recognize him as Messiah (Luke 19:41–44), the repentance required in the terms of Deuteronomy

30 would, from a Christian perspective, mean recognition of Jesus as Messiah. This would be the condition of return. Peter on the Day of Pentecost could say, 'This is that which was spoken of by the prophet' (Acts 2:16). But I have great difficulty in putting the return in the 19th and 20th centuries in the same category as the return in the sixth century. There are far too many significant differences!" (Colin Chapman, "One Land, Two Peoples—How Many States?" *Mishkan* 26 [1997], http://www.caspari.com/mishkan/zips/mishkan26.pdf [accessed Dec. 11, 2006]; also Colin Chapman, "Ten Questions for a Theology of the Land," in Philip Johnston and Peter Walker, eds., *The Land of Promise: Biblical, Theological and Contemporary Perspectives* [Leicester: Apollos (Inter-Varsity), 2000], 175–77).

47. John Hagee, *Final Dawn over Jerusalem* (Nashville: Nelson, 1998), 114.

48. Lindsey, *Late Great Planet Earth*, 53, 54.

49. Chuck Smith, *End Times: A Report on Future Survival* (Costa Mesa, CA: The Word for Today, 1978, 1980), 35. Unlike many date setters for the return of Christ (e.g., Wisenant, Camping), Smith and Lindsey left a tiny bit of wiggle room. Smith continues, "However, it is possible that Jesus is dating the beginning of the generation from 1967, when Jerusalem was again under Israeli control for the first time since 587 BC. We don't know for sure which year actually marks the beginning of the last generation. Nevertheless, we should live as though the Lord were coming today, because He just might. Be diligent about the things of the Lord and yet practical about your life. Don't quit your job. Don't quit school. But all the while look up and lift up your head, for your redemption is drawing near!" (idem, 35–36.)

50. Weber, *On the Road to Armageddon*, 173.

51. Ibid., 181–83.

52. Chuck Smith with David Wimbish, *Dateline Earth: Countdown to Eternity* (Old Tappan, NJ: Chosen, 1989), 49.

53. Ibid.; see also 26-27. After rebuking date-setters for falsely predicting the time of Christ's return, Smith writes, "I believe that the scene of redemption as previewed by the apostle John [in Revelation 4–5] will be occurring very soon—within the next 25 years at the maximum." Smith teaches that the scene in Revelation 4 and following will occur after the rapture of the church (see p. 43). So the newest date of 2014 is derived by adding twenty-five years to 1989 (the date Smith released *Dateline Earth*).

54. See video from "Jack Van Impe Presents" on You Tube.com at http://www.youtube.com/watch?v=-f3aRnkgOWs (accessed January 1, 2007), original date of airing unknown.

55. Weber, *On the Road to Armageddon*, 184.

56. Hagee, *Jerusalem Countdown*, 45.

57. Ibid., 47–49.

58. Chapman also lists Psalms 15:1; 48:1–2; 50:2; 132:7; 135:21. "In Psalm 87," Chapman writes, "Jerusalem is pictured as the city of God which is open to people from many nations. . . . People from . . . foreign, pagan nations, for whom the children of Israel had no warm feelings, would one day be included as citizens with full rights of Zion, the city of God" (Chapman, *Whose Holy City?* 31–32).

59. Ibid., 42.

60. Cf. Palmer Robertson, "A new-covenant perspective on the land," 138, in Philip Johnston and Peter Walker, eds., *The Land of Promise: Biblical, Theological and Contemporary Perspectives* (Leicester: Inter-Varsity, Apollos 2000).

61. Stephen Sizer, *Christian Zionism*, 170.

62. Chapman, *Whose Holy City?* 62. It is significant to note that the Crusaders who used force to further their creeds in the name of God were acting in direct opposition to the teachings of Christ.

63. Chapman, *Whose Holy City?* 63–64.
64. See notes 44–46 for a refutation of the dispensationalist contention that preliminary regathering must occur in the context of unbelief.
65. As thoroughly documented in *Whose Land, Whose Promise?* (pp. 130 and following), despite its laudable features as a democracy in the Middle East, the modern state of Israel is an exclusivist state that is guilty of stealing such basic goods as water and ancestral homes from Palestinian natives. Indeed, the official sanctioning of discrimination against Palestinians in Israel has led many social commentators and even the United Nations to identify Zionism as a racist philosophy (See Burge, *Whose Land, Whose Promise?* 141). Even former President Jimmy Carter has recently decried that "the persecution of the Palestinians now in the occupied territories under the occupation forces is one of the worst examples of human rights deprivation that I know" (Jimmy Carter, from interview on *Hardball* with Chris Matthews, November 28, 2006; transcript retrieved December 14, 2006, from MSNBC.com).
66. Psalm 110:1
67. Peter Walker, "Jesus and Jerusalem: New Testament Perspectives," in Naim Ateek, ed., *Jerusalem: What Makes for Peace?* 67, quoted in Colin Chapman, *Whose Holy City?*, 35.
68. Tim LaHaye, *The Beginning of the End* (Wheaton: Tyndale, 1972), 51.
69. Ibid.
70. Ibid., 58. See also the discussion in Weber, *On the Road to Armageddon*, 250–55.
71. Thomas Ice and Randall Price, *Ready to Rebuild: The Imminent Plan to Rebuild the Last Days Temple* (Eugene, OR: Harvest House, 1992), 131–32.
72. Rod Dreher, "Red-Heifer Days: Religion Takes the Lead," *National Review Online*, April 11, 2002, http://www.nationalreview.com/dreher/dreher041102.asp (accessed December 31, 2006); see also Weber, *On the Road to Armageddon*, 265.
73. Dreher, "Red-Heifer Days."
74. LaHaye, *The Beginning of the End*, 55–56.
75. Weber, *On the Road to Armageddon*, 263.
76. Ibid., 264.
77. Ibid.
78. Ibid., 265.
79. Ice and Price, *Ready to Rebuild*, 137–38.
80. Jim Combs, "The Olivet Discourse," in Tim LaHaye, ed., *Tim LaHaye Prophecy Study Bible* (Chattanooga: AMG Publishers, 2000), 1039.
81. Tom Wright, *Paul for Everyone: Galatians and Thessalonians* (Louisville: Westminster John Knox, 2004), 147–48.
82. I should note that the warning passages in Hebrews must be read in light of the entire book of Hebrews in order to see that they are largely warnings against returning to the types and shadows of the Old Covenant. Hebrews was written to Jewish believers who in the midst of suffering doubted the sufficiency of Christ's atoning sacrifice for sin and were being tempted to separate from the larger body of Christ and to return to the Judaism of unbelieving Israel.
83. LaHaye and Ice, *Charting the End Times*, 94–95.
84. Ibid., 97–98.
85. Quoting Jerry Hullinger, LaHaye and Ice, *Charting the End Times*, 95.
86. Thomas Ice, executive director of Tim LaHaye's Pre-Trib Research Center has exacerbated the problem by stating that without animal sacrifices in the

Millennium, Yahweh's holiness would be defiled. That, for obvious reasons, is blasphemous. Even a cursory reading of the book of Hebrews underscores in red that it is the blood of Christ that forever eradicates the barrier between sinful humanity and a holy God and renders a return to Old Covenant sacrifices an affront to the holiness of God (see Thomas Ice, "Literal Sacrifices in the Millennium," Pre-Trib Research Center Web site, http://www.pre-trib.org/article-view.php?id=39 [accessed January 2, 2007]; cf. LaHaye and Ice, *Charting the End Times*, 94–96).

87. N. T. Wright, *Jesus and the Victory of God*, vol. 2, *Christian Origins and the Question of God* (Minneapolis: Fortress, 1996), 205.

88. "Priest," in Leland Ryken, James C. Wilhoit, and Tremper Longman III, gen. eds., *Dictionary of Biblical Imagery* (Downers Grove, IL: InterVarsity, 1998), 662.

89. "Temple," in ibid., 849.

90. Wright, *Jesus and the Victory of God*, 205.

91. Ibid.

92. Sizer, *Christian Zionism*, 182.

93. Goppelt, *Typos*, 116.

94. Sizer, *Christian Zionism*, 182.

95. Ibid., 183.

Chapter 7: Scriptural Synergy

1. Ira J. Hadnot, "Last Disciple vs. Left Behind: New Take on Rapture Puts Authors in Apocalyptic Feud," *Dallas Morning News*, 2nd ed., November 6, 2004, 1G.

2. Ibid. See also my letter to the editor in response to this article at http://www.equip.org/abouthank/lettertoeditor.pdf.

3. Preterism, from the Latin *praeter*, meaning "past," is the view that biblical prophecy, to varying degrees, has already been fulfilled (usually with an emphasis on the events of the first century AD). No orthodox preterist holds that the second coming of Christ or the resurrection of the dead in Christ has already occurred. LaHaye's assertion that I believe Jesus returned in AD 68, with the implication that I believe the resurrection has already occurred, wrongly associates me with the heretical form of preterism.

   Formidable defenses of orthodox preterism include R. C. Sproul, *The Last Days According to Jesus* (Grand Rapids: Baker, 1998); Gary DeMar, *Last Days Madness: Obsession of the Modern Church*, 4th rev. ed. (Atlanta: American Vision, 1999); and Kenneth Gentry's contribution in Thomas Ice and Kenneth L. Gentry Jr., *The Great Tribulation: Past or Future?* (Grand Rapids: Kregel, 1999).

4. Hank Hanegraaff, *Resurrection* (Nashville: Word, 2000); and *The Third Day* (Nashville: W, 2003).

5. R. C. Sproul, *Knowing Scripture* (Downers Grove, IL: InterVarsity, 1977), 47.

6. Ibid., 46–47.

7. David Chilton, *The Days of Vengeance: An Exposition of the Book of Revelation* (Tyler, TX: Dominion, 1987), 66.

8. Sproul, *Knowing Scripture*, 46.

9. I first heard this metaphor from New Testament scholar N. T Wright. If we are not conscious of the music of the Old Testament playing in the background as we play that of the New, we are in danger of producing only discordant noise and not harmonious music at all. "Let him who has ears to hear . . . "

10. Leviticus 26:18, 21, 24, 28.

11. Even the two exceptions once worshiped the one true God of Israel. Nineveh was transformed through the preaching of Jonah (Jonah 3), and Tyre assisted Solomon in the construction of the Jewish temple (1 Kings 5). Their apostasy is associated with harlotry. See Chilton, *Days of Vengeance*, 424; cf. J. Massyngberde Ford, *Revelation* (Garden City, NY: Doubleday, 1975), 283–84.

Glossary

—⟨◊/◊/◊⟩—

allegory: a story in which the author intends to convey through symbols and metaphors a meaning that transcends its literal or surface meaning, as in John Bunyan's *The Pilgrim's Progress*. In allegory, the historicity of a detail is irrelevant to its hidden or transcendent meaning. Thus an allegorical interpretation of Scripture would neutralize the Bible's claim to convey historical events that form the basis of the Christian faith. (see pp. 29-30 and 171-72; also **Typological principle**)

apocalypse: (from the Greek word *apocalupsis*, meaning "uncover" from *apo* "away from" and *kalypto* "I cover, conceal") denotes an uncovering, a disclosure, a revelation. This term is found in the opening titular phrase of the introduction to the book of Revelation: "Ἀποκάλυψις Ἰησου Χριστου" (The Apocalypse of Jesus Christ).

apocalyptic: a literary genre used to describe prophetic literature composed in the highly metaphorical and symbolic language system used within post-exilic Judaism and early Christianity. (see **apocalyptic prophecy**)

apocalyptic prophecy: A category of prophetic pronouncement concerned with the eschatological hope in God's blessing and vindication of the redeemed, and His righteous judgment of the wicked. It often employs hyperbolic cosmic imagery (e.g., darkening sun, blood-red moon, stars falling from the sky, foreboding clouds) and fantasy imagery (e.g., red dragons with seven heads, locusts with human faces, leopards with bear's feet and lion's teeth) to invest earthly, historical, sociopolitical events with their full theological and eternal significance.

archetype: "An original model or type after which other similar things are patterned: a prototype" (*The American Heritage Dictionary of the English Language*, 3rd ed. [Boston: Houghton Mifflin, 1992], 95).

canon: (from the Greek word *kanon*, meaning "measuring rod" or "rule") the thirty-nine received books of the Old Testament and the twenty-seven of the New Testament officially recognized as inspired Holy Scripture by the early Christian Church.

Christian Zionism. a sociopolitical movement among fundamentalist Christians committed to the establishment of an autonomous Jewish state in Palestine with Jerusalem as its capital. Christian Zionism is largely

271

motivated by the **dispensationalist** contention that God has yet to fulfill his covenant with Abraham to give ethnic Jews **Eretz Israel**—from the river of Egypt to the river Euphrates. (See pp. 166ff; also **Zionism**)

dispensationalism: an eschatological viewpoint according to which God has two distinct peoples (the Church and national, ethnic Israel) with two distinct plans and two distinct destinies. Dispensationalism is distinctive for its teaching that the Church will be "raptured" from the earth in the first phase of Christ's second coming so that God can return to his work with national Israel, which was put on hold after Israel's rejection of Messiah. God's renewed working with Israel is thought by many dispensationalists to include a seven-year period of tribulation under the Antichrist in which two-thirds of the Jewish people will be killed, followed by the second phase of Christ's second coming in which Christ and the martyred "tribulation saints" will rule for a thousand years from a rebuilt Temple with a reinstituted sacrificial system. Dispensationalism was first conceived by John Nelson Darby in the nineteenth century and popularized by prophecy pundits such as Hal Lindsey and Tim LaHaye in the twentieth century.

Eretz Israel: (from the Hebrew phrase אֶרֶץ יִשְׂרָל, meaning "land of Israel") in Zionist parlance, Eretz Israel encompasses the land from the river of Egypt to the river Euphrates, or from Egypt to Iraq (see **Promised Land**).

eschatology: (from the Greek word *eschatos*, meaning "last, farthest," and *logos*, "speaking, word") eschatology is the study of last things or end times. Far from being a mere branch in the theological tree, eschatology is the root that provides life and luster to every fiber of its being. To study Scripture is to study eschatology, for all of God's work in redemption—past, present, and future—moves toward eternal redemption. Put another way, eschatology is the thread that weaves the tapestry of Scripture into a harmonious pattern.

exegesis: (from the Greek word *exegeisthai*, meaning "to explain, interpret, tell," from *ex-* "out," and *hegeisthai* "to lead, guide") exegesis is the method by which an author's intended meaning is understood. In sharp contrast, *eisegesis* is reading into the biblical text something that simply isn't there.

Exegetical Eschatology e^2 : I coined the phrase Exegetical Eschatology e^2 to underscore that above all else I am deeply committed to a proper *method* of biblical interpretation rather than to any particular *model* of eschatology. The plain and proper meaning of a biblical passage must always take precedence over a particular eschatological presupposition or paradigm. To highlight the significance of proper methodology, I use the symbol e^2 interchangeably with the phrase Exegetical Eschatology. Just as in mathematics the squaring of a number exponentially increases its value,

GLOSSARY

so too, perceiving eschatology through the prism of biblical exegesis will exponentially increase its value.

e^2 is a method of biblical interpretation whereby Scripture is read in light of Scripture and in accordance with historically proven rules of interpretation, namely, that any passage is to be interpreted in light of its literary, grammatical, historical, typological and broader context (as codified in the acronym **LIGHTS**); as a method of exegesis, e^2 begins primarily with methodological rather than substantive presuppositions, which is to say that the tools e^2 employs in order to discern the meaning of Scripture do not in themselves bear content to which Scripture must conform, but rather they reveal the content of Scripture itself. To put it plainly, method trumps model. Two significant presuppositions of e^2 are that the entire Bible is the inspired Word of God, and therefore coherent, and that eschatology is the thread by which God has woven together the tapestry of Scripture into a harmonious pattern.

gematria: an ancient practice of transforming names into numbers by assigning numerical values to letters such that the sum of the numerical values became associated with particular names (e.g., the Hebrew transliteration of the Greek form of Nero Caesar is associated with 666) (See also pp. 144-47 and p. 258 note 94).

Grammatical principle: ("G" in **LIGHTS**) an essential principle of biblical interpretation which holds that, as with any literature, a thorough understanding of the Bible cannot be attained without a grasp of the basic rules that govern the relationships and usages of words in language (including syntax, style, and semantics). (See chapter 4, pp. 70ff)

great tribulation: according to many dispensationalists, the great tribulation refers to a future seven-year period of incomprehensible horror following a secret rapture of the church. During this period, two-thirds of the Jewish people will die under the rule of an Antichrist. Biblically, however, the term "great tribulation" refers to the horrific persecution of Christians by the Beast beginning in AD 64 prophesied in the book of Revelation. (see Revelation 7:14; cf. Matthew 24:21; and also pp. 147-49)

heresy: a teaching that denies the essential tenets of the historic Christian faith as codified in the great, ancient ecumenical Creeds, such as the Apostles' Creed, Nicene Creed, or Creed of Athanasius.

hermeneutics: (from the Greek word *hermeneutes*, meaning "interpreter") the art and science of biblical interpretation. It is a science in that certain rules apply. It is an art in that the more you apply these rules, the better you get at it. In Greek mythology, the task of the god Hermes was to interpret the will of the gods. In biblical hermeneutics, the task is to interpret the Word of God.

Historical principle: ("H" in **LIGHTS**) an essential principle of biblical interpretation which holds that the biblical text is best understood and defended when one is familiar with the customs, culture, and historical context of biblical times. (See chapter 5, pp. 95ff)

idiom: (from the Greek word *idios*, meaning "personal, private") prevalent in all languages, including ancient Hebrew and Greek, an idiom is an expression unique to its own language that cannot be discerned from the meanings of its individual words and which often becomes incomprehensible when translated literally from one language into another (e.g., "coming on clouds," meaning divine judgment or vindication; or "flowing with milk and honey," meaning fertile).

Illumination principle: an essential principle of biblical interpretation which holds that though the Holy Spirit provides us with insights that can only be spiritually discerned, He does not supplant the scrupulous study of Scripture. As such, the Holy Spirit illumines what is *in* the text; illumination does *not go beyond* the text. (See chapter 3, pp. 37ff)

isopsephism: a grammatical "equation" in which one word or phrase is used alongside another word or phrase of equal numerical value according to the ancient letter-numbering system **gematria** (e.g., "count the numerical values of the letters in Nero's name, and in 'murdered his own mother' and you will find their sum is the same;" see p. 258 note 94).

L-E-G-A-C-Y: an acronym that codifies the basic factors historians consider in order to properly interpret a given book of the Bible, namely, Location, Essence, Genre, Author, Context, and Years (see pp. 98ff.).

L-I-G-H-T-S: an acronym that codifies the interpretive principles of **Exegetical Eschatology** $\boxed{e^2}$, namely, Literal principle, Illumination principle, Grammatical principle, Historical principle, Typological principle, and Scriptural Synergy.

Literal principle: ("L" in **LIGHTS**) an essential principle of biblical interpretation which holds that far from interpreting the Bible's various genres, figurative language, and fantasy imagery in a wooden, literalistic sense, we must interpret the Word of God in its most obvious and natural sense, just as we would interpret other forms of literature. Because the most natural sense of Scripture is not always obvious to us living in a different time and culture, the literal principle must be employed in conjunction with the other principles codified in the acronym **LIGHTS**. (See chapter 2, pp. 13ff.)

millennium: a thousand-year period mentioned in chapter twenty of the book of Revelation. Though mistaken by many as a semi-golden age of Christian history—leading to much debate over whether the return of

274

Christ will happen before (premillennialism) or after (postmillennialism)
the millennium, or whether the millennium is symbolic of the period of
time between Christ's first and second advents (amillennialism)—the
thousand years of Revelation are symbolic of the unique and ultimate
vindication (qualitative) that awaits the martyrs who died under the first-
century persecution of the Beast (for more see pp. 256-57 note 72).

Olivet Discourse: the prophetic and apocalyptic sermon Jesus delivered on
the Mount of Olives in which he lamented Israel's rebellion against God
and prophesied that he would bring judgment on Jerusalem before the
generation of his contemporaries had passed away—a prophecy
unambiguously fulfilled in AD 70 when the Roman army utterly destroyed
the temple and the city. Parallel accounts of the Olivet Discourse are found
in Matthew 24-25, Mark 13, and Luke 21; cf. Revelation 4-20.

preterism: (from the Latin word *praeter*, meaning "past") the view that
eschatological events prophesied in Scripture have already taken place.
Preterism manifests in two basic forms: partial- and hyper-preterism. The
former lies within the pale of orthodox Christianity in that it postulates
that the bodily return of Christ, the bodily resurrection of the dead, and
the final resolution of sin is yet future. The latter, however, is clearly
heretical in that it presumes all prophecy, including the second coming of
Christ and the resurrection of Christians, has been fulfilled.

pretribulational rapture: (see **rapture**)

Protocols of the Elders of Zion: A thoroughly discredited conspiracy theory
in which sinister Jews secretly scheme to seize global control by destabilizing
civil governments, disrupting world economies, and destroying Christian
civilization. The *Protocols* significantly stoked the embers of anti-Semitism.

Promised Land: (also known as *Eretz Israel* from the Hebrew "land of
Israel") the geographical region of the Middle East that God promised to
give Abraham's descendants on the condition that they remain faithful to
the Lord's commandments so that they might be a light and a blessing to
all the nations of the earth. It is instructive to note that the boundaries of
the Promised Land are variously described throughout the Hebrew
Scriptures. In some cases the land is described in terms of geographical
borders (see Genesis 15:18; Exodus 23:31; Deuteronomy 11:24). In other
cases the Promised Land is described in terms of the pagan nations who
previously occupied the territory (see Genesis 15:19-21; Exodus 3:8;
Joshua 9:1; Ezra 9:1). Just as the geographical markers admit divergence,
so the number of nations listed varies, demonstrating the folly of any
attempt to rigidly fix the boundaries of the Land of Promise.

prophecy: the verbal or literary expression of God's Word by human prophets. Prophecy is manifest in two forms—the *foretelling* of divinely revealed and eternally significant future earthly events and the *forthtelling* (or pronouncement) of God's already revealed Word into current historical realities. Prophecy in either form calls the wicked to repentance and the faithful to perseverance in light of God's holy nature and His impending judgment. While the prophets of the Old and New Testaments accurately foretold many events in which God specially intervened in human history, the normative way that God speaks to us today is through the infallible repository of redemptive revelation—the holy Bible.

rapture: (from the Latin word *rapio*, meaning "caught up") this word was used in Latin translations of the Bible to express Paul's teaching that believers living at the time of Christ's return would be "caught up . . . to meet the Lord in the air" (1 Thess. 4:17). As typically used by evangelical Christians today, however, the word "rapture" communicates the idea of a divine disappearing act in which Jesus Christ secretly returns to earth to take faithful believers out of this world just prior to a seven-year period of great tribulation. This understanding of rapture is referred to, for obvious reasons, as pretribulational rapture. If the question "Will there be a Rapture?" is taken to mean, "Will believers be 'caught up' to meet the Lord as Paul taught?" the answer is a resounding "yes." Conversely, if the question is "Will there be a pretribulational rapture as described above?" the answer is unambiguously "no." Far from teaching a pretribulational rapture of the church, the Bible teaches that the glorification of believers living at the time of Christ's return is a single event that will happen concurrently with the general resurrection of the dead (see esp. John 5:28-29, 1 Corinthians 15, 1 Thessalonians 4; also pp. 246-47 note 60).

resurrection: the raising of a body from death to eternal life; used to refer to the general resurrection of the dead—the just to eternal life and the wicked to eternal separation from God—that will occur at the time of Christ's future bodily return to earth (see John 5:28-29, 1 Corinthians 15, 1 Thessalonians 4); also used to refer to Jesus' resurrection from the dead as "the firstfruits of those who have fallen asleep" (1 Corinthians 15:20).

Scriptural Synergy: an essential principle of biblical interpretation which demands that individual Bible passages be interpreted in a way that harmonize with the whole of Scripture. Accordingly, complex passages of Scripture must be interpreted in light of the clear teachings of Scripture (see chapter 7, pp. 227ff.).

tribulation: (see **great tribulation**) trial, trouble, difficult or painful circumstance, persecution. As in the words of Jesus, "In this world you will have trouble. But take heart! I have overcome the world" (John 16:33).

Typology principle: A type (from the Greek word *typos*, meaning "impression, model, or image") is a person, event, or institution in the redemptive history of the Old Testament that prefigures a corresponding but greater reality in the New Testament. A type is thus a copy, pattern, or model that signifies a greater reality. The greater reality to which a type points, and in which it finds its fulfillment, is referred to as an *antitype* (from the Greek word *antitypos*, meaning "corresponding to something that has gone before"). For example, the antitype of the land is found in the Lord, the antitype of Jerusalem is found in Jesus, and the antitype of the majestic Temple is found in the Master Teacher. (See chapter 6, pp. 169ff)

YHWH: the four letters of the Hebrew Tetragrammaton (יהוה), representing the unspeakable personal name of God. YHWH carries with it the force of eternality and self-existence. Yahweh was derived by adding the vowel points of the Hebrew title Adonai (King of Kings and Lord of Lords) to the Tetragrammaton. In Romans 10, calling on YHWH and calling on Christ are equated, thus demonstrating that Jesus is Himself Almighty God.

Zionism: a sociopolitical movement which originated in nineteenth-century Europe and centered on the desire to establish an autonomous Jewish state. (see **Christian Zionism**)

Subject Index

―――❦❦❦――

abomination of desolation, 87–88, 208, 254n37
Abraham
  God's promise to, 49–50, 52–53, 175–177, 179, 183, 197, 200, 264n35
  land owned by, 176
  seed of, 49–51, 53
Abram, 51–53, 175
Acts, 102, 253nn24-25
Adam, 51–53
age, end of the, 82, 84–85
Ahijah, 205–206
allegorical biblical interpretation, 29–30, 172
allegories, 28, 29–30
Allen, Ronald, 265n45
Andrew, Brother, xxiv, 164, 241n34
Antichrist, the. *See* Beast, the
anti-Semitism, 41–42, 69, 97–98, 103–105, 162
antitype, 170, 172–174
Apocalypse Code (Lindsey), xvi–xvii
apocalyptic imagery, 21–22, 33, 105–108
apostles, 139, 257–258n82
Ariel, Yisreal, 209
ark of the covenant, 204, 218
Armageddon, 3–4, 47–48
Asia Minor, 110, 111
Augustine, 29
Augustus, 111
author, 100–101, 137–144, 252n18, 257–258n82, 258n86, 258n90

Babylon, 31–32, 66–67, 89, 135, 206

Baigent, Michael, 97
Balfour, James, 183, 264n42
Balfour Declaration, 183, 264n41-42
Barker, Dan, 250n9
Bauckham, Richard, 92, 119, 142, 251n28, 258n94
Beale, G. K., 128–129, 137
Beast, the
  description of, xix, 22–23, 32, 34–35
  Great Tribulation, 114, 147–152, 159
  identification of, 8, 242n13
  as imitation of Lamb, 35
  mark of, 10–12, 41
  Nero as, 8, 109, 114–115, 144, 147–149, 242n13, 255n43, 256n60
  number of, 8, 11, 144–147
  resurrection of, xix–xx, 20, 35, 239n16
  Roman pontiff as, 44–45
  symbol for, 34–35
  temple desecration by, 208, 211–212
  timing of demise of, 44–45
  as twenty-first-century character, 8
  wounding of, xix
Beginning of the End, The (LaHaye), xx, 240n22
Bell, L. Nelson, 189
Ben-Gurion, David, xxiii, 167

Bible
  accuracy of, 184–185
  Author of, 9–10
  classes of people in, 46, 240n19
  dating of writing of, 102–103
  English translations of, 80, 249n4
  included books in, 96–98
  interpretation of, xviii, 1–3, 13–20, 47–48, 72–73, 228–230, 236–237, 241n1, 249n4 (*see also* LIGHTS)
  learning to read, 1, 48, 241n1
  literary styles of, 14–15, 230–231
  origin and inspiration of, 35–36
  study of, 2, 241n2, 249n4
Birth of the Palestinian Refugee Problem, 1947-1949 (Morris), 162
Bloomberg, Craig, 142–143
Boaz, 122
Bone of Contention (Lubenow), 39
Bonhoeffer, Dietrich, 162
bride of Christ. *See* church, the
Brown, Dan, 97, 234
Burge, Gary, xxii–xxiii, xxiv–xxv, 165–166
Bush, George W., 168

Caesar, Julius, 111, 255n49
Caesar as Lord, 111–112

279

Scripture Index

289

Selected Bibliography

Books

Adams, Jay E. *The Time Is At Hand*. Woodruff, SC: Timeless Texts, 2000.

Adams, Jay E., and Milton C. Fisher. *The Time of the End: Daniel's Prophecy Reclaimed*. Woodruff, SC: Timeless Texts, 2000.

Armerding, Carl E., and W. Ward Gasque, eds. *A Guide to Biblical Prophecy*. Peabody, MA: Hendrickson, 1989.

Baigent, Michael. *The Jesus Papers: Exposing the Greatest Cover-Up in History*. San Francisco: HarperSanFrancisco, 2006.

Bauckham, Richard. *The Climax of Prophecy: Studies on the Book of Revelation*. Edinburgh: T. & T. Clark, 1993.

———. *The Theology of the Book of Revelation*. Cambridge, United Kingdom, 1993.

Beale, G. K. *The Book of Revelation: A Commentary on the Greek Text*. New International Greek Testament Commentary. Grand Rapids: Eerdmans, 1999.

Berkhof, Louis. *Principles of Biblical Interpretation*. Grand Rapids: Baker, 1950.

Blomberg, Craig. *The Historical Reliability of the Gospels*. Downers Grove, IL: InterVarsity, 1987.

———. *Jesus and the Gospels*. Nashville: Broadman & Holman, 1997.

Bock, Darrell L. *Luke 9:51-24:53*. Baker Exegetical Commentary on the New Testament. 4th ed. Edited by Moisés Silva. Grand Rapids: Baker, 2000.

Body, Gregory A. *Cynic Sage or Son of God?* Wheaton, IL: BridgePoint, 1995.

Bonhoeffer, Dietrich. *The Cost of Discipleship*. New York: Simon & Schuster, 1995. First published in German in 1937.

Brother Andrew [Anne van der Bijl], and Al Janssen. *Light Force: A Stirring Account of the Church Caught in the Middle East Crossfire*. Grand Rapids: Revell, 2004.

Metzger, Bruce M. *Breaking the Code: Understanding the Book of Revelation*. Nashville: Abingdon, 1993.

Burge, Gary M. *Whose Land? Whose Promise? What Christians Are Not Being Told about Israel and the Palestinians*. Cleveland: Pilgrim, 2003.

Caird, G. B. *The Language and Imagery of the Bible*. Grand Rapids: Eerdmans, 1980. Reprinted 1997. Page references are to the 1997 edition.

Carter, Jimmy. *Palestine Peace not Apartheid*. New York: Simon & Schuster, 2006.

Chapman, Colin. *Whose Promised Land? The Continuing Crisis over Israel and Palestine*. Grand Rapids: Baker Books, 2002.

———. *Whose Holy City? Jerusalem and the Future of Peace in the Middle East*. Grand Rapids: Baker Books, 2004.

Chilton, David. *Days of Vengeance: An Exposition of the Book of Revelation*. Tyler, TX: Dominion, 1987.

Craig, William Lane. "Did Jesus Rise from the Dead?" In *Jesus Under Fire: Modern Scholarship Reinvents the Historical Jesus*, edited by Michael J. Wilkins and J. P. Moreland, 147–153. Grand Rapids: Zondervan, 1995.

———. *Reasonable Faith: Christian Truth and Apologetics*. rev. ed. Wheaton: Crossway, 1994.

Crichton, Michael. *State of Fear*. New York: HarperCollins, 2004.

DeMar, Gary. *End Times Fiction: A Biblical Consideration of the Left Behind Theology*. Nashville: Nelson, 2001.

———. *Last Days Madness: Obsession of the Modern Church*, 4th rev. ed. Atlanta: American Vision, 1999.

Dershowitz, Alan. *The Case For Israel*. Hoboken, NJ: John Wiley & Sons, Inc., 2003.

Ehrman, Bart D. *Jesus: Apocalyptic Prophet of the New Millennium*. New York: Oxford University Press, 1999.

———. *Misquoting Jesus: The Story Behind Who Changed the Bible and Why*. San Francisco: HarperSanFrancisco, 2005.

———. *The New Testament: A Historical Introduction to the Early Christian Writings*. 3rd ed. New York: Oxford University Press, 2004.

Ellisen, Stanley A. *Who Owns the Land? The Arab-Israeli Conflict*. Revised by Charles H. Dyer. Wheaton: Tyndale, 2003.

Evans, Michael D. *The American Prophecies: Ancient Scriptures Reveal Our Nation's Future*. New York: Warner Faith, 2004.

Farrar, F. W. *The Early Days of Christianity*. New York, NY: Cassell & Company, 1889.

———. *The Expositor's Bible—Book of Daniel*. London: Hodder And Stoughton, 1895.

Farrer, Austin. *A Rebirth of Images: The Making of St. John's Apocalypse*. Westminster: Dacre Press, 1949.

———. *The Revelation of St. John the Divine: A Commentary on the English Text*. London: Oxford University Press, 1964.

Fee, Gordon D., and Douglas Stuart. *How to Read the Bible for All Its Worth: A Guide to Understanding the Bible*. 2nd ed. Grand Rapids: Zondervan, 1993.

Fruchtenbaum, Arnold G. "The Little Apocalypse of Zechariah." In *The End Times Controversy*, edited by Tim LaHaye and Thomas Ice, 251–81. Eugene, OR: Harvest House, 2003.

Funk, Robert W., Roy W. Hoover, and the Jesus Seminar. *The Five Gospels*. New York: Macmillan, 1993.

Gaebelein, Arno Clemens. *The Conflict of the Ages: The Mystery of Lawlessness, Its Origin, Historic Development, and Coming Defeat*. Vienna, VA: The Exhorters, n.d. Uncensored reprint edition.

Gaebelein, Frank E., ed. *Matthew, Mark, and Luke*. Vol. 8, *The Expositor's Bible Commentary*. Grand Rapids: Zondervan, 1984.

Geisler, Norman L., and Frank Turek. *I Don't Have Enough Faith to Be an Atheist*. Wheaton: Crossway, 2004.

Geisler, Norman L. *Church, Last Things*. Vol. 4, *Systematic Theology*. Minneapolis: Bethany House, 2005.

Gentry, Jr., Kenneth L. *The Beast of Revelation*. Atlanta: American Vision, 2002.

———. *Before Jerusalem Fell: Dating the Book of Revelation*. Atlanta: American Vision, 1998.

Gerstner, John H. *Wrongly Dividing the Word of Truth: A Critique of Dispensationalism*. Brentwood, TN: Wolgemuth & Hyatt, 1991.

Goppelt, Leonhard. *Typos: The Typological Interpretation of the Old Testament in the New.* Translated by Donald H. Madvid. Grand Rapids: Eerdmans, 1982.

Gregg, Steve, ed. *Revelation: Four Views.* Nashville: Nelson, 1997.

Gundry, Robert H. *The Church and the Tribulation.* Grand Rapids: Zondervan, 1973.

———. *First the Antichrist.* Grand Rapids: Baker, 1997.

Habermas, Gary R., and Antony G. N. Flew. *Did Jesus Rise from the Dead?* San Francisco: Harper & Row, 1987.

Habermas, Gary R., and Michael R. Licona. *The Case for the Resurrection of Jesus.* Grand Rapids: Kregel, 2004.

Habermas, Gary R. *The Historical Jesus: Ancient Evidence for the Life of Christ.* Joplin, Mo.: College Press, 1996.

Hagee, John. *Final Dawn over Jerusalem.* Nashville: Nelson, 1998.

———. *Jerusalem Countdown: A Warning to the World.* Lake Mary, FL, Frontline, 2006.

———. *Should Christians Support Israel?* San Antonio, TX: Dominion, 1987.

Hanegraaff, Hank. *The Bible Answer Book.* Nashville: Nelson, 2004.

———. *Resurrection.* Nashville: Word, 2000.

Hanegraaff, Hank, and Sigmund Brouwer. *The Last Disciple.* Wheaton: Tyndale, 2004.

Hendriksen, William. *More Than Conquerors: An Interpretation of the Book of Revelation.* Grand Rapids: Baker, 1998.

Hitchcock, Mark, and Thomas Ice. *The Truth Behind Left Behind: A Biblical View of the End Times.* Sisters, OR: Multnomah, 2004.

Hoekema, Anthony A. *The Bible And the Future.* Grand Rapids: Eerdmans, 1979.

Hutchins, Robert Maynard, ed. *Darwin.* Vol. 49, *Great Books of the Western World.* Chicago: Encyclopedia Britannica, 1952.

Ice, Thomas, and Kenneth L. Gentry Jr. *The Great Tribulation: Past or Future? Two Evangelicals Debate the Question.* Grand Rapids: Kregel, 1999.

Ice, Thomas, and Timothy Demy, gen. eds. *When the Trumpet Sounds.* Eugene, OR: Harvest House, 1995.

Johnson, Dennis E. *Triumph of the Lamb: A Commentary on Revelation.* Phillipsburg, NJ: P & R, 2001.

Josephus, Flavius. *Josephus: The Essential Works.* Translated and edited by Paul L. Maier. Grand Rapids: Kregel, 1988.

Keener, Craig. *The IVP Bible Background Commentary: New Testament.* Downers Grove: IVP, 1993.

Keith, Arthur. *Evolution and Ethics.* New York: Putnam, 1947.

Ladd, George Eldon. *The Blessed Hope.* Grand Rapids: Wm. B. Eerdmans, 1956

———. *A Commentary on the Revelation of John.* Grand Rapids: Eerdmans, 1972.

———. *The Gospel of the Kingdom: Popular Expositions on the Kingdom of God.* Grand Rapids: 2000. First printed 1959.

———. *The Presence of the Future.* Grand Rapids: Eerdmans, 1974. Revised and updated version of *Jesus and the Kingdom.* Harper and Row, 1964.

LaHaye, Tim. *The Beginning of the End.* Wheaton: Tyndale, 1972.

———. "Introduction: Has Jesus Already Come?" In *The End Times Controversy,* Edited by Tim LaHaye and Thomas Ice, 7–16. Tim LaHaye Prophecy Library. Eugene, OR: Harvest House, 2003.

————. *No Fear of the Storm*. Sisters, OR: Multnomah, 1992.

————, ed. *Tim LaHaye Prophecy Study Bible*. Chattanooga: AMG Publishers, 2000.

————. *Revelation Unveiled*. Grand Rapids: Zondervan, 1999.

LaHaye, Tim, and Jerry B. Jenkins. *Are We Living in the End Times?* Wheaton: Tyndale, 1999.

————. *The Indwelling: The Beast Takes Possession*. Wheaton: Tyndale, 2000.

————. *The Mark: The Beast Rules the World*. Wheaton: Tyndale, 2000.

LaHaye, Tim and Thomas Ice. *Charting the End Times*. Eugene, OR.: Harvest House, 2001.

LaHaye, Tim, and Thomas Ice, eds. *The End Times Controversy*. Eugene, OR: Harvest House, 2003.

Lenski, R. C. H. *Commentary on the New Testament: The Interpretation of St. John's Revelation*. Peabody, MA: Hendrickson, 2001. Originally published by Augsburg Press, 1943.

Lindsey, Hal. *Apocalypse Code*. Palos Verdes, CA: Western Front, 1997.

Lindsey, Hal, with C. C. Carlson. *The Late Great Planet Earth*. Grand Rapids: Zondervan, 1970.

Maier, Paul L. *The Flames of Rome*. Grand Rapids: Kregel, 1981.

Mathison, Keith A. *Dispensationalism: Rightly Dividing the People of God?* Phillipsburg, NJ: P & R, 1995.

Moffatt, James. *The Revelation of St. John The Divine*. Vol. 5, *The Expositor's Greek Testament*. Edited by W. Robertson Nicoll. rev. ed. Grand Rapids: Eerdmans, 1976.

Morris, Benny. *The Birth of the Palestinian Refugee Problem, 1947–1949*. Cambridge: Cambridge University Press, 1987.

Morris, Leon. *The First Epistle of Paul to the Corinthians: An Introduction and Commentary*. Leicester: InterVarsity, 1985.

Mounce, Robert H. *The Book of Revelation*. Grand Rapids: Eerdmans, 1977.

Osborne, Grant R. *The Hermeneutical Spiral: A Comprehensive Introduction to Biblical Interpretation*. Downers Grove, IL: InterVarsity, 1991.

Payne, J. Barton. *Encyclopedia of Bible Prophecy*. Grand Rapids: Baker, 1973.

Pentecost, J. Dwight. *Things to Come: A Study in Biblical Eschatology*. Grand Rapids: Zondervan, 1958.

Pearse, Meic. *Why The Rest Hates The West: Understanding The Roots of Global Rage*. Downers Grove, IL: InterVarsity, 2004.

Pinker, Steven. *The Language Instinct: How the Mind Creates Language*. New York: HarperPerennial, 1994.

Poythress, Vern S. *Understanding Dispensationalists*. Phillipsburg, NJ: P & R, 1994.

Pratt, Richard L. "Hyper-Preterism and Unfolding Biblical Eschatology." In *When Shall These Things Be? A Reformed Response to Hyper Preterism*, edited by Keith A. Mathison, 121-154. Phillipsburg, NJ: P & R, 2004.

Ramsey Michaels, J. *Revelation*. Downers Grove, IL: InterVarsity, 1997.

Riddlebarger, Kim. *A Case for Amillennialism: Understanding the End Times*. Grand Rapids: Baker, 2003.

Robinson, John A. T. *Redating the New Testament*. Eugene, OR: Wipf and Stock, 2000.

Ryrie, Charles C. *Dispensationalism*. Rev. ed. Chicago: Moody Press, 1995.

Ryken, Leland, James C. Wilhot, and Tremper Longman III, eds. *Dictionary of Biblical Imagery*. Downers Grove, IL: InterVarsity, 1998.

Schweitzer, Albert. *Out of My Life and Thought: An Autobiography*. New York: Henry Holt, 1933.

Scofield, C. I., ed. *The Scofield Study Bible*. readers ed. New York: Oxford University Press, 1917. Reissued 1996.

Sizer, Stephen. *Christian Zionism: Road-map to Armageddon?* Leicester: InterVarsity Press, 2004.

Smith, Chuck. *End Times: A Report on Future Survival*. Costa Mesa, CA: The Word for Today, 1978. Reprinted 1980.

Smith, Chuck, with David Wimbish. *Dateline Earth: Countdown to Eternity*. Old Tappan, NJ: Chosen, 1989.

Spilsbury, Paul. *The Throne, The Lamb & The Dragon*. Downers Grove, IL: InterVarsity Press, 2002.

Sproul, R. C. *Knowing Scripture*. Downers Grove, IL: InterVarsity Press, 1977.

———. *The Last Days According to Jesus*. Grand Rapids: Baker, 1998.

Strobel, Lee. *The Case for Christ: A Journalist's Personal Investigation of the Evidence for Jesus*. Grand Rapids: Zondervan, 1998.

Tan, Paul Lee. *The Interpretation of Prophecy*. Hong Kong: Nordica International, 1974. Reprinted 1993.

Taylor, John B. *Ezekiel*. Vol. 20, *Tyndale Old Testament Commentaries*. Edited by Donald J. Wiseman. Downers Grove, IL: InterVarsity, 1981.

Terry, Milton S. *Biblical Apocalyptics: A Study of the Most Notable Revelations of God and of Christ in the Canonical Scriptures*. Eugene, OR: Wipf and Stock, 2001.

———. *Biblical Hermeneutics: A Treatise on the Interpretation of the Old and New Testaments*. Grand Rapids: Zondervan, 1985. Reprinted Eugene, OR: Wipf & Stock, 2003.

Tregelles, S. P. *The Hope of Christ's Second Coming: How Is It Taught in Scripture? and Why?* 6th ed. Chelmsford, Eng.: The Sovereign Grace Advent Testimony, n.d. First edition, 1864.

Veith Jr., Gene Edward. *Reading Between the Lines: A Christian Guide to Literature*. Wheaton: Crossway, 1990.

Walvoord, John F. *The Blessed Hope and The Tribulation*. Grand Rapids: Zondervan, 1976.

———. *Every Prophecy of the Bible*. Colorado Springs, Chariot Victor, 1999.

———. *The Rapture Question*. Grand Rapids: Zondervan, 1957.

———. *The Revelation of Jesus Christ*. Chicago: Moody Press, 1966.

Walvoord, John F. and Roy B. Zuck, eds. *The Bible Knowledge Commentary: New Testament*. Colorado Springs: Victor Books, 1983.

———, eds. *The Bible Knowledge Commentary: Old Testament*. Colorado Springs: Victor Books, 1985.

Weber, Timothy P., *Living in the Shadow of the Second Coming: American Premillennialism, 1875–1982*. Chicago: University of Chicago Press, 1979. Revised editions 1983 and 1987. Page numbers quoted from the 1983 edition.

———. *On the Road to Armageddon: How Evangelicals Became Israel's Best Friend*. Grand Rapids: Baker, 2004.

Wilson, Dwight. *Armageddon Now!: The Premillenarian Response to Russia and Israel Since 1917*. Tyler, TX: Institute for Christian Economics, 1991.

Witherington III, Ben. *The Paul Quest: The Renewed Search for the Jew of Tarsus*. Downers Grove, IL: InterVarsity, 1998.

Woollcombe, K. J. "The Biblical Origins and Patristic Development of Typology." In *Essays on Typology*, edited by G. W. H. Lampe and K. J. Woollcombe, 39-75. Studies in Biblical Theology. Naperville, IL: Allenson, 1957.

Wright, N. T. *Jesus and the Victory of God*. Vol. 2, *Christian Origins and the Question of God*. Minneapolis: Fortress, 1996.

———. *Paul for Everyone: Galatians and Thessalonians*. Louisville: Westminster John Knox, 2004.

Young, Edward J., *The Prophecy of Daniel: A Commentary*. Eugene, OR: Wipf & Stock, 1998. Reproduced with permission from Wm. B. Eerdmans, 1977, rev ed.

Articles and Videos

Ari Shavit. "Survival of the Fittest? An Interview with Benny Morris." *Haaretz.com* http://www.haaretz.com/hasen/pages/ShArt.jhtml?itemNo=380986&contrassID=2 (accessed January 30, 2007).

DeMar, Gary. "Letting the Bible Speak for Itself—The Literal Meaning of 'This Generation': A Response to Ed Hindson's 'The New Last Days Scoffers,'—Part 6." American Vision. 2006. http://www.americanvision.org/articlearchive/06-17-05.asp# (accessed January 30, 2007).

Franz, Gordon. "The King and I: The Historical Setting of Revelation 1:9 and the Apostle John on Patmos." Pre-Trib Research Center. http://www.pre-trib.org/pdf/Franz-TheKingAnsITheHistor.pdf (accessed January 30, 2007).

Ice, Thomas. "The Death and Resurrection of the Beast." Pre-Trib Research Center. 2003. http://www.pre-trib.org/article-view.php?id=239 (accessed January 30, 2007).

———. "Why I Believe the Bible Teaches Rapture Before Tribulation." Pre-Trib Research Center. 2003. http://www.pre-trib.org/pdf/Ice-WhyIBelieveTheBibleTe.pdf (accessed January 30, 2007).

The White House, Office of the Press Secretary. November 19, 2003. "President Bush Discusses Iraq Policy at Whitehall Palace in London." http://www.whitehouse.gov/news/releases/2003/11/20031119-1.html.

The Gospel of Judas, DVD. National Geographic, 2006. Program aired April 16, 2006. More information available at http://channel.nationalgeographic.com/channel/gospelofjudas/index.html.

Veith Jr., Gene Edward. "Good Fantasy and Bad Fantasy." *Christian Research Journal* 23, no. 1 (2000): 12–22.

Wallace, Daniel B. "The Gospel of John: Introduction, Argument, Outline." *Bible.org*. http://www.bible.org/page.asp?page_id=1328 (accessed January 30, 2007).

Wright, N. T. "Farewell to the Rapture." *Bible Review*, August 2001. Available at http://www.ntwrightpage.com/Wright_BR_Farewell_Rapture.pdf (accessed January 30, 2007).

CONTACT CHRISTIAN RESEARCH INSTITUTE

By Mail

CRI United States
P.O. Box 8500
Charlotte, NC 28271-8500

CRI Canada
56051 Airways P.O.
Calgary, Alberta T2E 8K5

By Phone

U. S. 24–hour Toll–Free Customer Service: 1 (888) 7000-CRI
Fax: (704) 887-8299

Canada Toll-Free Credit Card Line: 1 (800) 665-5851
Canada Customer Service: (403) 571-6363

On the Internet

www.equip.org

During the *Bible Answer Man* Broadcast
Call in your questions toll free in the United States and Canada:
1 (888) ASK HANK (275-4265),
Monday through Friday, 5:50 p.m. to 7:00 p.m. Eastern Time

For a list of stations airing the *Bible Answer Man*
or to listen to the broadcast via the internet
Log on to our Web site at *www.equip.org*

If you would like Hank to speak in your church or in your area
Contact Paul Young at (704) 887-8222

DECIPHER THE CODE

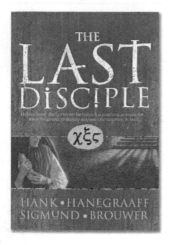 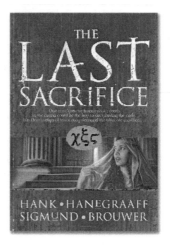

From Best-Selling Authors

HANK HANEGRAAFF

AND

SIGMUND BROUWER

✦ ✦ ✦

visit
www.decipherthecode.com
for more info